Spellbound Festive Beading
Two

A Spellbound Bead Co Book
Copyright © Spellbound Bead Co Publishing 2013

First Published in the UK 2013

Julie Ashford has asserted her right to be identified as author of this work in accordance with the Copyright, Designs and Patents Act, 1988.

All rights reserved. No part of this publication may be reproduced, stored in a retrieval system, or transmitted in any form or by any means, by photocopying, recording or otherwise, without prior permission in writing from the publisher.

The designs in this book must not be reproduced for resale or financial gain.

The author and publisher have made every effort to ensure that all the instructions in the book are accurate and safe, and therefore cannot accept liability for any resulting injury, damage or loss to persons or property, however it may arise.

Names of manufacturers, bead ranges and other products are provided for the information of readers, with no intention to infringe copyright or trademarks.

Printed in the UK by WM Print
for the Spellbound Bead Co

ISBN - 978-0-9565030-5-3

10 9 8 7 6 5 4 3 2 1

Editor: Jean Hall
Pattern Testing and Sample Production: Edna Kedge, Pat Ashford, Vicky Pritchard & Rowena Hayter
Photography: Spellbound Bead Co

Visit our website at www.spellboundbead.co.uk

Spellbound Bead Co
47 Tamworth Street
Lichfield
Staffordshire
WS13 6JW
England

Call 01543 417650 for direct sales
or your local wholesale distributor

Also available by this author:

Spellbound Festive Beading
ISBN 978-0-9565030-2-2

29 projects & inspirations in 15 chapters over 96 pages

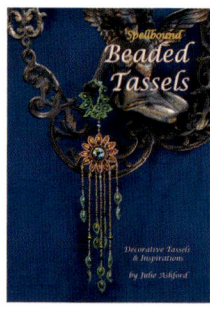

Spellbound Beaded Tassels
ISBN 978-0-9565030-4-6

Over 30 projects & inspirations - 112 pages

Acknowledgements

A special thank you to everyone who has contributed to this book - those who have tested, proofed and been kind about little hiccups, taken photographs, provided cake and counted lots & lots of beads.

Also a big thank you to all of our customers who have shown such marvellous enthusiasm for beads and baubles. This book is dedicated to them and to everyone who has a passion for beads, colour and all things that sparkle.

Contents

Introduction	4
Essential Ingredients	6
Tools & Useful Extras	7
Tips & Techniques	8
Beadwork Stitches for Beginners	10

The Projects

Constellation Stars	12
Frosted Fir Tree	18
Sweetheart Bauble	22
Rivoli Bauble	26
Astor Bauble	30
Christmas Tree Bauble	36
Nordic Bauble	42
Mistletoe Kisses Bauble	48
Poinsettia Bauble	54
Belle Époque Bauble	62
Christmas Pudding Bauble	68
Vintage Bauble	76
Garland Bauble	84
Sherwood Bauble	92
Ariel Tassel	99
Christmas Earrings	
Holly Wreath Earrings	104
Cracker Earrings	106
Rocking Robin Earrings	108
Index & Suppliers	112

Festive Beading Two

Designing a new beaded bauble pattern has become an annual Spellbound tradition. In the first Festive Beading book we looked back at some of the patterns we had developed over the preceding years and we added a few new ones that have become Spellbound classic designs.

That was three years ago and the first book has become a firm favourite with experienced beaders and beading newcomers alike. From the very start, we have been asked for a follow-up book to show the designs that just would not fit in the first book and some new creations too. This book continues where the last one left off.

The majority of the projects in this book use very basic equipment - just a needle and some beading thread. There are a couple of exceptions which are based on simple wirework so a pair of pliers and wire cutters will be needed just to finish off the connections.

All of the projects in the book are written in the same way that I approach workshop and kit instructions – from first principles. All of the main projects have full step-by-step instructions and there are lots of photos to give you ideas for new colourways.

The designs are graded for difficulty (see opposite) to help you to choose between a 'quick and easy' and a 'longer, more complex' project. If you have not done any beadwork before try one of the more simple projects first as they will make up quite quickly.

Throughout the book I have tried to use only readily available beading materials – there being nothing so frustrating as finding the perfect project and then being unable to find the beads to make it with!

Look out for the Extra Info boxes. They contain hints and tips on the techniques and materials you will be using in the projects.

Choose a Project to Suit Your Beading Experience

One Star - very easy - this project will be quick to make.

Two Stars - simple techniques - this project will take a little more time to complete.

Three Stars - getting a little more complex but manageable for a beginner with patience.

Four Stars - several stages building on top of one another. Each stage is straightforward, but there are more of them to follow, so it takes longer to get the desired result.

You will find quick and easy patterns like the Sweetheart Bauble and the Holly Wreath Earrings; three-dimensional wirework and little trees that will delight everyone. There are baubles with bows, berries and blossoms, geometric motifs and fringes. Elegant Mistletoe Earrings are made from tiny seed beads, cute robins made from Delica beads and bright Poinsettia blooms.

There are Inspiration projects within some of the chapters to help you to develop the theme further - just in case you have a few beads left over.

In addition to the Inspirations there are lots of small motifs - leaves, hearts, garlands and even a dragonfly - that would make fabulous earrings, pendants, stringing sequences for necklaces or even decorations for greetings cards and découpage. The only limit is the number of hours in the day.

Decision-making is often the most difficult part of any project, especially when there is lots of choice, but that is also a big part of the fun.

I do hope that you enjoy leafing through the book and picking out all of the projects you want to make - hopefully you will find it difficult to prioritise! I always find that a cup of tea and a bit of cake helps the decision-making go a lot more smoothly.

Happy beading.

Julie

August 2013

Essential Ingredients

The projects in this book all use a very simple selection of beads. For a lot of the designs you will need just two or three colours or sizes of seed beads, one size of bugle beads and a selection of fire polished faceted beads. This quick guide will give you an introduction to these basic supplies and the few extra items you might need for some of the patterns.

Seed Beads

These are the small glass beads used for weaving and stringing intricate patterns, tassels and fringes.

Seed beads are available in many sizes. These sizes are quoted on an inverse scale so size 6/0 is larger than a size 10/0.

These projects use size 6/0, size 8/0, size 10/0 and size 15/0 seed beads. You can substitute size 11/0 for size 10/0 seed beads for most of the projects if you wish.

Seed beads are manufactured in the Czech Republic or Japan. Czech seeds tend to be more rounded than the Japanese seeds so it is better not to mix the two types in the same project. All of the designs in the book are made with Czech seed beads.

Bugle Beads

Bugles are small glass tubes which are available in several lengths. Most of these projects use size 3 bugle beads which are 6-7mm long, or a size 2 bugle which measure 4-5mm in length.

Colours & Finishes

Crystal - a transparent plain glass that can have further effects added to it such as a silver lining or an AB coating.
Silver Lined - a metallic silver deposit on the inside of the hole which glistens through the glass and makes the beads sparkle more vibrantly.
AB - Aurora Borealis is a thin rainbow effect applied on top of the glass bead for extra glitz.
Frost - an acid-etched matt finish applied to a glass bead.
Ceylon - a pearlescent finish applied to a glass bead.

Fire Polished Faceted Glass

These hand-faceted beads are heated in a kiln to give a glossy finish to the glass. Plain finish beads can be made from over 100 colours of glass but special effects, surface dyes and combinations of two or more glass rods into each bead, means an almost unlimited range to choose from.

You will find a lot of 4mm and 6mm beads used in these patterns with a few 8mm and 12mm ones too.

Delica Beads™

These are tiny, cylinder-shaped glass beads used for accurate weaving as they will sit close together like bricks in a wall. They are available in several sizes and hundreds of colours. This book uses only size 11/0 Delicas.

Findings

You will need just a few items to complete the projects in the earring chapter:

Fishhook Earwires are comfortable to wear but you can substitute post & ball or clip earfittings if you prefer.

Jump Rings are the connecting links used in all sorts of jewellery designs.

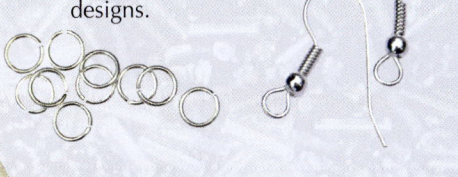

Twin Beads

Twin beads measure 2.5 x 5mm. They have two parallel holes which are suitable for a size 10 beading needle and a size D beading thread. They are manufactured by Preciosa in the Czech Republic. Please also see Tips & Techniques.

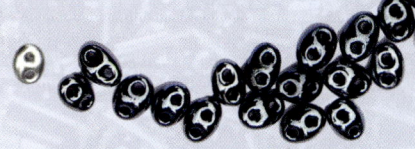

Beading Thread

Sold under many brand names such as Nymo and Superlon, beading thread is available in several thicknesses and many colours. These projects all use a size D thread.

Wire

Wire is commonly available but you need to make sure you pick the correct size and hardness as stated in the project.

Half-Hard Wire is used for structural shapes where it is important that the wire holds the shape firmly.
Soft Wire is used for weaving as it will snake through the bead patterns with ease.

Tools & Useful Extras

Threading Necessities

Beading Needles

Beading needles have a very narrow eye so they can pass through a bead with a small hole.
Size 10 Beading is a general beading needle that is suitable for most of the projects.
Size 12 Beading is a little finer for multiple passes of the thread through the bead holes.

Sharp Scissors to trim the threads close to the work are essential.

A Thread Conditioner such as Thread Heaven helps to smooth the kinks in the thread if you get into a knot or tangle.

A Fleecy Beading Mat with a slight pile will stop the beads from rolling around and it makes it easy to pick up small beads using the point of the needle.

Clear Nail Varnish is sometimes used to stiffen selected areas of stitched beadwork so that the desired shape is firmly retained.

Pliers

You will need pliers for the projects using wire and findings.

Round-Nosed Pliers for turning loops.

Cutters for trimming wire to length.

Chain-Nosed or Flat-Nosed Pliers for gripping and opening and closing jump rings.

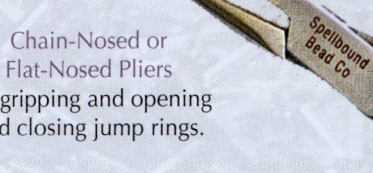

Tips & Techniques

There are a few basic techniques that you will need to know in order to work through the projects in the book. If you need a special technique for a particular project it will be explained within that chapter, but for the techniques that apply to most of the designs this is what you need to read.

Using a Keeper Bead

Before you start a piece of beadwork you will need to put a stopper at the end of the thread. The easiest stopper to use is a keeper bead.

A keeper bead is a spare bead, ideally of a different colour to the work, that is held on a temporary knot close to the end of the thread. Once the beading is completed the keeper bead is removed. That end of the thread is then knotted securely and finished neatly within the beadwork.

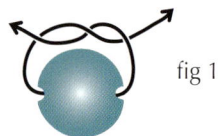

fig 1

To Add a Keeper Bead - Position the keeper bead 15cm from the end of the thread (unless instructed otherwise) and tie a simple overhand knot about the bead (fig 1). When you thread on the first beads of the pattern push them right up to the keeper bead - the tension in the thread will prevent the keeper bead from slipping.

When the work is complete untie the knot and remove the keeper bead. Attach the needle to this end of the thread and secure as shown opposite.

Correcting a Mistake

If you make a mistake whilst you are following a pattern remove the needle and pull the thread back until you have undone the work sufficiently. Do not turn the needle and try to pass it back through the holes in the beads - the needle tip will certainly catch another thread inside the beads and make a filamentous knot that is almost impossible to undo successfully.

If you are working with a double thread, carefully pull on the thread to bring the blunt end of the needle backwards through the beading. Take your time and the needle will be guided back through the exact path it had taken previously and you will not cause a knot.

Making A Wire Loop With Pliers

Hold the cut end of the wire in a pair of round-nosed pliers. With your other hand, grip the wire 8mm below the plier jaws to give firm support. Roll the wrist holding the pliers to form the loop. Make sure it is properly closed and centralise the loop above the beads with the tips of the pliers.

A Note About Baubles

Baubles are made by many different manufacturers - some are hand-blown, paper-thin glass and others are machine-made in both glass and plastic.

Hand blown baubles can vary a little in size from the stated diameter so you may need to adjust the bead count slightly if you are making a tightly-fitted design. The variety of neck sizes across all diameters of baubles, both hand-made and machine-made, is quite marked.

Most of the designs in the book require a close-fitted ring of beads around the neck so you may need to adjust your bead count accordingly. Guidance is given where necessary if you need to make adjustments.

Starting a New Thread

On occasion you will need to add a new thread to the work.

Work the old thread until you have no less than 15cm of thread remaining. Remove the needle from this thread end and leave the end hanging loose.

Prepare the needle with a new thread and tie a keeper bead 5cm from the end.

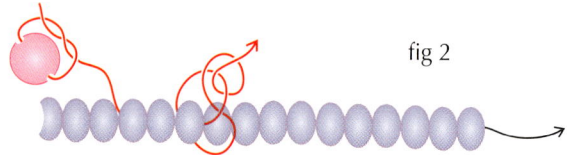

fig 2

Starting about 15 beads back from the old end of the thread pass the needle through 3 - 4 beads towards the old thread end.

Make a double knot here (fig 2). Pass the needle through a further 4 - 5 beads and repeat the knot. Pass the needle through to emerge alongside the old thread end and continue the beading.

When you have worked on a little, trim away the tail of thread and the keeper bead as close as possible to the beads for a neat finish.

A note of caution - before you make the knots, make sure that the needle does not have to pass through these beads again. If it does, just leave the new thread end attached to the keeper bead without any knots around the existing thread. You can return to the keeper bead later, remove it and attach the needle to this thread. The thread must now be secured as in "Finishing Off a Thread End' opposite.

Finishing off a Thread End

You will need to finish off a thread end neatly and securely.

Pass the needle through a few beads of the pattern. At that position pick up the thread between the beads with the point of the needle. Pull the needle through to leave a loop of thread 2cm in diameter. Pass the needle through the loop twice (fig 3) and gently pull down to form a double knot between the beads.

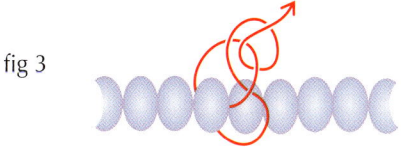

fig 3

Pass the needle through five or six beads of the pattern and repeat the double knot. Pass the needle through five or six more beads before trimming the thread end as close as possible to the work.

Do not finish off any thread ends until instructed to do so - you might need that thread end again or the needle might have to pass past that position again. See 'Knotty Problems' below.

Knotty Problems

Knots as Obstacles

Be careful where you tie your knots when adding a new thread to your work or finishing off an old thread end. Do not position the knots adjacent to, or inside beads that you have to pass the needle through again, because it will not fit through a hole blocked with thread. Sometimes it is better to leave an old thread end hanging loose and return to it later, than place a knot where it might cause an obstruction

Preventing Unwanted Knots

It can be very frustrating to get a knot in your working thread - especially if it keeps happening. There are a few things to try that can help to prevent these annoying knots.

Don't work with a thread that is too long for you - if the stated 1.8m is too much for you to manage use a shorter length and add in a new thread if necessary.

If you get a knot, undo it carefully and condition the thread to remove the distortions in the fibres. The thread will be less likely to re-knot in the same place.

Towards the end of a reel, the thread can be very curly. Cut a slightly shorter length of thread, pulling it between your fingers to help to release the curls, before you prepare the needle. An application of thread conditioner can help too. If it is very distorted be prepared to throw away the last metre or so, rather than spoil your project.

Twin Beads

Twin beads need to be threaded through the right hole in the correct direction.

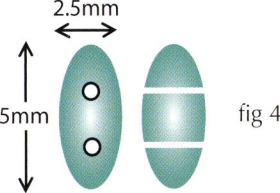

fig 4

Twin beads are eliptical in shape and have two parallel holes (fig 4).

This eliptical profile causes the beads to form a curve if threaded one against the other through the hole at one end (fig 5).

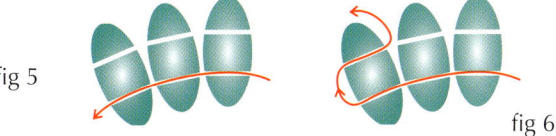

fig 5   fig 6

If you are instructed to pass through the second hole in a Twin bead you must ensure that the needle passes through this hole in the opposite direction bringing a strap of thread to the side of the Twin bead (fig 6). This reverses the direction of the needle and gives you access to the outer row of holes on the Twin beads of the previous row.

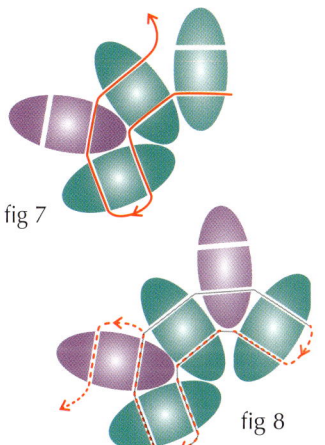

fig 7

fig 8

Adding a new Twin bead into the gap between the second, or outer holes, on the new row fills in the gap between the outer holes on the first row of Twin beads (fig 7).

You may have to take a long route back to reposition the needle.
Make sure it is pointing in the correct direction for the next row (fig 8).

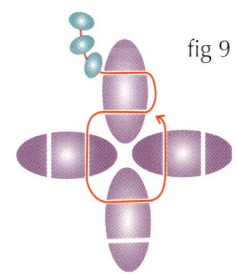

fig 9

Within a beading sequence the needle may pass from the outer hole to the inner hole of a new Twin bead allowing the development of a new motif (fig 9). Tension the thread carefully - don't pull too tightly or the motif will distort.

Extra Info....

When you thread on a new Twin bead check the other hole in the bead is well-formed. There are not many misshapes but an odd one or two might sneak in and can cause a lot of frustration.

Beadwork Stitches for Beginners

There are four basic beadwork stitches used in this book - Brick Stitch, Peyote Stitch, Square Stitch and Right-Angle Weave. The instructions for Brick Stitch are given in some detail below, as the Mistletoe Kisses Bauble calls for a shaped Brick Stitch motif. There is extra information about Square Stitch and Right-Angle Weave opposite which may be useful if you are new to either of these techniques. The Peyote Stitch technique is explained within the Cracker Earrings Project.

Brick Stitch

Brick stitch is so called because of the pattern the beads form as they line up, in staggered rows, giving the impression of a brick wall. It requires a starter row or 'foundation row' onto which the first row of brick stitch is worked.

1 The Ladder Stitch Foundation Row - This ladder of beads is worked so that all the holes of the beads are lined up perpendicular to the length of the row.

Prepare the needle with 1.5m of single thread and tie a keeper bead 15cm from the end. Thread on two beads. Pass the needle back down through the first bead and up through the second to bring the two beads alongside one another (fig 1).

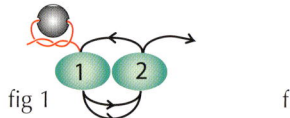
fig 1

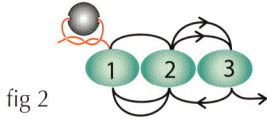
fig 2

2 Thread on a third bead; pass the neeedle back up bead 2 and back down bead 3 (fig 2) bringing bead 3 to sit alongside beads 1 and 2. Repeat for seven further beads to give you a row of ten (fig 3).

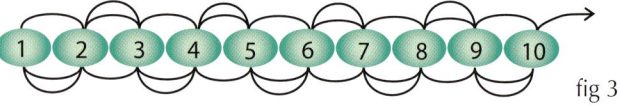
fig 3

3 Starting to Brick Stitch - Thread on two beads (11 & 12). Pick up the loop of thread between beads 10 and 9 and pass back up through bead 12 in the opposite direction (fig 4). This should bring the two new beads to sit alongside one another with bead 11 slightly overhanging the previous row.

4 Thread on bead 13. Pick up the loop of thread between beads 9 and 8 and pass back up bead 13 (fig 5). Repeat adding one bead at a time to the end of the row (ten beads in total).

fig 4   fig 5

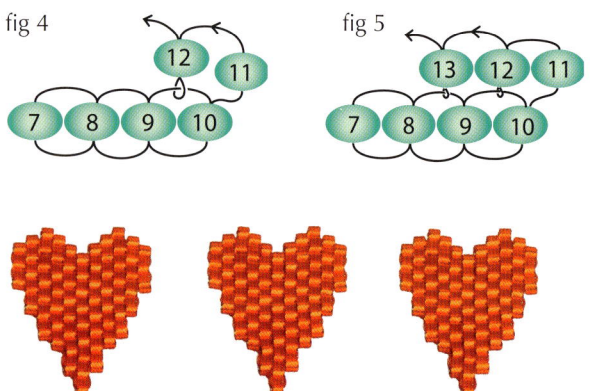

5 Pick up beads 21 and 22 to start the next row (fig 6) and work to the end of the row. Continue to work a further seven rows.

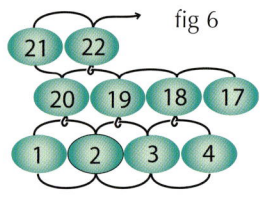
fig 6

Each row starts with a two bead stitch followed by eight single bead stitches. The beads of each row should sit right alongside one another and the rows should sit closely on top of one another. You should not be able to see the thread except at the top and bottom of the work.

You will also need to know how to shape the work by increasing and decreasing the length of the rows.

6 Decreasing at the Start of the Row - A plain brick stitch row starts with a two-bead stitch. If you pick up the first loop of thread along the previous row, the new row will overhang by half of one bead (as fig 4). If you pick up the second loop along the new beads will sit half a bead in from the end of the previous row (fig 7) decreasing the row length by one bead.

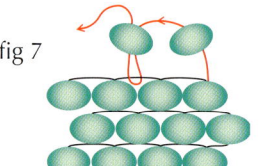
fig 7

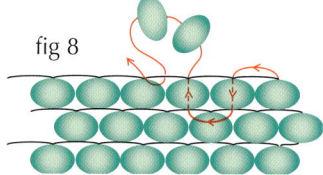
fig 8

If you need to make a bigger decrease you can weave the needle up and down through the beads of the previous row until you are in the correct place to start the new row with a two-bead stitch (fig 8). The new two-bead stitch can stretch across two bead loops (as fig 7) if necessary, to follow the pattern correctly.

This method of repositioning the needle to start the beading in the correct position, with the needle pointing in the correct direction to begin the stitch, is the main skill required to make a success of any brick stitch project.

7 Increasing at the End of the Row - Pick up one bead and pass the needle back up through the last bead of the row. Pass back down through the increase bead (fig 9) - this is just like making the foundation row.

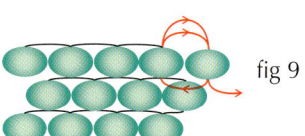
fig 9

In fig 9 the needle is emerging in the wrong direction to start the next row from the newly increased bead. Pass the needle through the previous bead of this row and start the new row with a two-bead stitch from this bead - make sure you have picked out the correct two beads for this location on the pattern. You can then backtrack to add any beads required at the start of the row above the increase bead.

Square Stitch

In square stitch the needle makes a square-shaped path through a newly added bead and the adjacent bead on the previous row. You can increase or decrease at the end of a row or within a row.

In the Rivoli, Belle Époque and Garland Bauble designs the square stitch increases within a row to produce a curve.

fig 10

To begin a block of square stitch you need a starter row of seed beads (fig 10).

Thread on the first bead of the new row.
Pass the needle through the last bead of the starter row in the same direction as before to bring the new bead alongside this bead with the holes parallel (fig 11).

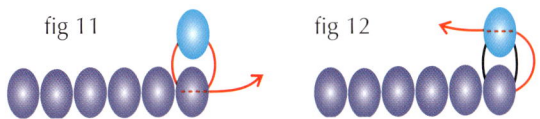

fig 11   fig 12

Pass the needle through the new bead in the same direction to complete the square stitch (fig 12).

Thread on a new bead and pass the needle through the next bead along the starter row and back through the new bead (fig 13) - note the square path of the thread.

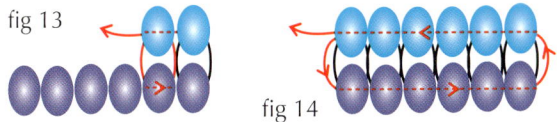

fig 13   fig 14

At the end of a row the needle should pass right through the previous row and back along the new row to bring all of the beads into line (fig 14).

fig 15   fig 16

To increase within a row - simply add two beads instead of one bead (fig 15).

To decrease within a row - add one new bead but pass through two beads on the previous row (fig 16).

Right-Angle Weave

Right-angle weave makes an openwork mesh that flexes and bends. This delicacy and flexibilty is used to make the bands around the bauble in the Poinsettia design. A narrower strip is strengthened to form the firm zig-zag band on the Nordic Bauble.

Simple right-angle weave starts with just four beads. The needle passes through the first bead to make a small ring (fig 17).

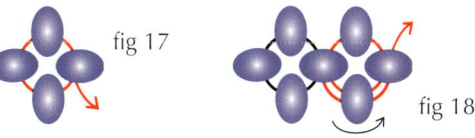

fig 17   fig 18

Three beads are added; the needle passes through the last bead of the previous stitch and the first two beads of the new stitch (fig 18).

This is repeated (fig 19). Each stitch completes a new ring of four beads.

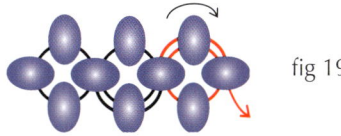

fig 19

Continuing like this will make a long strip two beads wide. To make a wider strip you need to turn a corner and start a new row.

Make the last stitch on the first row as before but just pass through the first of the three new beads (fig 20).

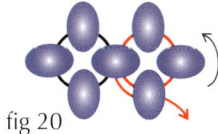

fig 20

Three new beads are threaded and the ring of four beads completed by passing through the bead of the previous stitch and the three beads of the new stitch (fig 21).

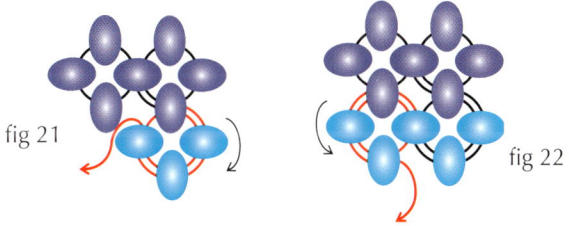

fig 21   fig 22

Just two beads are required to complete the next ring of four but the needle must be repositioned first. The needle passes through the adjacent bead on the previous row, the two beads are added and the needle passes through the last bead of the previous stitch and through the first three beads of this stitch (fig 22).

The technique depends upon deciding how many beads are needed to complete the ring of four and the position of the needle to start the next stitch.

A right-angle weave strap incorporating Twin beads.

Constellation Stars

You Will Need

Materials - Small Star

3g of size 6/0 silver lined crystal seed beads A
4g of size 8/0 silver lined crystal seed beads B
1g of size 10/0 silver lined crystal seed beads C
3g of size 3 silver lined crystal bugle beads D
3.4m of 0.4mm silver-plated soft wire
50cm of clear monofilament thread

Materials - Large Star

3g of size 6/0 silver lined crystal seed beads A
6g of size 8/0 silver lined crystal seed beads B
3g of size 10/0 silver lined crystal seed beads C
4g of size 3 silver lined crystal bugle beads D
Six 8mm crystal fire polished faceted beads E
Six 6mm crystal fire polished faceted beads F
Six 4mm crystal fire polished faceted beads G
4.1m of 0.4mm silver-plated soft wire
30cm of 0.8mm silver-plated half-hard wire
50cm of clear monofilament thread

Tools

A pair of wire cutters
A pair of round-nosed pliers

These very impressive three-dimensional stars are so easy to make – you don't even have to thread a needle. Get the family involved and make a whole host of stars to hang from the ceiling or use them to decorate a big bunch of silvery twigs for a contemporary take on the traditional Christmas tree.

The Decorations are Made in Several Stages

A cube of A beads is created to support the centre of the star.
A star point is added to each of the twelve edges of the cube.

If you are making a large star, an additional three straight rods of beads are pushed through the centre of the cube, to create a further six star points.

Extra Info....
You will be weaving both ends of the 0.4mm soft wire through the beads at the same time.

To form the pattern the wire ends need to pass through some of the beads in the same direction as each another and sometimes in opposite directions. Follow the diagrams carefully and pull the wire through the holes quite firmly to make a strong star shape.

The Small Star

1 Making the Cube – Cut 25cm of 0.4mm wire and smooth it out between your fingers.

Thread on 3A and place at the centre of the wire. Thread 1A onto one end of the wire and hold this bead 5cm from the end.

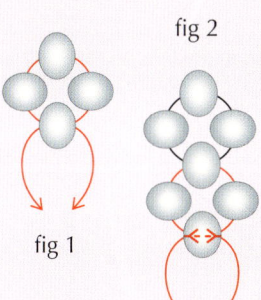

Pick up the other end of the wire and pass it through this A bead in the opposite direction so that the wires cross over inside the bead.

Pull equally on both ends of the wire so that the bead comes to rest against the 3A in the middle of the length to form a square (fig 1).

2 Thread 1A onto each end of the wire and let them run down to the edge of the square.

Thread 1A onto one end of the wire and as before, cross the other end through this A bead, pulling it down to complete a second square (fig 2).

Repeat step 2 to make a third square.

Thread 1A onto each end of the wire (fig 3).

You now have a strip of A beads ready to fold up into a cube shape.

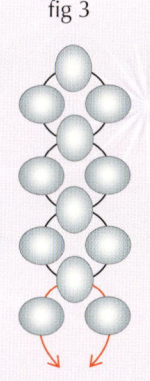

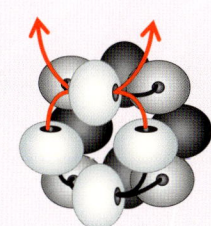

3 Curl the strip of A beads slightly so that the middle bead of the first 3A comes up towards the last two beads.

Following fig 4 pass the two ends of the wire in opposite directions through this middle A bead. Pull on both ends of the wire to bring the strip of beads into a cube (fig 5).

You have the two ends of the wire emerging from either side of an A bead. These two ends will be used to weave the first point of the star. You will then add separate wire lengths to each of the other eleven A beads of the cube to complete a point for each of the twelve edges of the cube.

4 Making the Points – For clarity fig 6 shows just one side of the cube. Referring to fig 6 thread 3B and 1A onto each end of the wire.

Choose one wire end and thread on 1B.

Pass the end of the wire through the last A bead threaded in the same direction as before to bring the new B bead to sit alongside the A bead.

Repeat with the other end of the wire (fig 6).

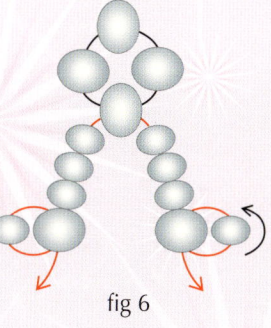

These single B beads will be used to form the side links to the neighbouring star points. The side links stabilise the three-dimensional shape of the star.

5 Thread 1C and 1D onto each end of the wire. Bring the ends of the wire together and thread them both in the same direction through 1B to form a diamond shape (Fig 7)

Separate the wire ends and thread 1B onto each end. Cross the two ends of the wire in opposite directions through 1B to complete a group of 4B (fig 8).

Thread 1D onto each end of the wire. Cross the two ends of the wire in opposite directions through 1B to complete a parallel section (fig 9).

Thread 1B onto each end of the wire. Cross the two ends of the wire in opposite directions through 1C to complete the bead sequence for the star point (fig 10).

Pull the wire ends tight to make this last group of beads firm.

To finish the wire ends pass them through the B beads to either side of the C bead (fig 11) and trim as close as you can.

See the Extra Info box opposite for tips about getting the ends neat.

fig 7

fig 8

fig 9

fig 10

fig 11

fig 12

6 Examine the cube at the base of the point. You need to make three more points around this face of the cube.

Cut 25cm of 0.4mm wire and thread it through the next A bead around the face of the cube to give you two ends of the same length.

Referring to fig 12 throughout, thread 3B and 1A onto each wire end.

Locate the link B beads, added in fig 6, to the previous star point. Working with the side of the wire adjacent to the last point, pass through this link B bead towards the cube. Now pass the wire end through the A bead on the new point in the same direction as before (fig 12). Pull on the wire to bring the two points together through the B bead.

Thread 1B onto the other end of the wire and pass through the A bead on that side once more, to create a new link B bead (fig 12).

Repeat step 5 to complete the star point.

Extra Info....
It's a tight fit to pass the wire in opposite directions through the C bead at the tip of the star point but it also makes the work firmer. Once the wire is passed back through the B beads (as in fig 11) and trimmed the star point will be strong enough for decorative uses.

If you want the star to withstand lots of handling swap the C bead at the tip for a 2mm French crimp. Carefully flatten the crimp with flat-nosed pliers to securely grip onto the wires.

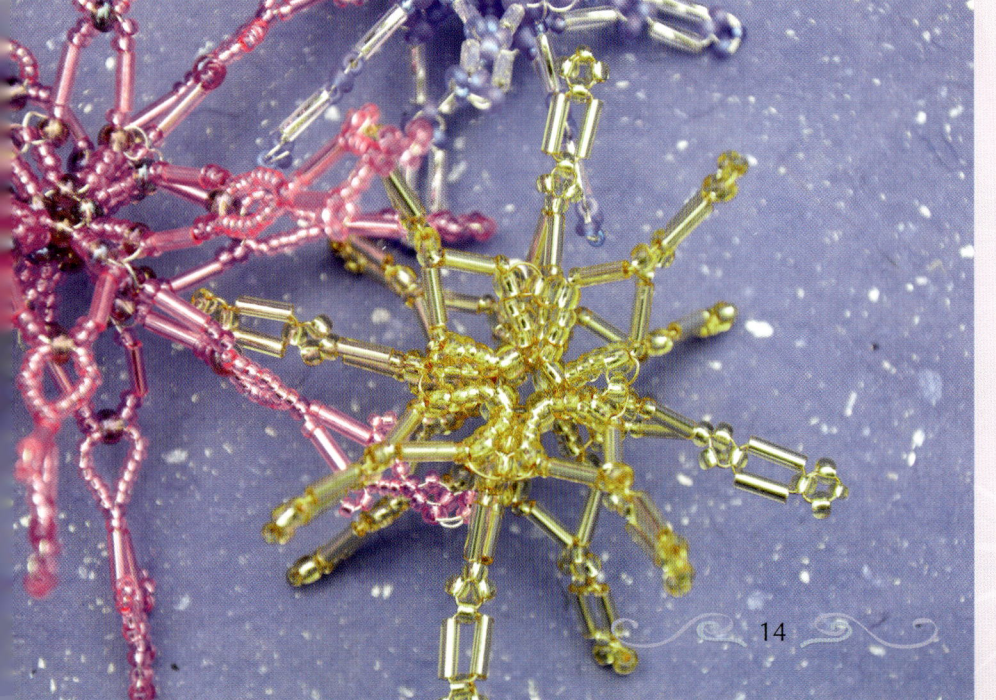

> **Extra Info....**
> Trimming the wire with cutters very close to the last bead can be difficult. Try this method instead.
>
> Fold the wire sharply against the side of the bead hole. Wiggle the wire backwards and forwards - this weakens the wire at the fold causing it to become brittle and to break where it has been under stress.
> You will now have a very neat finish with no nasty burr of wire on show.

7 Repeat steps 6 and 5 to make a third star point attached to the third side of the cube face.

Start the last point of this cube face along the fourth side with 3B and 1A on each end of the wire - the link B beads are already in place attached to the first and third points. Make the links as before to close up the set and complete this star point following step 5.

You will now have four points all coming from one side of the cube. As they are joined together through the B bead links, they lift up into a four-sided cup-shape from the face of the cube. You now have to make a similar cup-shaped set of four points from the opposite face of the cube.

8 Make four star points supported by the face on the opposite side of the cube.

The last four points are supported by the A beads of the cube between the two opposite faces of the cube (see fig 13). These new points join up to the B bead links on the star points to either side.

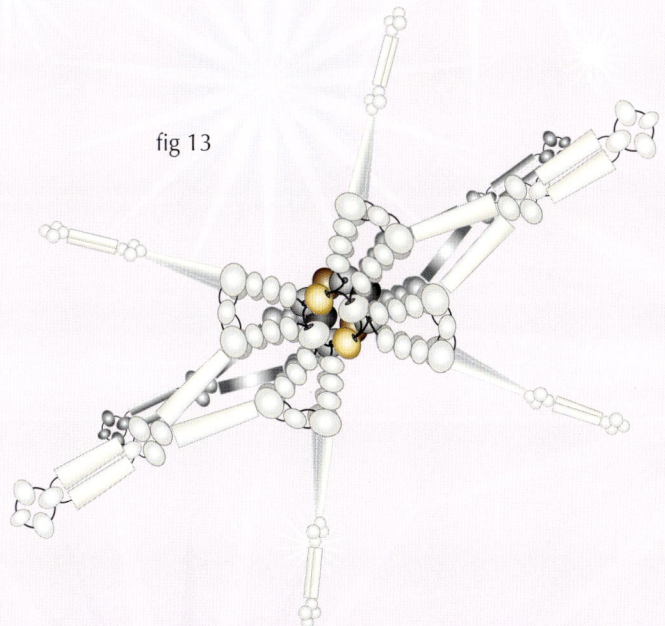

fig 13

Make the A bead cubes in berry colours to weave into festive foliage arrangements.

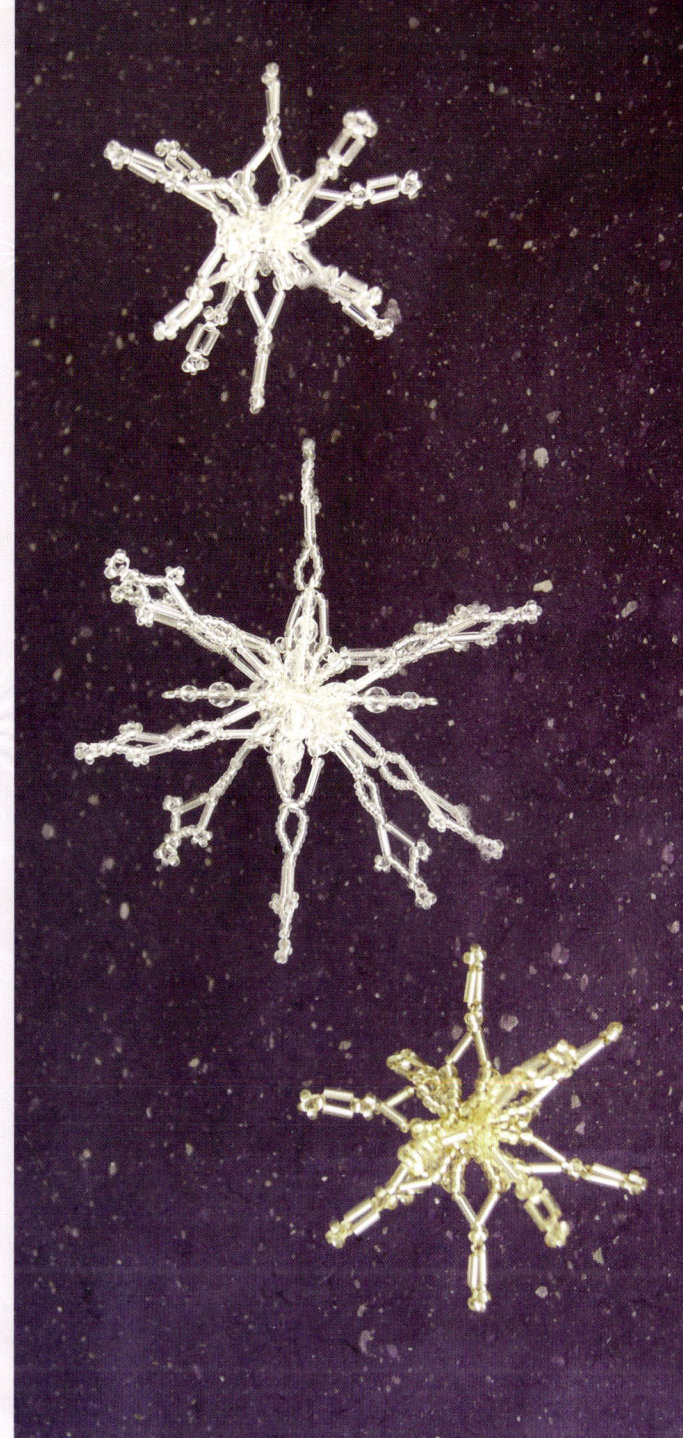

9 Cut 25cm of 0.4mm wire and thread through one of these vacant A beads on the cube. You are working at 90° to the two faces of the cube previously worked.

Thread the first 3B and 1A to each end of the wire. Look to either side of this new point and locate the existing B bead links. Working one side at a time pass the wire down through the B bead of the adjacent link and up through the new A bead. That B bead now links three points together. Repeat with the other end of the wire linking it to the adjacent B bead on that side.

Make the remainder of the point as before.

10 Repeat to add a point to each of the remaining three A beads of the cube (twelve points in total).
Suspend the completed star from a loop of monofilament thread.

The Large Star

If you have not made the Small Star before making this larger version,
read through steps 1-10 to familiarise yourself with the technique.

11 Starting the Large Star - Using 40cm of wire, instead of the stated 25cm, work steps 1- 4 inclusive to make a cube of A beads and to start the first star point.

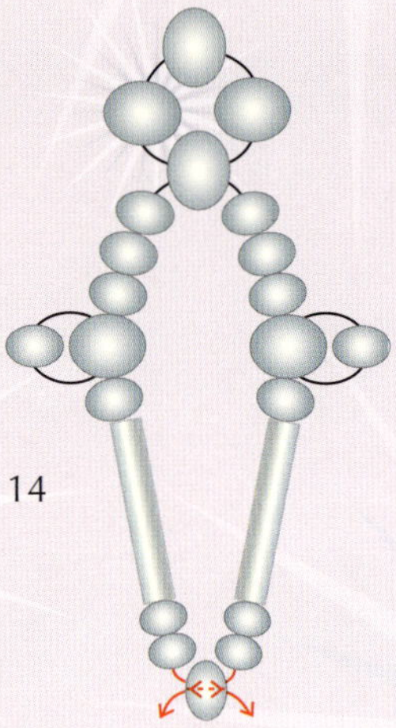

fig 14

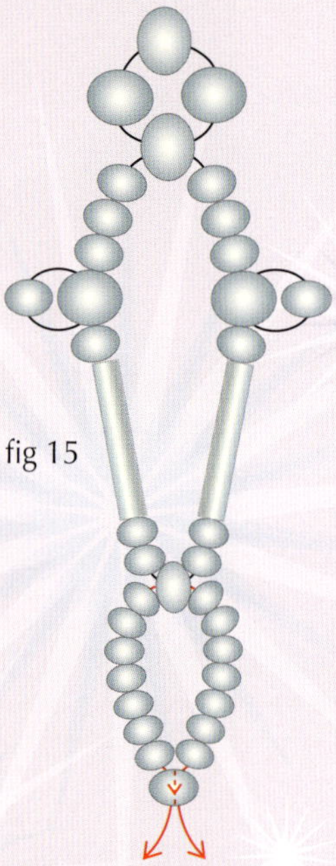

fig 15

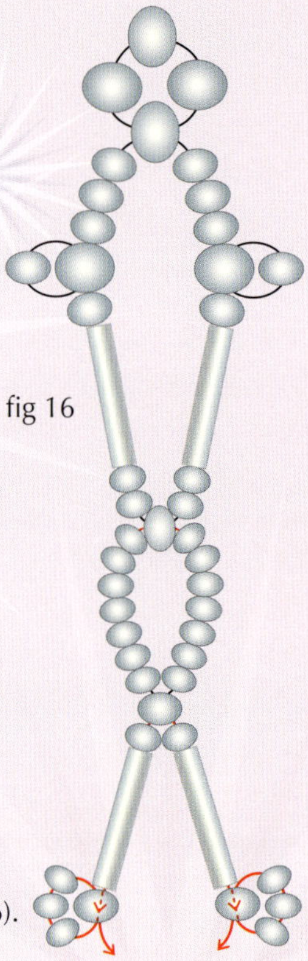

fig 16

fig 17

12 Thread 1B, 1D and 2C onto each end of the wire.
Cross the two ends of the wire in opposite directions through 1A bead to form a diamond shape (fig 14).

Thread 7C onto each end of the wire. Bring the ends of the wire together and thread them both in the same direction through 1B to form a teardrop shape (fig 15).

Thread 1C, 1D, 1B and 3C onto each end of the wire. Pass each wire end through the B bead just added in the same direction as before to make a strap of C beads to the outer edge of the point (fig 16).

Referring to fig 17 throughout -
Thread 3C onto each end of the wire. Bring the the ends of the wire together and thread them both in the same direction through 1B.
Thread 1C onto each end of the wire and cross the wire ends in opposite directions through1B.
Thread 1B onto each wire end and cross in opposite directions through 1C (fig 17).

Pull the wire ends tight to make this last group of beads firm.

Pass the ends of the wire through the previous B beads (as fig 11) and trim as close as you can. See the Extra Info box on page 15 for an alternative method for making your work neat.

You have completed the first star point on the large star.

13 Examine the cube at the base of the point. You need to make three more points around this face of the cube.
Cut 30cm of 0.4mm wire and thread it through the next A bead around the face of the cube to give you two ends of the same length.

Referring to fig 12 throughout, thread 3B and 1A onto each wire end. Locate the B bead link, added in fig 6, to the previous star point. Working with the side of the wire adjacent to the last point, pass through this link B bead towards the central cube. Now pass the wire end through the A bead on the new point (fig 12). Pull on the wire to bring the two points together through the B bead.

Thread 1B onto the other end of the wire and pass through the A bead on that side once more, to create a new link B bead (fig 12).

Repeat step 12 to complete the star point.

14 Repeat steps 13 and 12 to make a third star point attached to the third side of the cube face.

Start the last point of this cube face along the fourth side with 3B and 1A on each end of the wire - the B bead links are already in place attached to the first and third points. Make the links as before to close up the set and complete this star point following step 12.

15 You will now have four points all coming from one side of the cube. As they are joined together, through the B bead links, they lift up into a four sided cup-shape from the face of the cube.

Make a similar cup-shaped set of four points from the opposite face of the cube to give you eight points so far.

Repeat steps 8, 9 and 10 using 30cm lengths of wire and the bead sequences as in step 12 to complete twelve star points in total.

16 Adding Extra Star Points - Examine the cube of A beads at the centre of the star.

Each cube face has a central hole which lines up with the central hole on the opposite cube face.

The stiffer 0.8mm wire will thread through these holes to support the final six star points.

fig 18

Cut 10cm of 0.8mm wire and make a 3mm loop at one end with your round-nosed pliers.

Thread on 1C, 1G, 2C, 1F, 1C, 1B and 1E.

Pass the unlooped end of the wire though the central hole on one face of the cube and out through the opposite hole.

Thread on 1E, 1B, 1C, 1F, 2C, 1G and 1C and push the beads up snugly to the cube at the centre of the star.

Trim the excess 0.8mm wire to 6-8mm from the last bead and roll a loop to secure the work (fig 18). You have added two more points to the star.

17 Repeat step 16 to make two more points from each of the remaining two pairs of opposite faces on the cube (six additional points in total).

18 To Complete the Star - Straighten out all of the 0.4mm star points so that each point is flat and in one plane (as fig 17). Now twist the end sections added in figs 16 and 17 through 90° on the same axis (see photos) - this adds six more planes of decoration to the design creating a more pleasing effect.

Suspend the completed star from a loop of monofilament thread.

Constellation Stars Inspiration

Making the Large Constellation Star just a bit bigger creates this stunning tree-topper

Galaxy Tree Topper

Crystal beads have been added for extra sparkle, but this also adds extra weight, so for stability and strength the twelve woven arms are made with 0.5mm soft wire. The extra star points are made with 1.2mm half-hard wire.

The end of the last 1.2mm point forms into a spiral socket to slip over the top-most branch of the tree.

Right - Finally to stabilise the star, a long length of 0.5mm wire is used to link the woven arms together forming a beaded cage 3cm from the central A bead cube.

Frosted Fir Tree

You Will Need

Materials

3g of size 10/0 frosted transparent green seed beads A
2g of size 10/0 ceylon white beads B
2g of size 10/0 silver lined crystal seed beads C
1.5g of size 3 silver lined bronze bugle beads D
Three 4mm green fire polished faceted beads E
One 4mm crystal AB fire polished faceted bead F
One gold plated 50mm headpin
20cm of 0.6mm gold plated half-hard wire
2m of 0.2mm gold plated soft wire
50cm of transparent monofilament thread
A reel of white size D beading thread

For the red tree replace -
A with frosted transparent red and B with silver lined red
C and D with silver lined gold
E with red and F with topaz

For the white tree replace -
A with frosted transparent crystal
D with silver lined crystal and E with crystal AB
and swap the wires and headpin to silver

Tools

A size 10 beading needle
A pair of scissors to trim the threads
A pair of wire cutters & a pair of round-nosed pliers

As a child there are few things more magical than waking up to see snowflakes drifting past the window. As an adult, although we may grumble a little about the inconveniences of the weather, a fresh fall of snow brings a touch of awe and wonder at the beauty it creates; turning even a humble conifer into a sparkling showstopper.

The Decoration is Made in Four Stages

The tree boughs are made in four separate layers.
The trunk is made from bugle beads.
The star is made for the top of the tree.
The tree is assembled using the 0.6mm wire and is suspended on the monofilament thread.

1 The Boughs - There are four layers of bough - all made with the same technique but with different bead counts. You will be using 0.2mm wire - it is important that you keep this wire smooth as kinks can weaken it and cause breakage.

2 The First Layer - Cut 60cm of 0.2mm wire. Thread 5A onto the wire and hold these beads 10cm from the far end. Pass the long end of the wire through the first A bead threaded to bring the beads into a ring (fig 1).

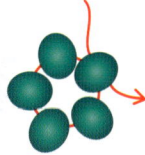
fig 1

3 Thread on 10A, 5B and 2C.

Leaving aside the last C bead threaded to anchor the strand, pass the wire back down through the other beads just added and the next A bead around the ring of 5A to make a rod of beads (fig 2).

fig 2

Do not pull the wire too tightly - you will need to get a needle in and out between the beads so leave about 1mm of play along the length.

Repeat around the ring to make five rods in total (fig 3).

fig 3

4 The two ends of the wire will now be adjacent to one another - twist them together twice close to the ring of 5A. Be careful not to block the holes in the beads of the ring.

Do not trim yet.

5 Prepare the needle with 1.5m of single thread and tie a keeper bead 15cm from the end.

Pass the needle up through one of the rods of beads to emerge just before the last B bead of the sequence. Pull the thread through so the keeper bead pulls up to the ring end of the rod. The fronds of the boughs are added on this thread.

6 Thread on 1C. Pass the needle back through the second B bead from the end of the bough (fig 4).

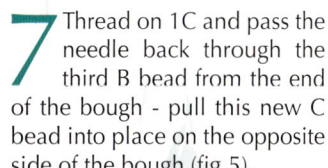
fig 4

7 Thread on 1C and pass the needle back through the third B bead from the end of the bough - pull this new C bead into place on the opposite side of the bough (fig 5).

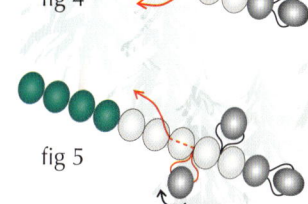
fig 5

8 Thread on 1B and 1C. Pass the needle back down the new B bead to bring the C bead into an anchor.

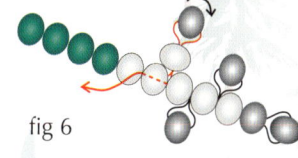
fig 6

Pass back through the fourth B bead from the end of the bough positioning the new frond on the opposite side of the bough (fig 6).

Extra Info....

The 0.2mm wire will just fit through the eye of a size 10 beading needle. If you like to use a needle it can make steps 2 to 4 a bit faster and very satisfying to do.

Make sure the end of the wire is trimmed very crisply and thread just the first 6-8mm of the wire through the eye. As you work, the wire will become fatigued and it may break at the eye, but all you need to do is rethread the end and continue as before.

9 Referring to fig 7 you can see the bead sequences for the remaining fronds on the bough. The next frond is made with 1B and 1C. Follow the sequence in fig 7 until you have made the last frond between the third and fourth A beads of the bough.

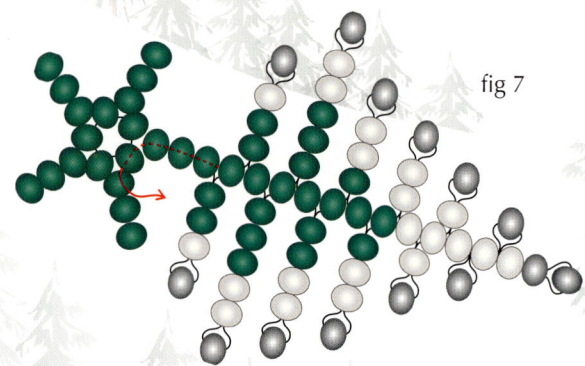
fig 7

10 Pass the needle down through the remaining 3A of the bough and the next A bead around the ring at the base of the bough (as shown in fig 7).

You are now in the correct position to pass the needle up towards the tip of the next bough along.

Work this bough as for the first. Repeat until all five boughs are complete.

11 Pass the needle through the 5A beads of the central ring. Pull the thread quite tightly to bring the beads of the ring as close together as possible.

Finish off the thread end neatly and securely. Remove the keeper bead and finish off this end in a similar fashion.

Return to the wire ends. Separate the ends and thread them through an adjacent bead or two before trimming neatly.

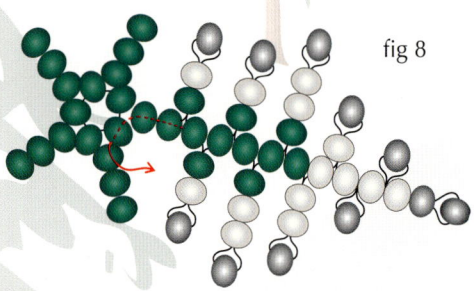
fig 8

12 The Second Layer - Using 50cm of 0.2mm wire start as for the first layer with a ring of 5A. This time the boughs need to be slightly shorter.

Make five boughs as before using the 0.2mm wire with 7A, 4B and 2C.

Fig 8 shows the bead sequence for the frond. Following this diagram complete each bough as before using your needle and thread.

Finish off the thread and the wire ends as before.

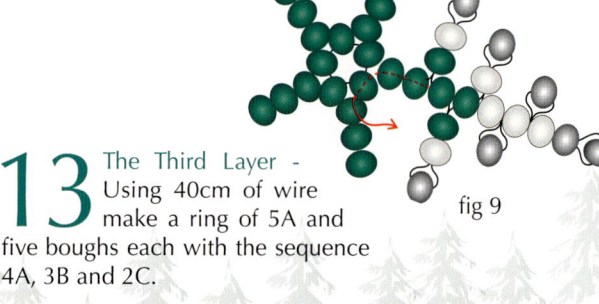
fig 9

13 The Third Layer - Using 40cm of wire make a ring of 5A and five boughs each with the sequence 4A, 3B and 2C.

Fig 9 shows the beads sequences for the fronds to be added to each bough with needle and thread.

Finish off the thread and the wire ends as before.

14 The Fourth Layer - Using 30cm of wire make a ring of 5A and five boughs each with the sequence 2A, 2B and 2C.

Fig 10 shows the bead sequences for the fronds to be added to each bough with needle and thread.

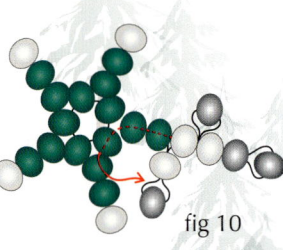
fig 10

Finish off the thread and the wire ends as before.

Set the four layers aside for the moment.

15 The Trunk - This is made from three identical sections which stack one on top of the other.

fig 11

Cut 15cm of 0.2mm wire. Thread 2D onto the wire and hold 5cm from the far end. Pass the long end of the wire through the first D bead threaded to bring the two beads parallel to one another.
Pass the long end back through the second D bead (fig 11).

fig 12

16 Thread on 1D and pass the wire back up the previous D bead and down the new bead to bring it up parallel to the other beads (fig 12).

Repeat step 16 twice to make a 5D length. Curve the block of 5D into a tube so that the first D bead is touching the fifth D bead.

Link the first and fifth D beads together by passing the wire up and down through these two beads until the join is firm. Trim the two ends of the wire as close as you can to the beads.

Repeat to make two more 5D bead tubes.

17 The trunk is assembled onto a headpin. Thread on 1A, 1D bead tube (up through the central hole), 1A, 1D bead tube, 1A, 1D bead tube and 1A.

Trim the excess headpin length down to 8mm and turn a loop. Set aside for the moment.

18 The Star - Prepare the needle with 75cm of thread and tie a keeper bead 15cm from the end.

fig 13

fig 14

Thread on 1F and 4C. Pass the needle through the F bead a second time to bring the C beads into a strap around the F bead (fig 13).

Thread on 4C and pass through the F bead again to make a second strap to the other side of the F bead (fig 14).

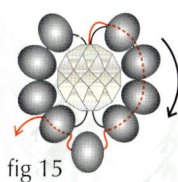

fig 15

19 Pass the needle through the 4C beads to one side of the F bead and thread on 1C. Pass the needle through the first C bead of the other strap to bring the new bead into the gap (fig 15).

Pass the needle through the following 3C and thread on 1C. Pass the needle through the following C bead of the other strap to bring this new bead into the gap at this end of the F bead (fig 16).

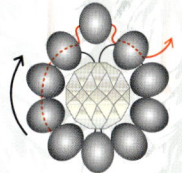

fig 16

20 Thread on 1C. Pass the needle through the C bead on the strap that the needle emerged from to square stitch the new C bead to the C bead on the strap. Pass the needle through the next 2C of the strap (fig 17).

fig 17

fig 18

Thread on 1C and repeat making a square stitch between the new C bead and the C bead on the strap. Pass the needle through the next 2C around the F bead.

You have now added two points on the star. Add a third point at the current needle position; one 2C further around the F bead and a final one 2C further on from that (fig 18).

Finish off both thread ends neatly and securely within the C beads around the central F bead - do not block the hole in the F bead with knots or thread ends.

21 Assembling the Tree - The boughs of the tree are linked together, through the central rings using 0.6mm wire.

Make a 4mm diameter loop at the end of the 0.6mm wire.

Join this loop onto the loop at the top of the trunk made in step 17. Thread the wire up through the 5A ring on the first layer of boughs - if the loop pulls through the 5A ring, go back and make a bigger loop, so that it cannot pull through.

22 Thread on 1E. Trim the excess wire to 8mm above the bead and make a loop.

As before, make a 4mm diameter loop on the end of the piece of 0.6mm wire. Join this loop to the loop above the E bead. Thread on the second layer and check that the loop is not pulling through. Thread on an E bead. Trim to 8mm and loop the wire above the E bead.

Make a loop at the end of the 0.6mm wire and link onto the loop above the E bead. Thread on the third layer and 1E; trim to 8mm and loop the wire.

Make a 4mm loop at the end of the 0.6mm wire and thread on the fourth layer and 5A.

Pass the end of the wire up through the hole in the F bead at the centre of the prepared star - you will have to push the C beads surrounding the F bead slightly to the side so the wire can pass. Push the star down to the top of the A beads. Trim the wire above the star to 8mm and make a loop.

Suspend the completed tree from a loop made from the monofilament thread.

fig 19

23 Shape the wire-threaded boughs of each layer into a gentle arch as shown in fig 19 to complete the tree.

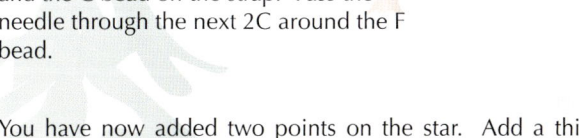

Sweetheart Bauble

You Will Need

Materials

For the Frosted Silver Bauble
One 40mm frosted silver glass bauble
10g of size 10/0 silver lined crystal seed beads A
5g of size 6/0 frost silver lined crystal seed beads B
3g of size 10/0 metallic silver colour seed beads C
One 8mm crystal AB fire polished faceted bead D
A reel of white size D beading thread

For the Frosted Lilac Bauble
One 40mm frosted lilac glass bauble
10g of size 10/0 silver lined pale tanzanite seed beads A
5g of size 6/0 ceylon white seed beads B
3g of size 10/0 transparent crystal AB seed beads C
One 8mm crystal AB fire polished faceted bead D
A reel of white size D beading thread

Tools

A size 10 beading needle
A pair of scissors to trim the threads

This simply sweet bauble design is quite quick to make and looks gorgeous with red bows too. You could also ring the changes by adding heart-shaped beads instead of the mistletoe leaves or a series of crystal drops. If you want a larger decoration see the Mistletoe Kisses Bauble on page 48.

The Decoration is Made in Four Stages

A foundation row around the neck of the bauble is made.
The strands of mistletoe and the bow loops are added.
The swags and the bow tails connect the strands together.
The hanging loop is added to the top of the bauble.

1 The Foundation Row - Prepare the needle with 1.5m of single thread with a keeper bead 15cm from the end.

Thread on four repeats of 1B and 6A. Pass the needle through the first B bead to bring the beads into a ring (fig 1).

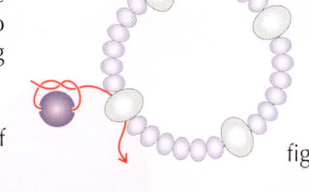
fig 1

Drop this ring over the top of the bauble (fig 2).

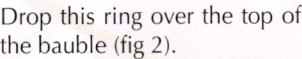
fig 2

The ring needs to fit the neck of the bauble snugly so you may need to adjust the bead count.

If you need to adjust the bead count add or subtract the same number of A beads from each quarter to keep the B beads equally spaced around the neck.

Pass the needle through the beads of the ring again to make it firmer. Finish with the needle emerging from a B bead (as fig 2).

2 The Mistletoe Strands and Bow Loops - Thread on 10A, 1C and 40A for the main stem.

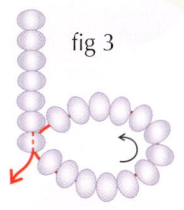
fig 3

3 Thread on 13A. Pass the needle through the last A bead of the main stem in the same direction as before - try to keep the stem bead vertical at the end of the strand (fig 3).

Thread on 13A and pass through the A bead at the end of the main stem (fig 4).

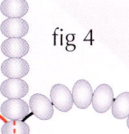
fig 4

fig 5

fig 6

4 Pass the needle through the first and last A beads of the first loop and the last A bead of the main stem in the same direction as before (fig 5).

Repeat with the first and last beads of the second loop (fig 6).

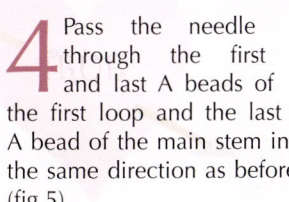
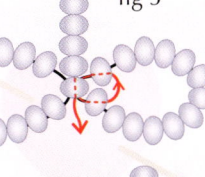

fig 7

5 Referring to fig 7 pass the needle down through the first bead of the first loop, up the first bead of the second loop and through the bottom A bead of the main stem in the opposite direction (fig 7).

The stitches in steps 4 and 5 pinch the loops into a more narrow shape and provide a support for the berry beads.

6 Thread on 1B and pass the needle up through the last A bead of the main stem (fig 8).

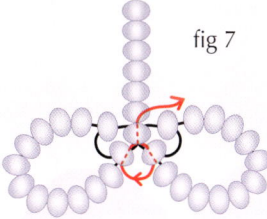

fig 8
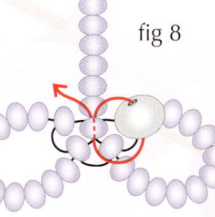

fig 9
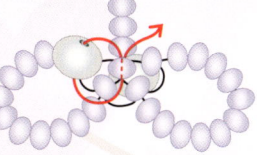

Flip the work over and add 1B bead to this side of the bottom A bead of the main stem (fig 9).

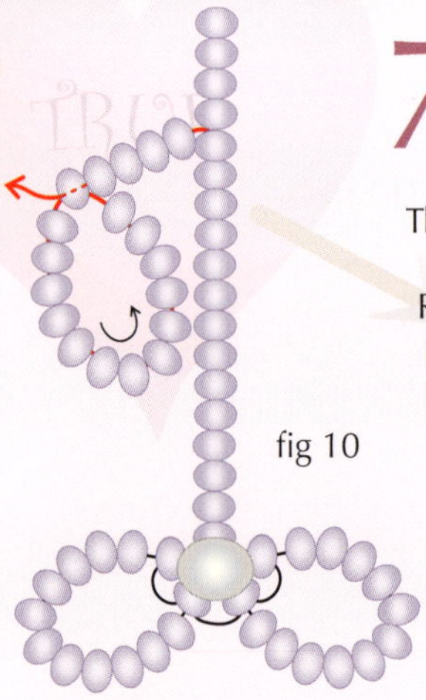

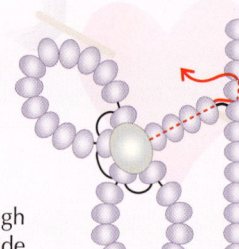

7 Pass the needle up through the following 14A beads of the main stem.

Thread on 5A for the first side stem.

Repeat steps 3 to 6 to complete a new set of leaves with attached berries (see figs 10 and 11).

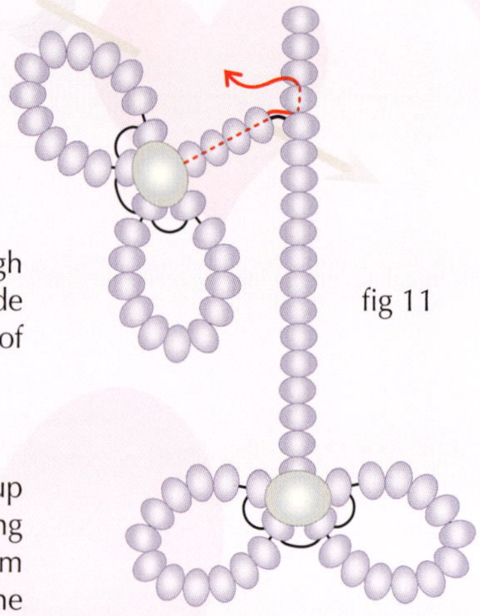

fig 10

Pass the needle up through the following 4A of the side stem and the first A bead of the main stem (fig 11).

fig 11

8 Pass the needle up through the following 11A beads of the stem and thread on 5A for the second side stem.

Repeat steps 3 to 6 to make the third set of leaves with attached berries.

Pass the needle up to the top of the side stem and through the following 14A beads of the main stem and the following 1C.

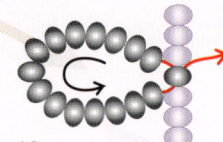

fig 12

9 Thread on 15C.

Pass the needle up through the C bead on the main stem to make a bow loop (fig 12).

Referring to fig 13 thread on 15C and pass the needle up through the C bead on the main stem. Pass up through the following 8A and thread on 2A.

Pass the needle through the B bead on the foundation row in the same direction as before (fig 13).

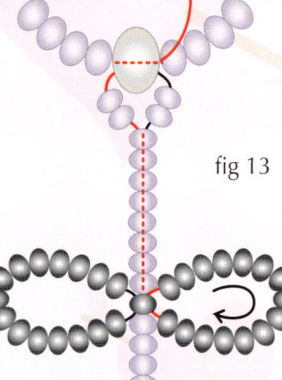

fig 13

10 Pass the needle through the following A beads of the neck ring to emerge from the next B bead around the ring.

Repeat steps 2 to 10 three more times to add mistletoe strands and bow loops to each of the four B beads around the neck of the bauble.

11 **The Swags & Bow Tails** - If necessary pass the needle though the beads of the neck ring to emerge from the first B bead.

Referring to fig 14 pass the needle down through the first 10A and 1C of the main stem and the following 2C of the lower edge of the first bow loop (fig 14).

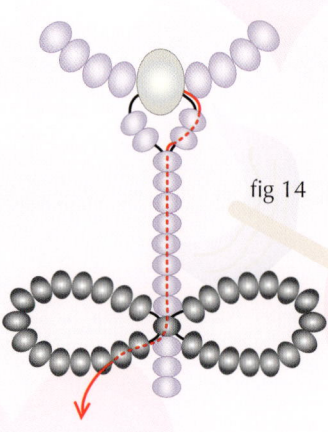

fig 14

12 Thread on 7C, 4A, 1B, 2A, 1B, 2A, 1B, 4A and 7C.

Locate the next set of bow loops around the bauble - the swag now attaches to this set of bow loops.

Referring to fig 15 pass the needle through the last 2C beads of the second bow loop, up through the C bead on the main stem and the first 2C of the first bow loop (fig 15).

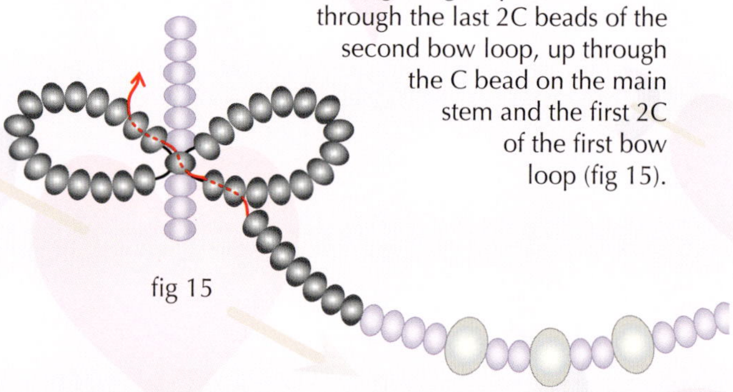

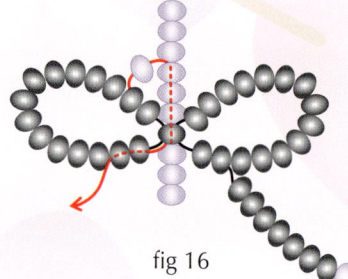

fig 15

13 Thread on 1A.

Referring to fig 16 pass the needle down the 3A main stem beads above the bow, the C bead on the main stem and the following 2C of the lower edge of the first bow loop (fig 16).

fig 16

The needle is now in the correct place to start the next swag.

Repeat steps 12 and 13 three times to complete the first row of swags. The needle should finish as in fig 16.

14 Pass the needle through the first 7C of the following swag. *Thread on 10A, 1B, 2A, 1B, 2A, 1B and 10A for the first of the longer swags.

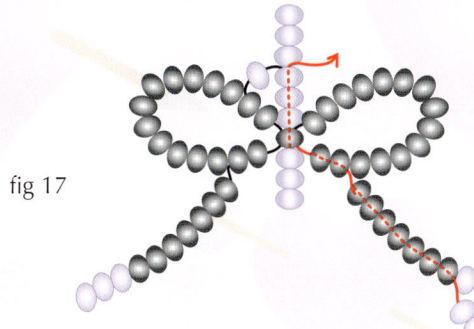

fig 17

15 Referring to fig 17 pass the needle up through the adjacent 7C of the next bow around the bauble, the following 2C of the bow loop, the C bead on the main stem and the following and 3A.

Thread on 1A.

Referring to fig 18 pass the needle down through the 2C beads of the top of the bow loop, the following C bead of the main stem, 2C of the opposite bow loop and 7C beads of the next swag (fig 18).

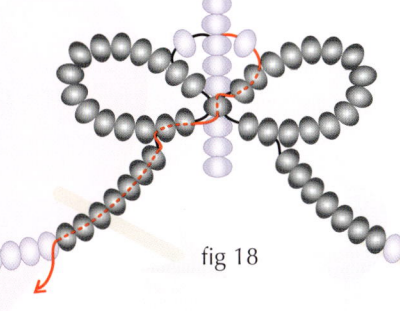

fig 18

The needle is now in the correct position to make the next swag.

16 Repeat from the * in step 14 to the end of step 15 twice to complete two more swags.

Repeat from the * in step 14 to fig 17.

This final bow is missing one of the single A beads between the main stem and the top of the bow loops.

17 Thread on 1A. Pass the needle down through the 2C beads of the unattached adjacent bow loop and through the following C bead on the main stem (refer to fig 18) to complete the bow.

Finish off this thread end and all remaining thread ends neatly and securely.

18 **The Hanging Loop -** Prepare the needle as in step 1 and thread on 1D and 4A to make a short length of main stem.

Repeat step 3 to make two 13A bead loops on each side of the end of the stem (fig 19).

Thread on 1A and pass the needle through the loop at the top of the bauble.

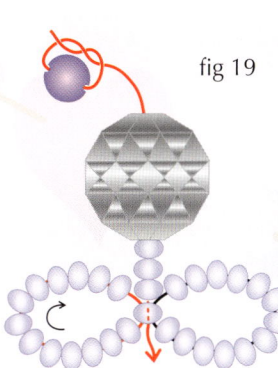

fig 19

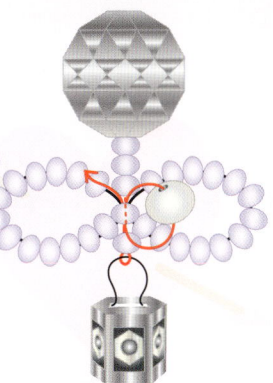

fig 20

19 Pass the needle back up through the 1A just added and the following 1A (see fig 20). Thread on 1B and pass through the last A bead again to pull the berry bead into place as before (fig 20).

Repeat to add a B bead berry to the other side of the leaf loops as before.

Pass the needle up through the following 3A and 1D.

20 Thread on 1A, 1B, 1A, 3C and 1A. Thread on 50A for the loop and pass the needle back down the last A bead and the following 1C of the previous sequence.

Thread on 1C and pass down through the first C bead threaded to draw the new C bead alongside the middle C bead of the 3C (fig 21).

21 The connection to the bauble and the 50A loop both need to be strengthened.

Pass the needle down through the beads to the bauble loop, through the loop and back up through the first A bead. Add 2B berries to this A bead as before and pass back up to the bottom of the main hanging loop.

Pass through the 50A of the hanging loop and back down the main stem. If possible repeat (without adding more berries) to make the connection stronger.

Finish off all remaining thread ends neatly and securely.

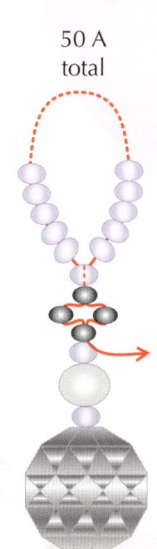

50 A total

fig 21

Paris was the centre of the artistic and literary world in the late 19th Century. Baron Haussmann's re-modelling of the city had caused hardship and heartbreak, but by then it looked truly wonderful, with elegant boulevards, river promenades and chic boutiques along the Rue de Rivoli. If you like this style take a look at the Belle Époque Bauble for yet more inspiration.

The Decoration is Made in Six Stages
A fringed rosette is made first.
This links to the next two rosettes with the first swags.
The second layer of swags is added.
The third layer of swags is added.
A fitted ring is made for the bauble neck which links to the top of the rosettes.
The hanging loop completes the decoration.

1 The Rosette - Prepare the needle with 1.5m of single thread and tie a keeper bead 15cm from the end. Thread on 1J and 7A.

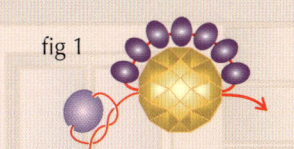
fig 1

Pass the needle through the J bead to bring the A beads into a strap to one side (fig 1).

2 Thread on 7A and pass the needle through the J bead again to make a second strap on the opposite side of the J bead (fig 2).

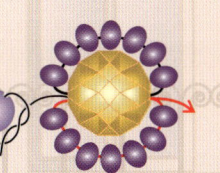
fig 2

Pass the needle through the first 2A beads of the new strap (fig 3).

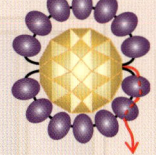
fig 3

fig 4

3 Thread on 9B, 1A, 1C, 1E, 1C, 1A, 1D, 1A, 1F, 1A and 3B.
Leaving aside the last 3B beads to anchor the strand, pass the needle back up through the last 1A bead and the following beads to emerge 1B bead from the top of the strand (fig 4).

Thread on 1B and pass through the A bead at the top of the strand and the following 1A (fig 5). This centres the strand beneath the A bead.

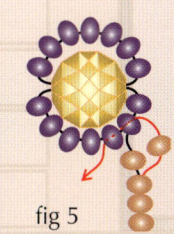
fig 5

4 Thread on 12B, 1A, 1C, 1E, 1C, 1A, 1D, 1A, 1F, 1A and 3B. As before, leave aside the last 3B beads to anchor the strand and pass back up through the beads just threaded to emerge 1B bead from the top.

fig 6

Referring to fig 6 pass the needle through the adjacent B bead at the top of the previous strand, through the A bead at the top of this strand and the following 1A.

fig 7

5 Thread on 16B, 1A, 1C, 1E, 1C, 1A, 1D, 1A, 1F, 1A and 3B. Referring to fig 7 and using the same technique complete the strand.

Repeat to make a strand as in step 4 and a strand as in step 3 (fig 7).

fig 8

6 Pass the needle through the J bead and the 7A beads of the top strap (fig 8).

7 The First Swags - Thread on 15A, 1F, 5A, 1F, 5A, 1F, 22A and 1J.

Pass the needle through the last 7A beads in the same direction as before to bring them into a strap around the J bead (fig 9).

This J bead is the central bead of the next rosette.

fig 9

8 Pass the needle through the J bead and thread on 7A. Pass the needle through the J bead again and the following 2A (fig 10).

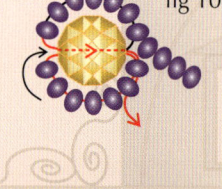
fig 10

You are now in the correct position to make the first fringe strand of this rosette.

Repeat steps 3 to 8 inclusive.
Repeat steps 3 to 6 inclusive.

9 Thread on 15A, 1F, 5A, 1F, 5A, 1F and 15A. Pass the needle through the first 6A beads of the top strap around the first J bead (fig 11). This will bring the swags and rosettes into a circle.

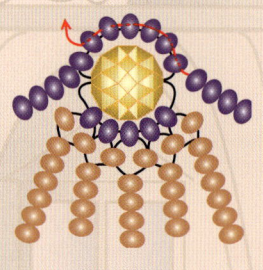
fig 11

10 Row Two Swags - Thread on 1B. Pass the needle through the last A bead passed through in the same direction and the new B bead to make a square stitch (fig 12).

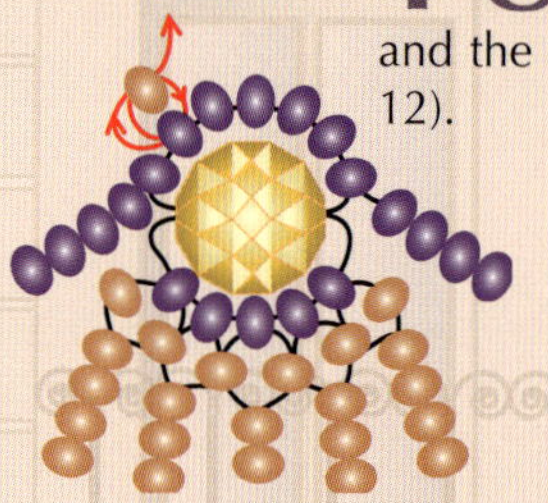

11 Repeat to add 1B to the next A bead with a square stitch (fig 13).

Thread on 2B. Pass the needle through the next 1A and back through the 2B (fig 14).

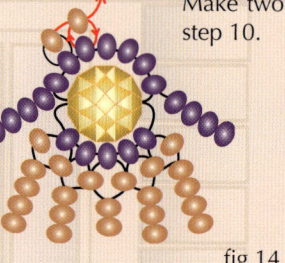
fig 12

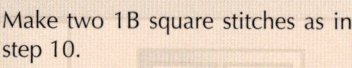

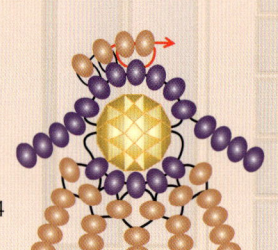
fig 13   fig 14

Make two 1B square stitches as in step 10.

12 Thread on 12B, 1G, 3B, 1G, 3B, 1G and 13B to make the first swag of the second layer.

Locate the next rosette around the work.

Pass the needle through the second A bead of the top strap on this rosette to bringing the needle through to point towards the first A bead of the strap.

Pass the needle through the last B bead threaded to complete a square stitch (fig 15).

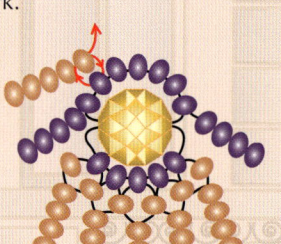
fig 15

Repeat steps 11 and 12.
Repeat step 11.
Thread on 12B, 1G, 3B, 1G, 3B, 1G and 12B.

Pass the needle through the first 5B beads added to the first rosette in steps 10, 11 and 12 to close up this layer of swags (fig 16).

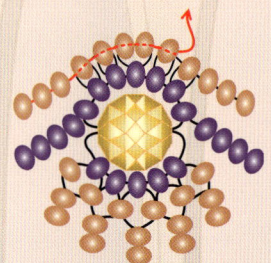
fig 16

13 Row Three Swags - Thread on 1C and square stitch this bead to the last 1B bead passed through (fig 17).

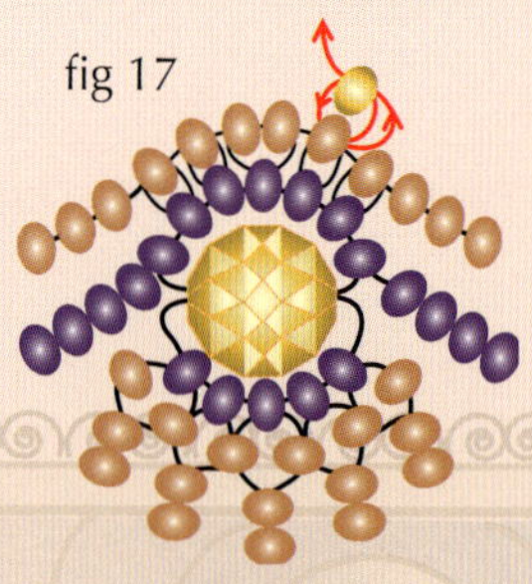

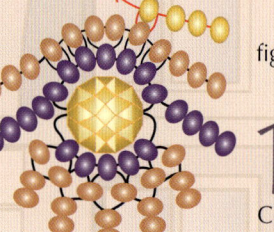
fig 17

Referring to fig 18 throughout:

Make one 1C square stitch.
Make one 2C square stitch.
Make one 1C square stitch
(5C attached to 4B in total).

Thread on 11C, 1H, 1C, 1H, 1C, 1H and 12C.

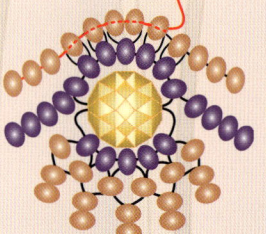
fig 18

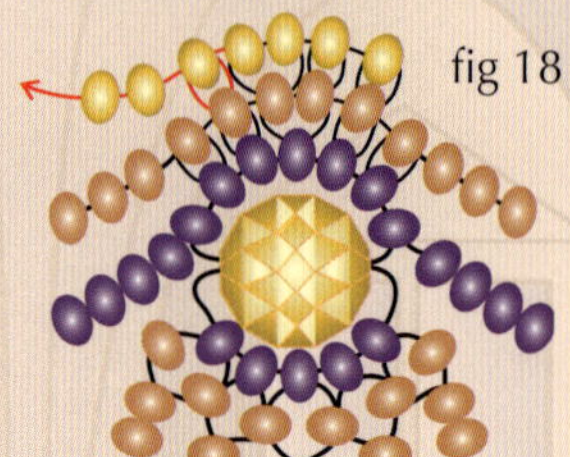

fig 19

14 As before, locate the next rosette around and square stitch the last C bead threaded to the second B bead of the rosette (fig 19).

Make a 1C stitch, a 2C stitch and a 1C stitch as in fig 18.

15 Make a swag as in step 13 and repeat step 14 to make the four square stitches.

Thread on 11C, 1H, 1C, 1H, 1C, 1H and 11C for the last swag. Pass the needle through the 4C beads on the first rosette to close up the layer.

Finish off all thread ends neatly and securely.

16 The Neck Ring - Prepare the needle as in step 1 and thread on three repeats of 1D, 1A, 1C, 4B, 1C and 1A.

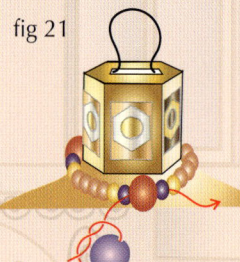
fig 20

Pass the needle through the first 1D and 1A to bring the beads into a ring (fig 20).

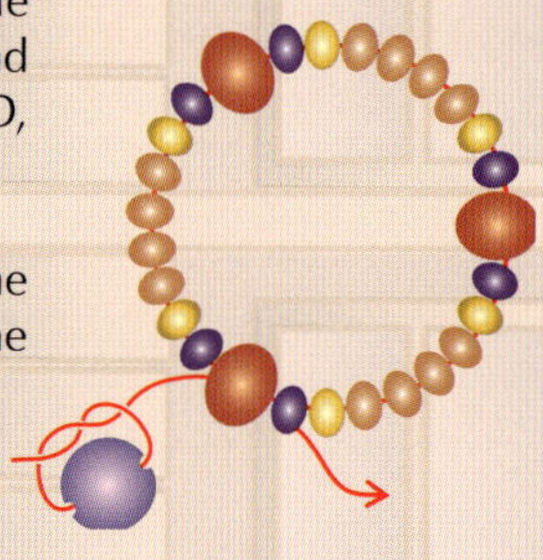

fig 21

Drop the ring over the neck of the bauble (fig 21).

The ring needs to fit quite snugly so you may need to adjust the bead count.

If you need to make an alteration, add or subtract B beads equally from the three 4B sections, to keep the 3D beads evenly spaced around the neck.

17 Pass the needle through the beads of the ring again to make it firm. Make sure the needle is emerging as in fig 21 from an A bead following a D bead.

20 The Hanging Loop - Repeat steps 1 and 2 to add two straps of A beads around a J bead.

Referring to fig 24 (which shows the J bead vertical) pass the needle to the end of the new strap and thread on 1A.

Pass the needle through the beads of the first strap and thread on 1A.

Pass the needle through the first 1A of the following strap (fig 24).

Pass the needle through the following 7A beads to emerge from the first of the single A beads just added (fig 25).

fig 24

fig 25

21 Thread on 1B, 1K, 1B, 1A and 1D. Pass the needle through the loop at the top of the bauble.

Referring to fig 26 pass the needle back up through the D bead and the four beads above it. Pass through the A bead on the ring in the same direction as before to centre the bauble beneath the J bead.

Pass the needle up and down through the connection to the bauble two more times to make it strong. Pass the needle through the following 5A beads around the J bead (fig 26).

fig 26

18 Thread on 5A, 1B, 1C, 1F, 1C and 1B.

Referring to fig 22 drape the swags around the bauble and pass the needle through the middle C bead at the top of the first rosette.

Thread on 1B and pass the needle up through the last 1C, 1F, 1C and 1B beads (fig 22).

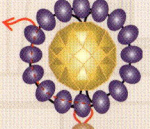

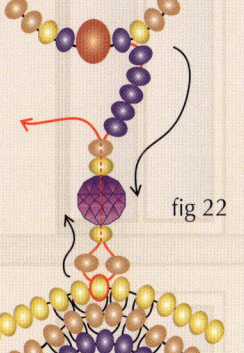

fig 22

22 Repeat steps 10 and 11 to add two 1B square stitches and one 2B square stitch to the A beads around the J bead (fig 27).

Make a 1B square stitch.
Make a 2B square stitch.
Make two 1B square stitches to give a curved line of 9B in total (see fig 28).

Pass the needle back through the 7A beads underneath the 9B beads and the first 5B beads just added (fig 28).

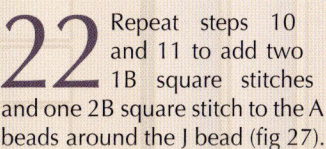

fig 27

fig 28

fig 23

19 Referring to fig 23 thread on 5A. Pass the needle through the 1A, 1D and 1A bead on the neck ring and the following beads to emerge from the last A bead of the next grouping around the bauble neck (fig 23).

Repeat steps 18 and 19 twice to complete the connections to the remaining two rosettes.

Finish off the thread ends neatly and securely.

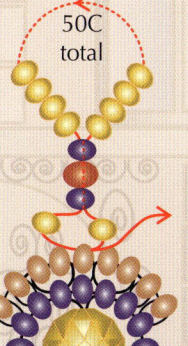

50C total

23 Thread on 1C, 1A, 1D, 1A and 50C. Pass the needle back down the last A bead threaded and the following 1D and 1A to pull the 50C up into a loop.

Thread on 1C and pass the needle through the fifth B bead above the J bead in the same direction as before (fig 29).

The loop needs to be strengthened.

Pass the needle through the link to the loop and the 50C beads twice more. Pass the needle through the last 4B beads above the J bead.

Finish off the thread ends neatly and securely.

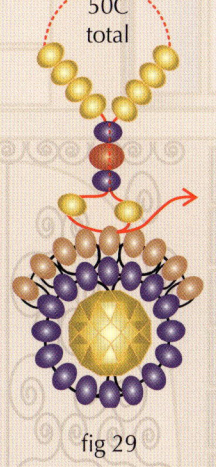

fig 29

Astor Bauble

You Will Need

Materials

One 40mm frosted pale blue glass bauble
5g of size 10/0 silver lined frosted blue seed beads A
3g of pearly pale grey Twin beads B
2.5g of size 3 silver lined crystal bugle beads C
5g of scarab blue Twin beads D
2.5g of size 10/0 silver lined crystal seed beads E
Twenty-one 6mm pale blue AB fire polished faceted beads F
Twenty 4mm crystal AB fire polished faceted beads G
Two 4mm pale blue fire polished faceted beads H
A reel of white size D beading thread

Tools

A size 10 beading needle
A pair of scissors to trim the threads

Flapper dresses with glistening beaded fringes, the chink-chink of cocktail glasses and a smokey haze suffused the fabulous parties of the new intellectuals and the social élite as they mingled with the Astors at their grand parties in the 20's & 30's. Taking a cue from those gorgeous drop-waisted dresses this bauble design has an understated elegance and looks stunning in all colourways.

The Decoration is Made in Six Stages

First you make the foundation row.
The second row creates four six-petal flower motifs.
Four straps to support the flower swags are made next.
The flower swags are created to link up the straps.
The fringing is added to the flower swags.
The hanging loop completes the decoration.

1 The Foundation Row - Prepare the needle with 1.8m of single thread and tie a keeper bead 15cm from the end.

Thread on twelve repeats of 1A and 1B. Drape the beads around the neck of the bauble. You need the 12B beads to be evenly distributed around the neck with the ring fitting snugly and the thread not showing between the beads.

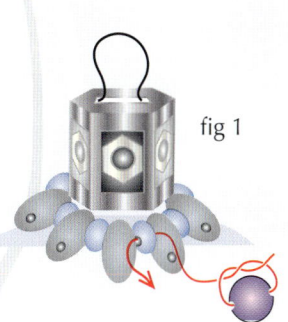

fig 1

If it is too tight try four repeats of 1A, 1B, 2A, 1B, 2A, 1B or four repeats of 1A, 1B, 3A, 1B, 3A, 1B. If you use one of these longer repeats you will need to make a very small adjustment in step 5 but the remainder of the beading will follow the same pattern.

2 Pass the needle through the first A bead to draw the beads into a circle around the base of the bauble neck (fig 1). Pass the needle through the same holes around the ring once more to make it a little more firm. Make sure the needle is emerging as fig 1 before moving on.

3 Following fig 2 pass the needle through the top hole of the following B bead; turn the needle and pass it through the bottom hole of the same B bead.

The needle is now in the correct position to start the second row.

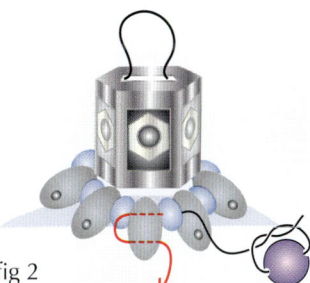

fig 2

Extra Info....

Twin beads are used in this design to make links and flower motifs. It is very important to pass in the right direction through the correct hole in the Twin beads. The figs show this clearly but if you have not used Twin beads before, read through the 'Twin Beads' information on page 9.

4 The Six-Petal Flower Motifs - Thread on 1B. Referring to fig 3 pass the needle through the bottom hole on the next B bead around the ring and thread on 10A and 1B. Pass the needle through the bottom hole on the new B bead. This B bead is the first petal on a flower motif

Thread on 5B. Following fig 4 pass the needle through the bottom hole on the first B bead of the flower motif in the same direction as before and the top hole on the same B bead.

Thread on 10A and pass the needle through the bottom hole on the second B bead around the top ring (fig 5).

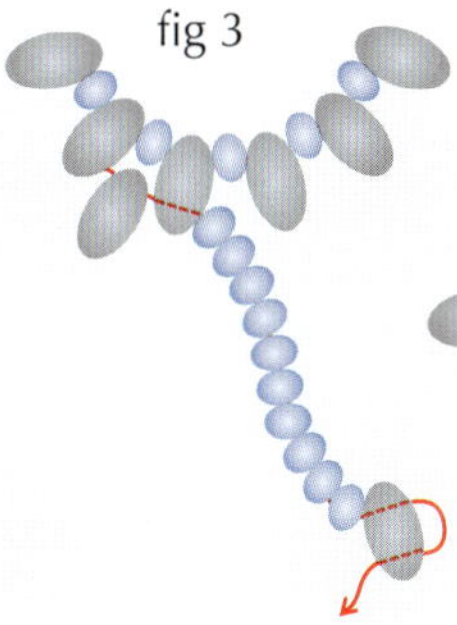

fig 3

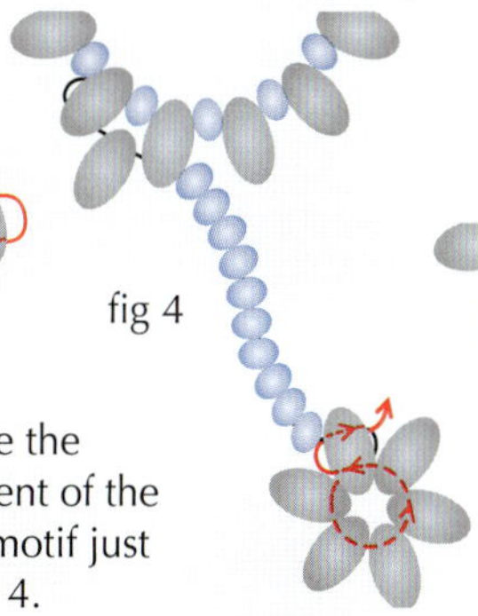

fig 4

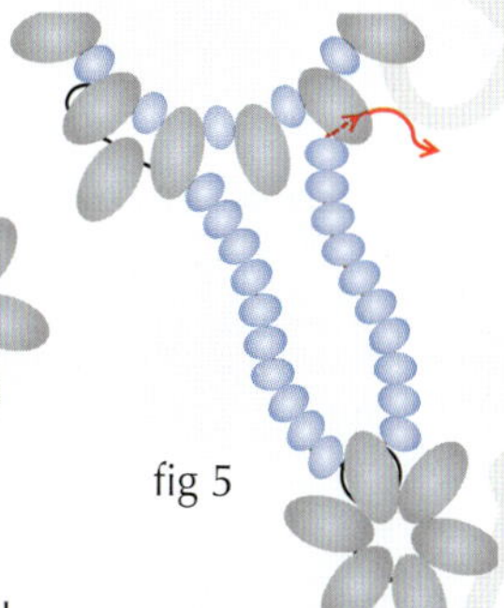

5 Examine the placement of the flower motif just made in step 4.

fig 5

If you have added extra A beads to the top ring the two straps that connect the flower to the top ring will be slightly further apart than shown in fig 5.

The flower motif will thus be slightly too high on the bauble surface. Ideally the centre of the flower needs to sit just above the equator of the bauble - if your flower is too high you will need to add 1A or 2A to the 10A straps.

If you need to make the adjustment remove the needle from the thread and unpick the motif carefully. Reattach the needle and make the motif again with straps of 11A, 12A or 13A so the flower sits in the correct place on the bauble. You will need to repeat this adjusted count on the remainder of this row but the rest of the pattern will be unaffected by the changes made.

6 Repeat step 4 three more times to add four single B beads and to complete four flower motifs in total. You may find that the straps supporting the flower motifs tend to cross over - it will depend on the tension in your thread - you will be able to arrange them as you prefer once the completed bauble is displayed.

Referring to fig 6 pass the needle through the top hole of the next B bead, turn the needle and pass through the bottom hole of the same bead (this is the first B bead added in fig 3).

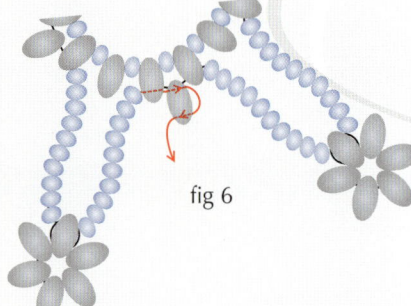

fig 6

The first strap to support the flower swags will hang from this position.

7 The Swag Supports - Thread on 6A, 1C, 1A, 2B, 1D and 1B. Referring to fig 10 pass the needle through the second hole in the first B bead just threaded to draw the three previous beads into a picot (fig 7) - make sure you have passed through the B bead in the correct direction so that it sits horizontally above the picot (see fig 7).

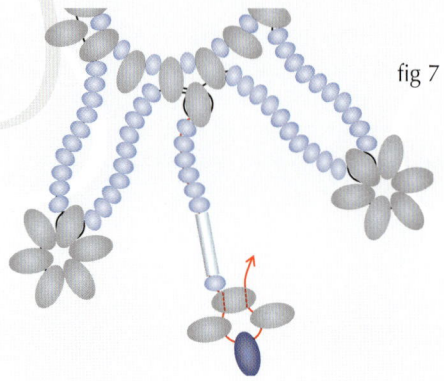

fig 7

8 Thread on 1A, 1C and 6A. Referring to fig 8 pass the needle through the bottom hole of the B bead of the previous row to complete the support strap - note how the support strap hangs from either side of the B bead.

The needle now needs to be repositioned for the next strap.

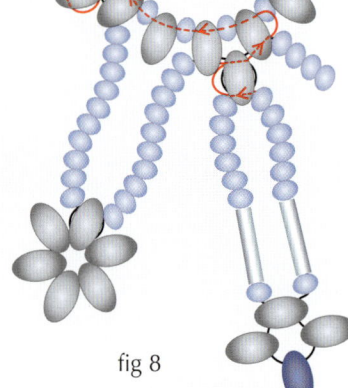

Referring to fig 8 pass the needle through the top hole of this B bead and the bottom hole of the following 1B.

Pass through the top hole of this B bead and the following eight beads of the top ring to emerge from the top hole of the fifth B bead around the ring.

fig 8

Pass the needle through the bottom hole of this B bead, the top hole of the following B bead and out through the bottom hole on the same B ready to make the next support strap (fig 8).

Repeat steps 7 and 8 three more times to complete four straps in total. The needle should be emerging from the B bead at the top of the first strap when you have completed the repeats.

9 Pass the needle down through the beads of the first strap as shown in fig 9 to emerge from the bottom hole of the D bead - this is the correct position to begin the flower swags.

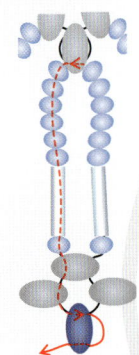

fig 9

32

10 **The Flower Swags** - Thread on 3D. Pass the needle through the bottom hole of the D bead at the bottom of the swag support in the same direction as before to pull the 3D beads up into a picot.

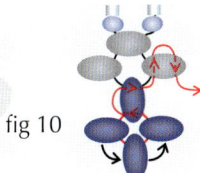
fig 10

Pass the needle through the top hole on this D bead, up through the adjacent hole on the following B bead and down the other hole on this B bead (fig 10).

You will notice that the 3D beads just added have completed a four-petal flower motif with the D bead from the bottom of the swag support. The remaining flowers on the swag will all have four petals as well.

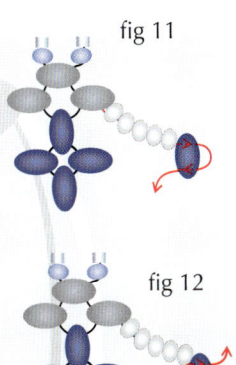
fig 11

fig 12

11 Thread on 5E and 1D. Pass the needle through the second hole on this last D bead (fig 11).

Thread on 3D. Pass the needle through the bottom hole on the first D bead of this motif to draw up the four-petal motif and pass the needle through the top hole on the same D bead (fig 12).

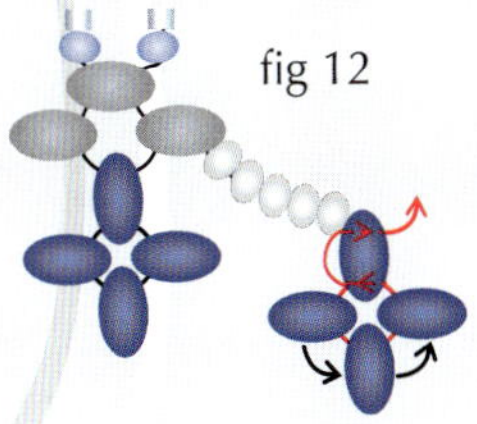

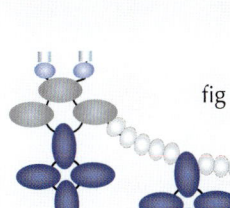
fig 13

12 Thread on 5E and 1D. Pass the needle through the second hole on the D bead (fig 13).

As before thread on 3D and pass the needle through the bottom hole on the first D bead to draw up the flower motif. Pass the needle through the top hole on this D bead (fig 14).

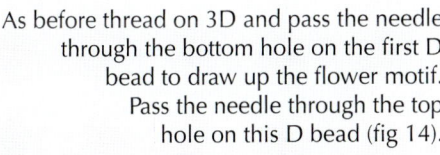

Repeat step 12 one more time to create a third flower motif hanging from the E bead string.

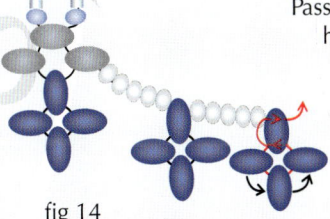
fig 14

13 Thread on 5E. Locate the next swag support around the bauble.

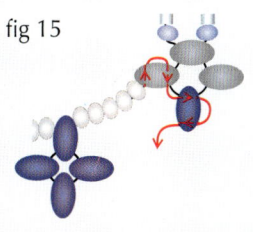
fig 15

Following fig 15 pass the needle up through the outer hole on the closest B bead on this support.

Pass down through the second hole in this B bead, the following top hole on the D bead and the bottom hole in the D bead (fig 15). The needle is now in the same position as fig 9 on the new swag support.

Repeat steps 10 to 13 three times to complete a row of flowers which link together the four swag supports.

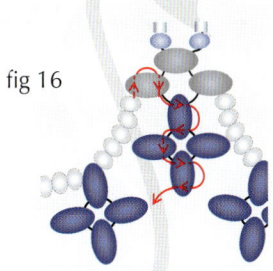
fig 16

14 Referring to fig 16 reposition the needle through the D beads of the first four-petal flower motif to emerge from the bottom hole of the lowest D bead.

The lower edges of the four-petal flowers are now linked together to complete the swags.

15 Referring to fig 17 thread on 1E.

Pass the needle down through the outer hole on the adjacent side petal of the closest flower motif.

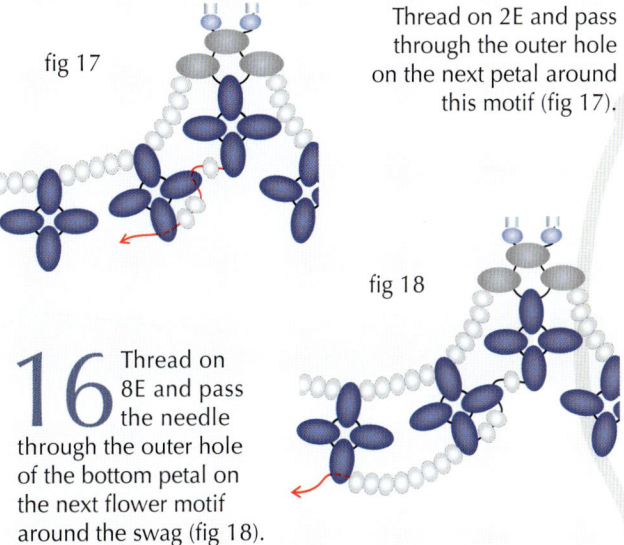
fig 17

Thread on 2E and pass through the outer hole on the next petal around this motif (fig 17).

fig 18

16 Thread on 8E and pass the needle through the outer hole of the bottom petal on the next flower motif around the swag (fig 18).

Repeat this step once more to make a link to the next flower motif.

17 Referring to fig 19 thread on 2E.

Pass the needle through the outer hole on the next D bead of this flower motif.

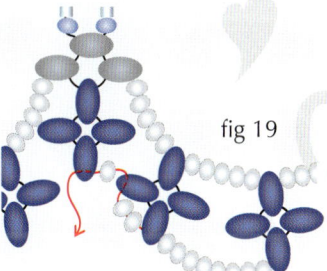
fig 19

Thread on 1E and pass though the outer hole on the bottom D bead of the next swag support (fig 19).

Repeat steps 15 to 17 to complete the remaining three swags.

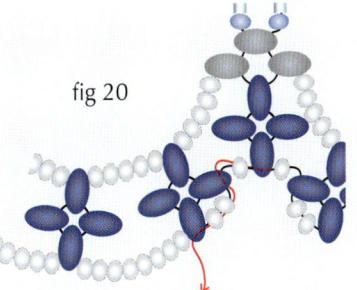
fig 20

Pass the needle through the following 1E, 1D, 2E and 1D beads of the lower row of the swags just completed (fig 20).

The first fringe strand will hang from this position.

18 The Fringe Strands - Thread on 13A, 1E, 1A, 1C, 1A, 1E, 1A, 1G, 1A, 1F, 1A, 1E, 1D, 1E, 1D, 1E, 1D and 1E.

Pass the needle up through the last 1A bead and the following 1F to pull the bottom seven beads into a modified picot (fig 21).

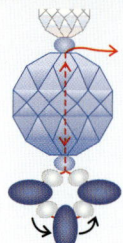

fig 21

19 Pass the needle up through the remaining beads of the strand to emerge from the top A bead.

Pass the needle through the bottom hole in the D bead in the same direction as before to centre the strand beneath the D bead (see fig 22).

Pass the needle through the following 5E beads (fig 22).

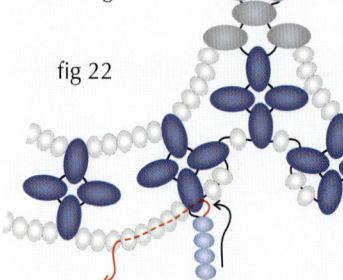

fig 22

Thread on 15A, 1E, 1A, 1C, 1A, 1E, 1A, 1G, 1A, 1F, 1A, 1E, 1D, 1E, 1D, 1E, 1D and 1E.

Make the modified picot at the bottom of the strand as in fig 21.

20 Pass the needle back up through the remaining beads of the strand bringing the needle through to emerge 1A bead before the top of the strand.

Thread on 1A.

Pass the needle through the E bead on the swag where you started this fringe strand in the same direction as before to centre the strand beneath this E bead (see fig 23).

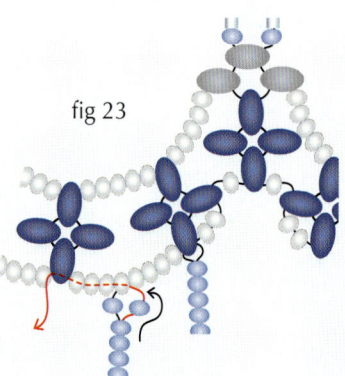

fig 23

Pass the needle through the following 3E and 1D (fig 23).

21 Make a new fringe strand from this position with 21A, 1E, 1A, 1C, 1A, 1E, 1A, 1G, 1A, 1F, 1A, 1E, 1D, 1E, 1D, 1E, 1D and 1E.

Pass the needle right to the top of the fringe strand and through the hole in the D bead to centre the strand beneath the bead as in fig 22.

22 Pass the needle through the following 4E beads and make a 15A, 1E, 1A, 1C, 1A, 1E, 1A, 1G, 1A, 1F, 1A, 1E, 1D, 1E, 1D, 1E, 1D and 1E strand as before. Do not forget to bring the needle out 1A bead before the top of the strand so you can add the extra A bead as in fig 23.

Pass the needle through the E beads of the swag to emerge from the D bead at the bottom of the third flower motif.

Make a fringe strand from here with 13A, 1E, 1A, 1C, 1A, 1E, 1A, 1G, 1A, 1F, 1A, 1E, 1D, 1E, 1D, 1E, 1D and 1E to match the first fringe strand.

Pass the needle through the E and D beads of the lower swag edge to emerge from the bottom D bead of the first flower motif on the next swag (as fig 20) and repeat to make a matching set of fringe strands.

Repeat to complete the fringe stranding on the remaining two swags.

Finish off the thread end neatly and securely. Remove any remaining keeper beads and finish off these ends in a similar fashion.

23 The Hanging Loop - Prepare the needle with 1.2m of single thread and tie a keeper bead 15cm from the end.

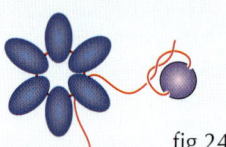 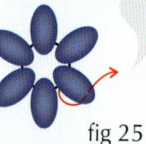

fig 24 fig 25

Thread on 6D. Pass the needle through the same hole on the first 1D bead in the same direction to draw up the beads into a six-petal flower motif (fig 24). Pass the needle through the outer hole of the same D bead (fig 25).

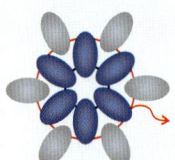

fig 26

24 Thread on 1B and pass through the outer hole on the next D bead around the flower.

Repeat to add 1B bead into each gap (fig 26).

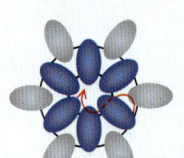

fig 27

The needle will be emerging from a D bead. Pass the needle through the inner hole on this D bead to emerge at the centre of the flower (fig 27).

25 Locate the D bead on the opposite side of the flower centre. Thread on 1H and pass the needle through the inner hole of the opposite D bead to pull the H bead to sit across the centre of the flower (see fig 28).

fig 28

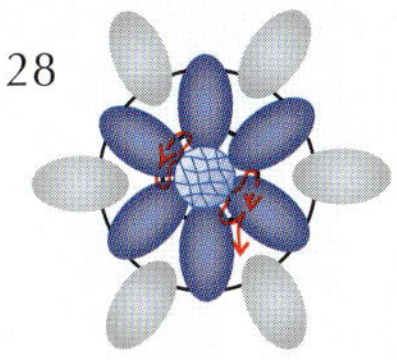

Pass the needle back through the H bead in the opposite direction and the inner hole of the first D bead in the same direction as before - this will bring the H bead down snugly into the flower centre (fig 28).

Flip the flower over and pass the needle through the central space in the flower so you are looking at the reverse of the flower.

Add an H bead to the centre of the flower on this side as before.

fig 29

Pass the needle through the outer hole on the D bead, the following hole on the B bead and the outer hole on the B bead to emerge at the edge of the flower (fig 29).

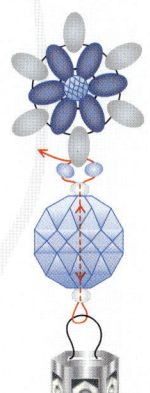

fig 30

26 Thread on 1A, 1E, 1F and 1E. Pass the needle through the wire loop at the top of the bauble.

Pass the needle back up through the 1E, 1F and 1E beads before threading on 1A. Pass the needle through the B bead to centre the connection above the loop on the bauble (fig 30).

This connection will need to be made more firm. Pass the needle down and up through this bead sequence three more times to reinforce the work.

27 Pass the needle through the B and D bead holes to emerge from the outer hole of the topmost B bead (fig 31).

Thread on 3A, 1E, 1D, 1E, 50A and 1E.

Pass the needle down through the second hole in the D bead and thread on 1E and 3A.

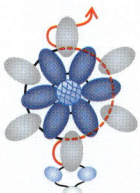

fig 31

Pass the needle through the outer hole of the topmost B bead once more (fig 32). Make sure the new D bead is sitting horizontally as in fig 32.

This bead loop needs to be made more firm. As before pass the needle through the bead sequence just created three more times before finishing off the thread end neatly and securely.

Remove the keeper bead. Secure and neaten this end in a similar fashion.

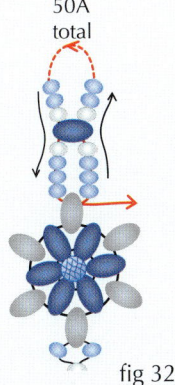

fig 32

Astor Inspiration

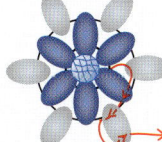

Clivedon Bauble

This is a very decadent interpretation of the Astor design to drape over a 60mm bauble.

There are five flower swags - each with seven fringe strands; larger flower motifs and an additional small motif hanging from the neck ring.

Christmas Tree Bauble

You Will Need

Materials

One 140mm frosted green tree-shaped glass bauble
10g of size 10/0 green scarab seed beads A
10g of size 10/0 silver lined gold seed beads B
4g of size 8/0 silver lined red seed beads C
Twenty-six 6mm red fire polished faceted beads D
A reel of green size D beading thread

Tools

A size 10 beading needle
A pair of scissors to trim the threads

This tiered design is made over a hand-blown, tree-shaped bauble. The tree is part of a huge catalogue of traditional glass ornaments created in the region of the Czech Republic formerly known as Bohemia. If you cannot obtain one of these fabulous glass baubles, there are additional instructions to show you how to make a tree from scratch - once it's beaded it's difficult to tell the difference.

The Decoration is Made in Five Stages

A foundation row is created around the bottom tier.
A series of loops drop down from this row to give the impression of the tree boughs.
The baubles and swags are added to the edge.
This is repeated on each tier.
The hanging loop and star are added to the top.

> **Extra Info....**
> As these baubles are handmade, there is a little variation in the exact dimensions of each tier.
>
> The bead counts are given as 'ideal amounts' but you may have to adjust the counts for your particular ornament. Guidance is given where necessary but you will find a pen and paper useful to note down any adjustment needed.

1 The Foundation Row - Prepare the needle with 1.8m of single thread and tie a keeper bead 15cm from the end.

Thread on 48A. Drape the beads around the top of the biggest tier of the tree.

The beads need to fit snugly with no thread showing between them. You may need to adjust the bead count to get a satisfactory fit.

When you have the correct count for your bauble, pass the needle through the first A bead to draw the ring up tight to the bauble (fig 1). Make a note of the number of beads used.

Pass the needle through the entire row again to make the work firm.

2 The row needs to be divided into eight sections.

If you have a row of 48A then the row will divide easily into eight sections of 6A. If, for example, you have 51A you will need to divide it into five sections of 6A and three sections of 7A. Make your calculation.

Now you need to plan the row. If you have 51A, as suggested above, the three 7A sections need to be separated out along the sequence - for example - 6A, 7A, 6A, 7A, 6A, 6A, 7A, 6A. Make a note of your sequence.

The following instructions will assume eight sections of 6A but you will need to follow your planned sequence when counting around the row.

3 The Tree Boughs - Thread on 15A and 4B. Pass the needle through the first B bead in the same direction as before to bring the 4B into a small ring (fig 2).

Thread on 15A and pass the needle through the sixth A bead along the foundation ring (see your sequence) (fig 3).

fig 3

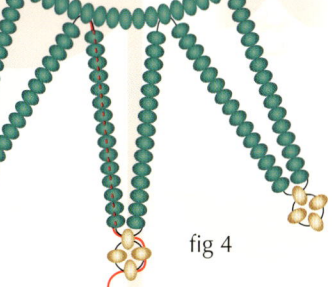

fig 2

Repeat step 3 around the foundation row to make eight loops in total.

4 Pass the needle through the first 15A of the first loop and the following 3B of the first ring (fig 4).

Note the needle is pointing in the opposite direction.

fig 4

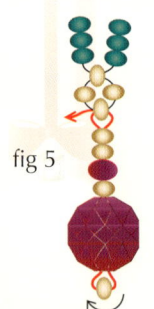

fig 5

5 **The Baubles and Swags** - Thread on 2B, 1C, 1B, 1D and 1B.

Leaving aside the last B bead to anchor the strand, pass the needle up through the D bead and the following four beads.

Pass the needle through the B bead at the bottom of the ring in the same direction as before to centre the strand below the bough loop (fig 5).

6 Thread on 23B. Pass the needle through the bottom B bead of the next 4B ring around the bauble (fig 6).

Be careful not to pull too hard on the thread - the D bead strand and the swag need to fall softly over the edge of the bauble.

Repeat steps 5 and 6 seven more times to complete the row.

Finish off the thread ends neatly and securely.

fig 6

7 **The Second Tier** - Prepare the needle as in step 1 and thread on 42A for the foundation row. Try this bead count for size around the next tier of the bauble.

Make any necessary adjustment to the count as before and pass the needle through the first A bead to draw up the ring around the bauble. Pass the needle through the beads of the ring again to make it firm.

This tier has seven tree boughs, so if you have 42A in your foundation row, you will have seven repeats of 6A. Make your calculations as before and write down the sequence for the spacing of the bough loops along the row.

8 Thread on 13A and 4B. Pass the needle through the fourth B bead in the same direction as before to bring the 4B into a small ring (as fig 2).

Thread on 13A and pass the needle through the sixth A bead along the foundation ring (see your sequence) (fig 7).

Repeat to the end of the row.

9 Repeat step 5.

Repeat step 6 using 21B beads for the swag.

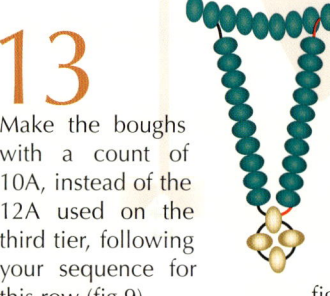

fig 7

Repeat step 9 six more times. Finish off the thread ends neatly and securely.

10 **The Third Tier** - Prepare the needle as in step 1 and thread on 36A for the foundation row. Try this bead count for size around the next tier of the bauble.

Make any necessary adjustment to the count as before and pass the needle through the first A bead to draw up the ring around the bauble. Pass the needle through the beads of the ring again to make it firm.

This tier has six tree boughs, so if you have 36A in your foundation row, you will have six repeats of 6A. Make your calculations as before and write down the sequence for the spacing of the bough loops along the row.

11 Make the boughs with a count of 12A (instead of the 13A used on the second tier) following your sequence for this row (fig 8).

Make the D bead strands and the swags as for the second tier.

Finish off the thread ends neatly and securely.

fig 8

12 **The Top Tier** - Prepare the needle as in step 1 and thread on 28A for the foundation row. Try this bead count for size around the top tier of the bauble - it needs to sit at the base of the bauble cap.

Make any necessary adjustment to the count as before and pass the needle through the first A bead to draw up the ring around the bauble. Pass the needle through the beads of the ring again to make it firm.

This tier has four tree boughs so if you have 28A in your foundation row you will have four repeats of 7A.

Make your calculations as before and write down the sequence for the spacing of the bough loops along the row.

13 Make the boughs with a count of 10A, instead of the 12A used on the third tier, following your sequence for this row (fig 9).

fig 9

Make the D bead strands and the swags as for the second layer.

Finish off the thread ends neatly and securely.

14 **The Hanging Loop** - Prepare the needle with 1.5m of single thread and tie a keeper bead 15cm from the end. Thread on 1D, 2A and 14B.

Pass the needle through the fifth B bead just added in the same direction as before to make a ring of 10B (fig 10).

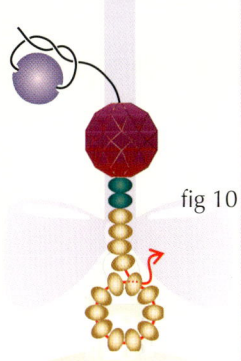
fig 10

fig 11

15 Thread on 4B. Leaving aside the last B bead to form an anchor, pass the needle through the next B bead in the opposite direction and thread on 2B.

Pass the needle through the second B bead around the ring (fig 11). This completes the first star point.

Repeat step 15 to make a second star point (fig 12).

fig 12

16 Thread on 3A.

Pass the needle through the loop at the top of the bauble and back up through the 3A beads just added.

Pass the needle through the B bead on the ring in the same direction as before (fig 13).

This connection needs to be reinforced.

Pass the needle down the 3A, through the bauble loop and up to the ring twice more. Finish with the needle emerging as in fig 13.

fig 13

fig 14

17 Repeat step 15 twice to make two more star points. Thread on 2B and pass the needle up through the 2B beads immediately before the 2A added in step 14 (fig 14).

Pass the needle through the following 2A and the D bead.

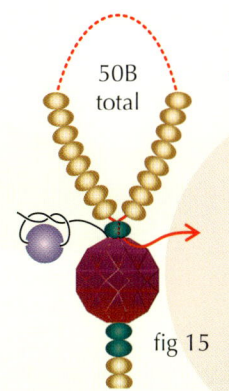
50B total
fig 15

18 Thread on 1A and 50B. Pass the needle down through the A bead to draw the 50B into a loop (fig 15).

The loop needs to be reinforced.

19 Pass the needle down through the D bead and into the beads of the star.

Referring to fig 16 pass the needle through to the 10B beads of the ring at the centre of the star and back up to emerge from the top of the D bead.

Pass the needle through the beads of the loop to reinforce.

Repeat once more.

Finish off all remaining thread ends neatly and securely.

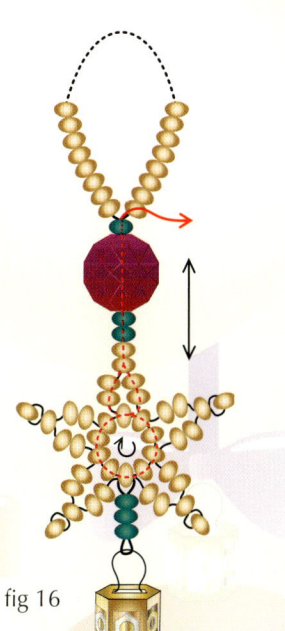
fig 16

39

Christmas Tree Inspiration

This decoration is made with a similar beading technique and bead count to the glass bauble on the previous pages. If you cannot obtain a shaped glass bauble this version makes a very good alternative.

Crafty Christmas Tree

You Will Need

Materials

An A4 sheet of 120gsm red card
10g of size 10/0 silver lined red seed beads A
10g of size 10/0 silver lined gold seed beads B
4g of size 8/0 silver lined purple seed beads C
Twenty-six 6mm purple AB fire polished faceted beads D
Eight 6mm red fire polished faceted beads E
One 12mm red fire polished faceted bead F
One 20 x 6mm purple lustre tubular glass bead H
A reel of red size D beading thread
A little PVA glue and some sticky tape

The Decoration is Made in Six Stages

A series of cardboard cones are made first.
A foundation ring is decorated with a series of loops to give the impression of the tree boughs.
The baubles and swags are added to the ends of the loops.
This is repeated three times to fit the different-sized cones.
The cones are strung together to form the 'tree'.
The hanging loop and star are added to the top.

20 The Cones - You need to draw four circles on the card

One circle 45mm in diameter
One circle 55mm in diameter
One circle 60mm in diameter
One circle 70mm in diameter

Mark the centre point on each circle.
Carefully cut out the circles. Make a single straight cut from the edge to the centre on each circle (fig 17).

21 Make a mark on the edge of the largest circle a quarter of the way around the circle from the cut.

Repeat on the next two circles.

Make a mark one third of the way around on the smallest circle.

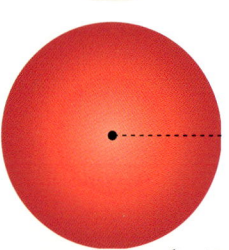

fig 17

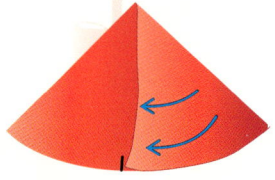

fig 18

Working on one circle at a time bring the far cut edge around to the mark to create a cone (fig 18).

Use a small piece of sticky tape on the inside of the cone to hold the card in place.

Use a little PVA glue to stick down the edge on the outside of the cone - you may find a paper clip useful to hold the flap down until the glue dries.

22 The Foundation Row - In step 1 the foundation row is applied directly to the bauble. The beading for the cones is prepared separately and then dropped over the cones. Otherwise the bead counts and techniques are exactly the same for the three largest cones, as for the three lower tiers of the bauble.

For the largest cone - Prepare the needle with 1.8m of single thread. Thread on 48A. Pass the needle through the first A bead in the same direction to make a ring. Pass the needle through the following 48A again to reinforce the row.
Work steps 3 to 6 inclusive to make a beaded tier to fit over the largest cone.

For the next largest cone - Prepare the needle as before and thread on 42A. Make the beads into a ring as above and follow steps 7 to 9 to complete this tier.

For the next cone - Prepare the needle as before and thread on 36A. Make the beads into a ring as above and follow steps 10 and 11 to complete this tier.

23 For the smallest cone make a ring of 8A as above. Thread on 15A and 4B. Pass the needle through the first B bead as before and thread on 15A. Pass the needle through the second A bead around the ring.

Pass the needle down the last 4A beads of the previous stitch (fig 19). Thread on 11A and 4B.

Pass the needle through the first B bead as before and thread on 15A. Pass the needle through the second A bead around the ring.

Repeat step 23 once.

fig 19

fig 20

Pass the needle down the last 4A beads of the previous stitch (as fig 19). Thread on 11A and 4B.

Pass the needle through the first B bead as before and thread on 11A.

Pass the needle up through the first 4A of the first loop (fig 20).

24 Pass the needle through the following 1A on the ring and down through the A beads of the first loop to emerge from the bottom B bead ready to add the D bead strands and the swags.

Add the D bead strands and the swags as for the previous layers.

25 Drop the layers into place over the cones. You will see that the decoration on the lower three cones tends to slide off-centre.

Starting with the largest cone, use a 50cm length of single thread to make a few simple stitches through the card, to hold the foundation rows in place The swags should hang evenly around the edges of the cone.

Repeat on each of the three larger cones.

26 Assembling the Tree - Prepare the needle with a 1m length of doubled thread with a keeper bead 15cm from the ends.

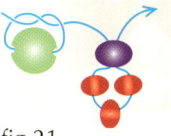

fig 21

Thread on 1C and 3A. Pass the needle through the C bead in the opposite direction to bring the 3A into a picot (fig 21).

27 Referring to fig 22 throughout thread on 1F, 1C, 1H, 4C and 1E. Pass the needle up through the centre of the largest cone, piercing the card if necessary.

Thread on 1E, 4C and 1E. Pass the needle up through the centre of the second-largest cone.

Thread on 1E, 4C and 1E. Pass the needle up through the centre of the third-largest cone.

Thread on 1E, 4C and 1E. Pass the needle up through the centre of the smallest cone.

Pass through the ring of 8A in the centre of the top tier beading and thread on 1E and 3A.

28 Leaving aside the last 1A bead to anchor the strand, pass the needle down through the 2A beads above the E bead, through the cone and all of the following beads and cones to emerge alongside the keeper bead.

Remove the keeper bead and tie the needle thread to the tail threads pulling the knots snugly between the beads.

Neaten all of the thread ends by passing them up through the F bead before trimming.

29 The Hanging Loop - Refer to steps 14 and 15 to start to make the hanging loop and star for the top of the tree.

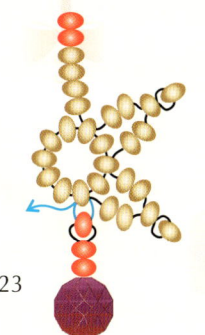

fig 23

Pass the needle through the A bead at the very top of the tree. Pass the needle through the B bead on the star again to make the connection (fig 23).

Pass the needle through this link twice to make it strong.

Complete the decoration by following steps 17 to 19.

fig 22

Nordic Bauble

You Will Need

Materials

One 60mm frosted grey glass bauble
10g of ceylon white Twin beads A
5g of gunmetal grey Twin beads B
5g of metallic silver Twin beads C
9g of size 10/0 gunmetal grey seed beads D
4g of size 10/0 ceylon white seed beads E
5g of size 10/0 metallic silver seed beads F
1g of size 3 gunmetal bugle beads G
Nine 4mm gunmetal fire polished faceted beads H
Four 6mm gunmetal fire polished faceted beads J
One 8mm gunmetal fire polished faceted bead K
A reel of grey size D beading thread

Tools

A size 10 beading needle
A pair of scissors to trim the threads

Scandanavian folk designs have a wonderful simplicity, especially those seen in woven and knitted textiles. The classic 'Ski Jumper' has bounced in and out of fashion for decades, but the classic design elements - the rondelle, the interlocked zig-zag and the falling snow - can be re-visited and re-invented in so many different ways. Here Twin beads are used to make the rondelles and the snowflakes.

The Decoration is Made in Six Stages
The four Twin bead rondelles are made first.
The zig-zag band is made separately.
The fringe strands are attached to the zig-zag band.
A foundation row for the neck of the bauble is made.
Connections from the foundation row to the rondelles and the zig-zag band join the elements together.
The hanging loop completes the decoration.

Extra Info....
This design looks fabulous in lots of different colourways. If you want to swap the colours around make sure you choose a D bead that contrasts with Twin bead A. Also note that -
A matches E
B matches D
C matches F

1 The Twin Bead Rondelle - Prepare the needle with 1.8m of single thread and tie a keeper bead 15cm from the end.

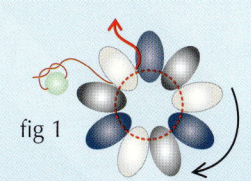
fig 1

Thread on 1A, 1B and 1C. Repeat twice. Pass the needle through the first A bead to bring the beads into a tight circle (fig 1). Pass the needle through the same holes in the beads again to make the circle firm. Make sure the needle is emerging from the A bead as fig 1.

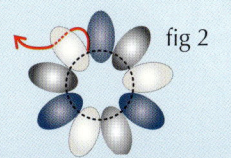
fig 2

2 Pass the needle through the outer hole in the A bead in the opposite direction to make a strap of thread to the side of the A bead (fig 2). Note that the needle is now pointing in the opposite direction.

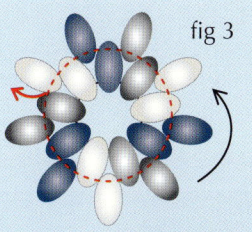
fig 3

3 Referring to fig 3 thread on 1A and pass through the outer hole on the next C bead around. Thread on 1C and pass through the outer hole on the next B bead around. Repeat in the next gap to add 1B bead passing though the outer hole on the A bead.

Repeat around the circle to add nine beads in total.

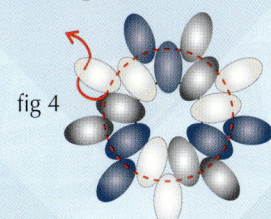
fig 4

Pass the needle through the inner hole on the first A bead added in this row (fig 3).

4 Reposition the needle as in step 2 (fig 4) - note that the needle has changed direction again.

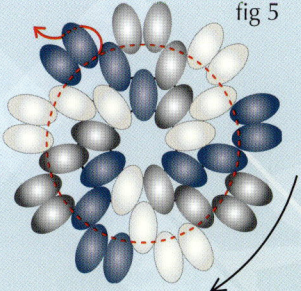
fig 5

Referring to fig 5 thread on 2B and pass through the outer hole on the next B bead around.
Thread on 2C and pass through the outer hole in the next C bead around and thread on 2A for the next gap.
Pass through the outer hole on the next A bead to complete the stitch.

Repeat twice (18 beads in total).

Finish with the needle emerging from the second B bead of the first stitch.

Reposition the needle through the outer hole of this bead as in step 2 (fig 5).

5 Referring to fig 6 thread on 1B and pass though the outer hole of the next bead. Thread on 1B and repeat. Thread on 1A for each of the next two gaps and 1C for the following two gaps.

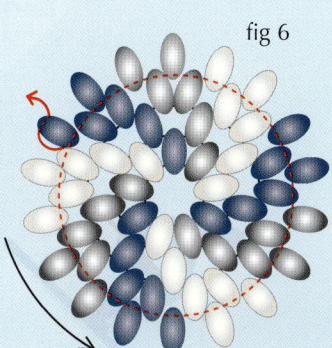
fig 6

Work around the rondelle as before to add 18 beads in total.

Finish the row by passing through the second B bead of the row.

Reposition the needle through the outer hole in this bead as in step 2 (fig 6).

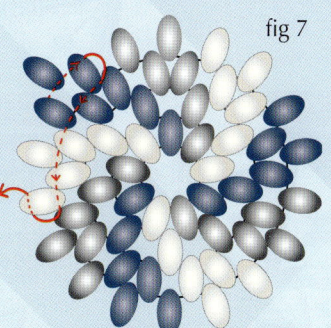
fig 7

6 Referring to fig 7 thread on 1B. Pass the needle through the outer hole of the next B bead around the rondelle.

Pass the needle through the inner hole of the same B bead in the opposite direction and the following six beads to emerge from the inner hole of the fourth bead around (an A bead).
Pass the needle through the outer hole of this A bead in the opposite direction (fig 7).

fig 8

Using the same method add an A bead in this gap and a C bead in the gap between the next 2C beads (see fig 8).

Repeat around the rondelle to add nine beads in total (fig 8).

Pass the needle through the last row once more to make it firm and finish off both thread ends neatly and securely.

Repeat steps 1-6 three more times to make four rondelles in total.

7 The Zig-Zag Band - The zig-zag is made from a simple repeat of plain band sections and corner blocks. The band changes direction at the corner blocks: Turn X 'zigs' it up, Turn Y 'zags' it down.

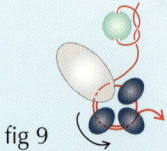
fig 9

Prepare the needle as in step 1 and thread on 1A and 3D. Pass the needle through the same hole in the A bead and the following 2D beads again to bring them into a small ring (fig 9).

8 Thread on 3D. Pass the needle through the middle D bead on the first ring and the following 2D from the new stitch (fig 10).

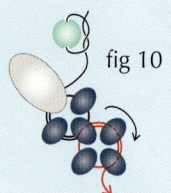
fig 10

Repeat this stitch twice (see fig 11). This is a simple right-angle weave.

Thread on 1D, 1E and 1D. Make the stitch as before bringing the needle through the E bead a second time to complete the stitch (fig 11).

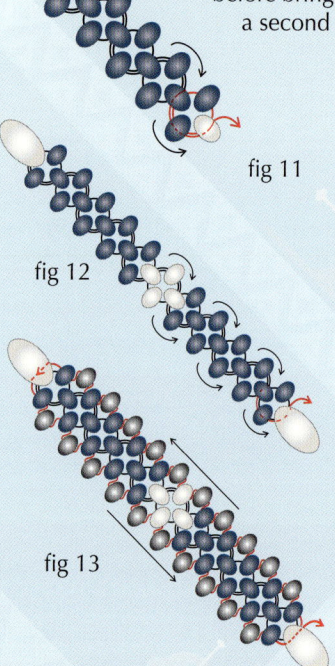
fig 11

fig 12

fig 13

9 Referring to fig 12 make one stitch with 3E and four stitches with 3D.
Make one stitch with 1D, 1A and 1D bringing the needle through the same hole in the A bead to complete the stitch (fig 12).

10 Referring to fig 13 pass the needle through the following 1D bead of the row and thread on 1F. Pass through the next D bead along this edge of the band.

Repeat all the way along this edge.

Pass the needle through the A bead at the far end of the band and repeat along the other edge of the band to embellish and strengthen the work. Finish with the needle emerging from the A bead as before (fig 13).

11 Making a Corner Block - Pass the needle through the other hole in the A bead (see fig 14) and thread on 3A. Pass the needle through the second hole in the original A bead to draw the beads into an X-shape (fig 14).

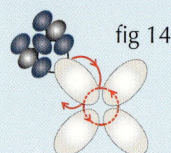
fig 14

12 Referring to fig 15 pass the needle through the first hole in the same A bead and thread on 2D. Pass the needle through the outer hole on the next A bead (fig 15).
Thread on 2D and pass through the outer hole on the next A bead around.

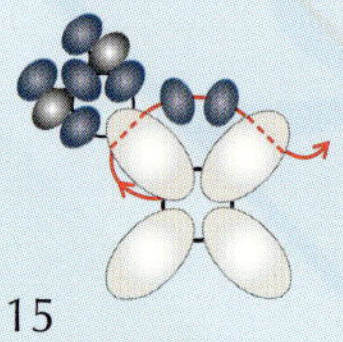

Repeat this stitch twice to complete the block sequence (fig 16).

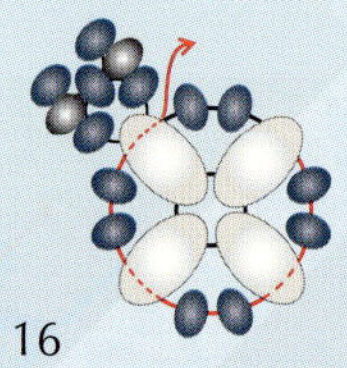

fig 15

fig 16

13 Turn X - Pass through the following 2D and 1A to emerge 1A bead around the X-shape from the starting position pointing away from the previous row (fig 17). fig 17

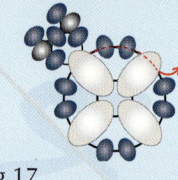
fig 18

14 Thread on 3D and pass through the same hole in the A bead (fig 18). This is the first stitch of the new row (compare to fig 9).

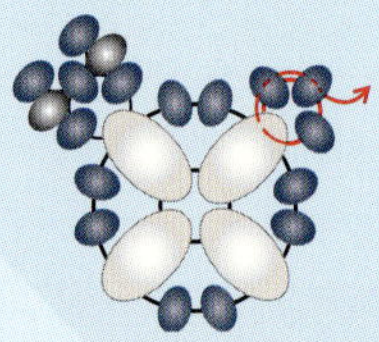

Repeat steps 8 to 12 inclusive to make the next row and corner block.

You now have to change the direction of the band to continue the zig-zag.

15 Turn Y - Pass the needle through the following 2D, 1A, 2D, 1A and 2D and 1A.
The needle should be emerging from the fourth A bead of the corner block pointing towards the previous row (fig 19) - this is the correct place to start the new row - (see fig 20 with the new row in shade).

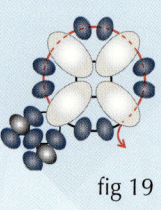
fig 19

fig 20

Repeat step 14.
Make Turn X and repeat step 14.
Make Turn Y and repeat step 14.
Make Turn X and repeat step 14.
Make Turn Y and repeat step 14.
Make Turn X and add 3D as in fig 18.
Repeat steps 8 to 10.

44

16 You should now have an eight band zig-zag with an A bead at either end. These two A beads now need to be joined together to create the final corner block.

It is important there are no twists in the band. Lay the whole band out flat. Fold the two ends into the centre to meet one another so the two A beads just touch together.

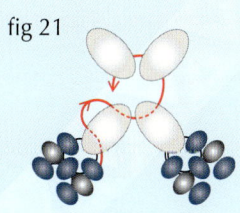
fig 21

Referring to fig 21 pass the needle through the other hole in the current A bead. Pass the needle through the outer hole on the A bead at the other end of the band and thread on 2A.

Pass the needle through the first A bead of the four to bring the beads into the X-shape (fig 21).

Pass the needle through the other hole in the A bead and add 2D into the gaps around the corner block as before to complete the band. Leave the needle attached.

17 The Fringe Strands - These hang from the lower points of the zig-zags.

As you reposition the needle through the beads of the band between the points, you need to pass through the beads along the top edge of the band - this will tighten up this edge a little and make the work firmer.

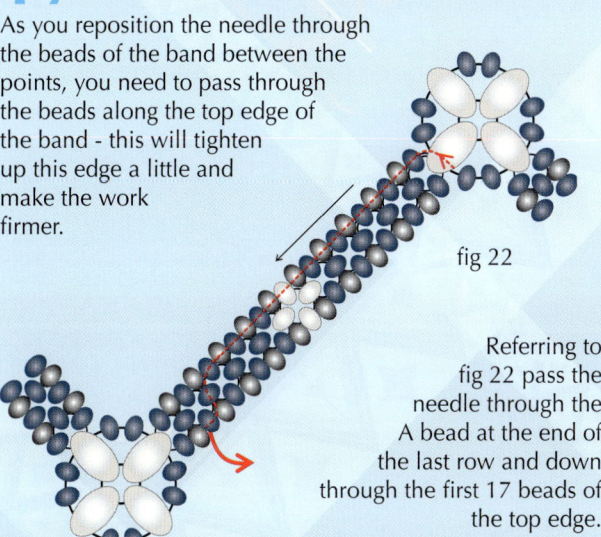
fig 22

Referring to fig 22 pass the needle through the A bead at the end of the last row and down through the first 17 beads of the top edge.

Work the needle across the band to emerge from the D bead just before the last F bead of the bottom edge (fig 22).

18 Thread on 2E, 1F, 1G, 1F, 1E, 2D and 1A. Pass the needle through the other hole on the A bead (fig 23).

Thread on 4A and pass through the same hole on the first A bead again to draw up a five bead ring (see fig 24). Pass the needle through the inner holes on the next 3A beads and out through the outer hole on the fourth A bead (fig 24).

fig 23

fig 24

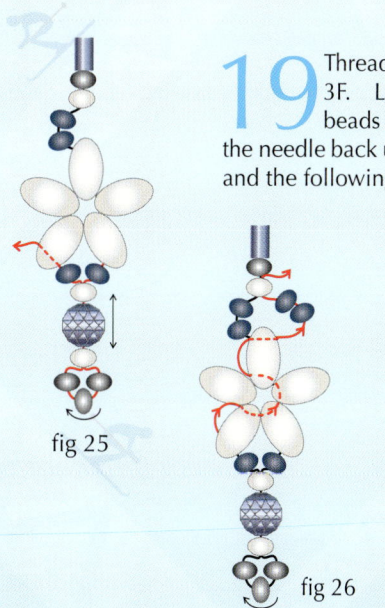

19 Thread on 1D, 1E, 1H, 1E and 3F. Leaving aside the last 3F beads to anchor the strand, pass the needle back up through the last E bead and the following 1H and 1E.

Thread on 1D.

Referring to fig 25 pass the needle through the outer hole of the third A bead of the ring to bridge the dangle between the third and fourth A beads (fig 25).

fig 25

fig 26

20 Referring to fig 26 pass the needle through the other hole in this A bead, through the inner holes of the next 3A beads and the outer hole of the first A bead.

Thread on 2D and pass up through the E bead below the bugle bead (fig 26).

45

21 Pass the needle up to the top of the strand.

Referring to fig 27 pass the needle through the adjacent F bead.

Pass the needle through the following D and A beads to emerge between the 2D beads at the bottom of the corner block (fig 27).

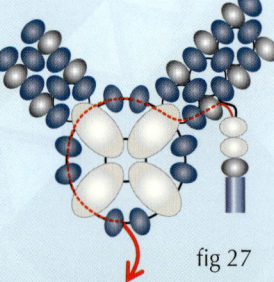

fig 27

22 Thread on 4E, 1F, 1G, 1F, 1E, 2D and 1A to start the central strand. Make this strand as for the previous strand using a larger J bead instead of the H bead.

At the top of the strand refer to fig 28 to reposition the needle through the A and D beads of the corner block and the first 1D and 1F of the lower edge of the next band around.

Make a fringe strand identical to the first strand from this position.

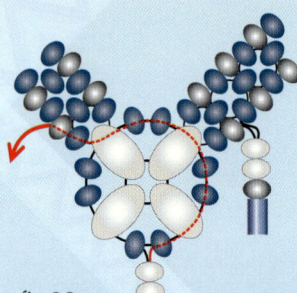

fig 28

23 Reposition the needle through the beads to the top edge of the band in a mirror image of the technique used in step 17. Pass the needle around the beads of the next corner block and down through the top edge beads of the next band (as fig 22) to be in the correct position to start the next set of three fringe strands.

Repeat from step 18 three times to complete four sets of three strands.

Pass the needle along the top edge of the last band so all eight bands have been strengthened similarly and finish off the thread end neatly and securely. Finish off any remaining thread ends similarly.

24 The Foundation Row - Prepare the needle as in step 1 and thread on 1C and 6D.

Repeat this sequence three more times and pass the needle through the same hole on the first A bead to bring the beads into a ring (fig 29).

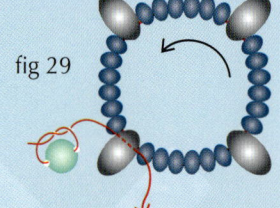

fig 29

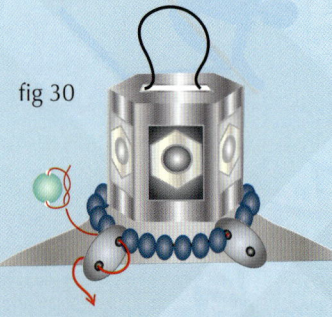

fig 30

Drop the ring over the neck of the bauble (fig 30) - it needs to fit quite snugly.

If it does not fit well, adjust the D bead counts equally around the ring until you have the four C beads evenly distributed around the neck (see fig 30).

Make sure the needle is emerging from the first C bead (as in fig 29). Pass the needle through the other hole in this C bead (fig 30).

25 Making the Links - The first links are made to the top corner blocks of the zig-zag band.

Thread on 2D, 1E, 18D and 1B.

Pass the needle through the top 2D beads of the first corner block (see fig 31).

Pass the needle up through the other hole in the B bead and thread on 18 D.

Pass the needle up through the E bead and thread on 2D.

Pass the needle through the lower hole of the C bead on the foundation row in the same direction as before (fig 31).

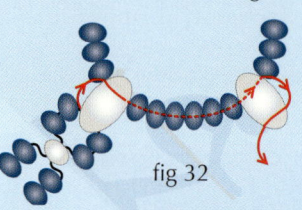

18D total

fig 31   fig 32

26 Pass the needle through the top hole of this C bead, the following D beads, the top hole of the next C bead and the lower hole of the same bead (fig 32).

Repeat steps 25 and 26 three more times to make links to the four top corner blocks of the zig-zag band.

27 The rondelles are now linked into place. Make sure the needle is emerging from the lower hole on the last C bead (as fig 32) and thread on 10D.

Pass the needle through the outer hole of one of the A bead points on the first rondelle.

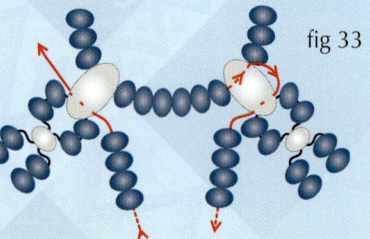

fig 33

Thread on 10D and pass the needle through the lower hole on the next C bead around the foundation row (fig 33).

Repeat to add the remaining three rondelles. Finish off all the remaining thread ends neatly and securely.

46

28 **The Hanging Loop -** Prepare the needle as in step 1 and thread on 9C. Pass the needle through the first C bead to make a ring (as in fig 1).

Pass the needle through the outer hole of the first C bead (as fig 2).

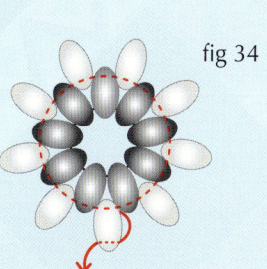

fig 34

Add 1A bead into each gap (as fig 34).

Pass the needle through the outer hole of the last A bead passed through (fig 34).

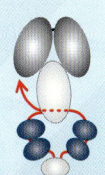

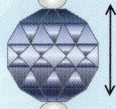

fig 35

29 Thread on 2D, 1E, 1K and 1E. Pass the needle through the loop at the top of the bauble and back up through the three beads above it.

Thread on 2D. Pass the needle through the A bead in the same direction as before (fig 35).

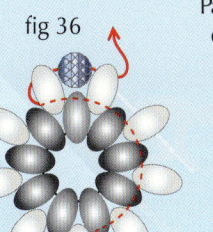

fig 36

Pass the needle up and down this connection two or three more times to make it strong.

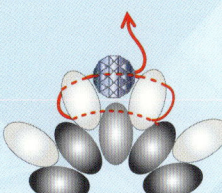

fig 37

30 Referring to fig 36 pass the needle through the other hole of this A bead and the following ten beads to emerge from the fifth A bead around the ring.

Pass through the outer hole of this A bead and thread on 1H.

Pass through the outer hole in the previous A bead to draw the H bead across the gap (fig 36).

Reinforce the H bead as shown in fig 37.

31 Thread on 1F, 1D, 1E and 50D. Pass the needle back down the E bead to draw up the loop and thread on 1D and 1F.

Pass the needle through the H bead (fig 38).

Pass the thread through the beads just added two or three more times to make the loop strong.

Finish off all remaining thread ends neatly and securely.

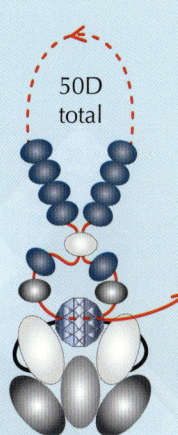

50D total

fig 38

Nordic Inspiration

Tromsø Tassel

A simple adaptation of the Twin bead rondelle.

The hanging loop connects to the inside edge of the top two points with an extra ring of eight Twin beads to taper the design.

The graduated fringe strands have a single Twin bead at the bottom.

Make four Tromso Tassels adding the hanging loops just up to the small rings. Link these rings together around the neck of a bauble for a stunning interpretation of the Nordic theme.

47

Mistletoe Kisses Bauble

You Will Need

Materials

One 60mm frosted turquoise glass bauble
3g of DB684 semi-matt silver lined red Delica beads A
15g of size 10/0 silver lined lime green seed beads B
8g of size 6/0 ceylon white seed beads C
5g of size 10/0 silver lined crystal seed beads D
4g of size 3 silver lined crystal bugle beads E
One 8mm red fire polished faceted bead F
A reel each of red and white size D beading thread

Tools

A size 12 beading needle
A pair of scissors to trim the threads

Mistletoe is harvested from the orchards of Herefordshire and Worcestershire in great quantities to be sold at the annual Mistletoe Market in Tenbury Wells. A small sprig can cost just a few pennies but choose one with lots of berries as you need to forfeit one each time you win a kiss. The main project is made in bright colours but use a silvery bauble and the same beads to give a more subtle effect.

The Decoration is Made in Five Stages

First you make the hearts.
The foundation row and the supports for the X-shaped kisses are made next.
The mistletoe strands and the swags are added.
The foundation row is embellished.
The hanging loop completes the decoration.

1 **The Hearts** - Fig 1 shows the brick stitch grid for the hearts. If you have not used brick stitch before please refer to the instructions on page 10.

Prepare the needle with 1.2m of single red thread and tie a keeper bead 15cm from the end.

Start with the central row as indicated and work the nine A beads in ladder stitch.

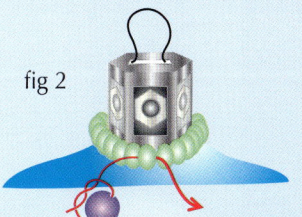

fig 1
start here

Work out from either side of this row in brick stitch to complete the heart. Finish off the thread ends neatly and securely.

Repeat step 1 three more times to make four hearts in total and set these aside for the moment.

2 **The Foundation Row with Frame Supports** - Prepare the needle with 1.8m of single white thread and tie a keeper bead 15cm from the end.

Thread on 32B. Pass the needle through the first bead in the same direction as before to bring the beads into a ring.

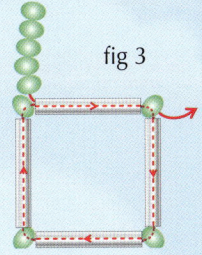

fig 2

Drop this ring over the top of the bauble (fig 2). The ring needs to fit the neck of the bauble snugly so you may need to adjust the B bead count.

If you need to adjust the bead count, do so in multiples of 4B, so the final bead count is divisible by four.

The following instructions will assume a bead count of 32B but you will need to make allowance for any adjustment you may have made to the count.

3 Thread on 20B, 1E, 1B, 1E, 1B, 1E, 1B, 1E and 1B.

Pass the needle through the first E and the following B bead in the same direction as before to make a square of E beads (fig 3).

4 Thread on 7D. Pass the needle through the diagonally opposite B bead (fig 4).

Pass the needle through the 7D in the opposite direction and the B bead in the corner in the same direction as before. Pass the needle through the following 1E and 1B (fig 5).

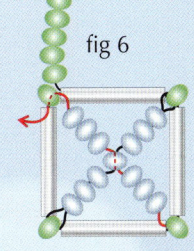

5 Thread on 3D.

Referring to fig 6 pass the needle up through the middle D bead of the first diagonal and thread on 3D. Pass the needle through the B bead in the diagonal corner (fig 6).

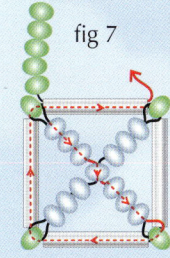

6 Referring to fig 7 pass the needle through the last 3D beads, the central bead of the first diagonal and the following 3D in the opposite direction.

Pass the needle through the B bead in the corner and the following 1E, 1B, 1E, 1B and 1E beads (fig 7).

7 Thread on 19B. Referring to fig 8 pass the needle up through the first B bead of step 3, the first B bead of the foundation ring and the following 8B to emerge a quarter of the way around the ring (fig 8).

8 Repeat steps 3 to 7 inclusive three times (fig 9).

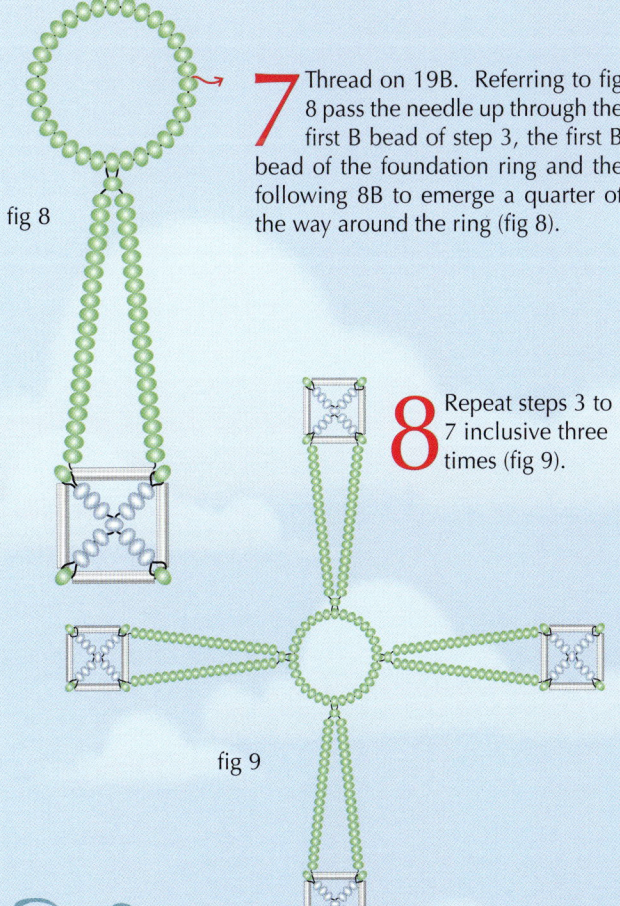

49

9 **The Mistletoe Strands** - Pass the needle down through the first 1B of the first frame support made in step 3 and the following 19B of the left-hand row.

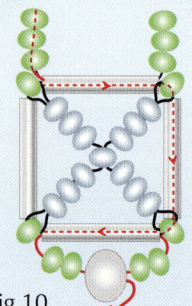

fig 10

Referring to fig 10 pass the needle through the top E bead and the following 1B, 1E, 1B and 1E.

Thread on 2B, 1C and 2B. Pass the needle through the last E bead and the following 2B and 1C beads again (fig 10). The mistletoe strands will hang from this C bead.

Thread on 53B for the stem.

10 Thread on 13B. Pass the needle through the last B bead of the stem in the same direction as before - try to keep the stem bead vertical at the end of the strand (fig 11).

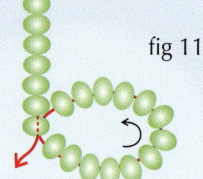

fig 11

Thread on 13B and pass through the B bead at the end of the stem (fig 12).

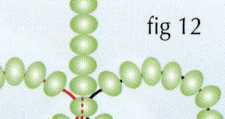

fig 12

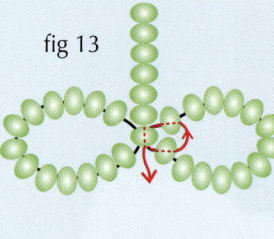

fig 13

11 Pass the needle through the first and last B beads of the first loop and the last B bead of the stem in the same direction as before (fig 13).

Repeat with the first and last beads of the second loop (fig 14).

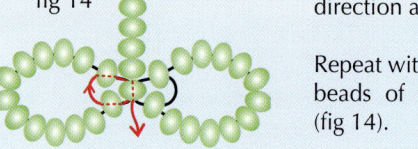

fig 14

12 Referring to fig 15 pass the needle down through the first bead of the first loop, up the first bead of the second loop and through the bottom B bead of the stem in the opposite direction (fig 15).

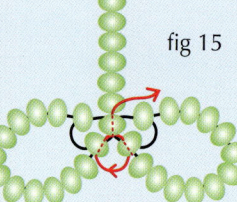

fig 15

The stitches in steps 11 and 12 pinch the loops into a more narrow shape and provide a support for the berry beads.

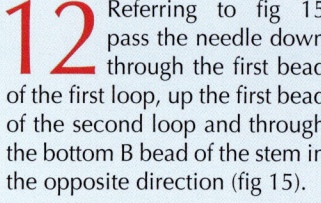

fig 16

13 Thread on 1C and pass the needle up through the last B bead of the stem (fig 16).

Flip the work over and add 1C bead to this side of the bottom B bead of the stem (fig 17).

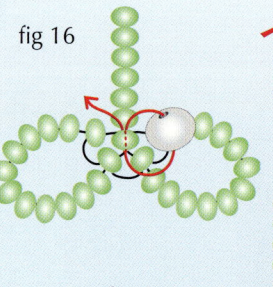

fig 17

fig 18

14 Pass the needle through the following 21B beads of the stem.

Thread on 7B for the first side stem.

Repeat steps 10 to 13 to complete a new set of leaves with berries (see figs 18 and 19).

Pass the needle up through the following 6B of the side stem and the first B bead of the main stem (fig 19).

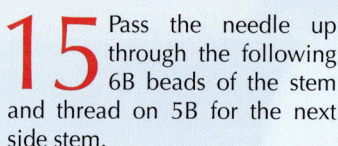

fig 19

15 Pass the needle up through the following 6B beads of the stem and thread on 5B for the next side stem.

Repeat steps 10 to 13 to make the third set of leaves with berries.

Pass the needle up to the top of the side stem and through the first B bead of the main stem (as fig 19).

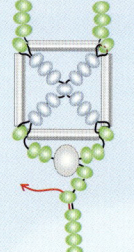

fig 20

16 Pass the needle up the following 21B beads of the main stem to emerge 2B from the top of the strand (fig 20).

Thread on 2B and pass the needle through the C bead at the top of the strand in the same direction as before.

Pass through the following 3B to be in the correct position to make the second stem (fig 21).

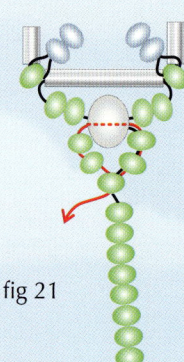

fig 21

17 Thread on 25B. Repeat steps 10 to 13 to complete a new set of leaves with berries.

fig 22

Pass the needle up through the following 11B and thread on 6B for the first side stem.

Repeat steps 10 to 13 to complete a new set of leaves with berries.

Pass the needle up through the remaining 5B beads of the side stem and the following 10B of the main stem.

Thread on 5B for the final side stem.

Repeat steps 10 to 13 to complete a new set of leaves with berries.

Pass the needle up through the remaining 4B beads of the side stem and the following 4B to emerge from the B bead which links the two mistletoe strands (fig 22).

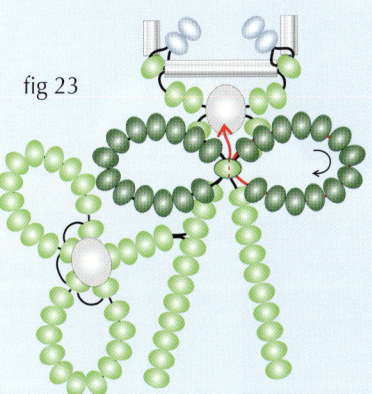
fig 23

18 Thread on 13B and pass the needle through the link bead.

Repeat the last stitch to add a second 13B loop to this bead (fig 23).

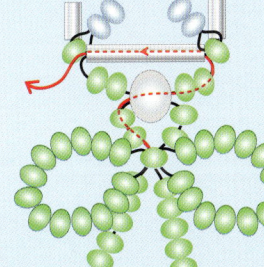
fig 24

19 Referring to fig 24 pass the needle through the following 2B, 1C, 2B and the bottom E bead of the frame (fig 24).

Thread on 40B.

fig 25

20 Pass the needle through the E bead at the bottom of the next frame around the bauble.

Referring to fig 10 thread on 2B, 1C and 2B. Pass the needle through the bottom E bead of the frame once more and the first 2B and 1C just added. (fig 25).

The needle is now in the correct position to start the next set of mistletoe strands.

21 Thread on 53B. Repeat from step 10 to step 20.

Thread on 53B to start the third set of strands and repeat from step 10 to step 20.

Thread on 53B and repeat steps 10 to 19.

Pass the needle through the bottom E bead of the first frame to close up the first swag series around the bauble. Pass the needle through the first B bead of the first swag (fig 26).

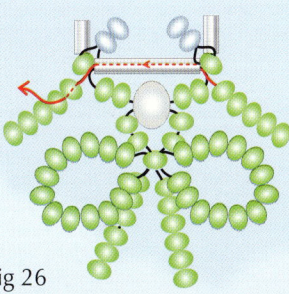
fig 26

22 Thread on 43D. Pass the needle up through the last B bead of the first swag, through the bottom E bead of the second frame and the following 1B of the next swag (fig 27).

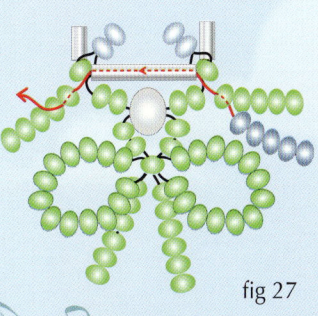
fig 27

Repeat step 22 three times to complete the decoration around the lower part of the bauble.

Finish off this thread end neatly and securely.

23 **Embellishing the Foundation Row** - Prepare the needle with 1.2m of single thread and tie a keeper bead 15 cm from the end.

Pass the needle through the beads of the foundation row to emerge from the middle B beads between the two frame attachments (fig 28). See the Extra Info box if you adjusted your bead count in step 2.

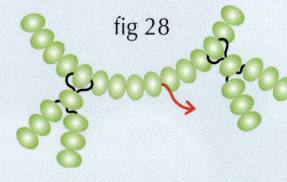
fig 28

26 Thread on 13B. Pass the needle through the B bead on the foundation row in the opposite direction (fig 32).

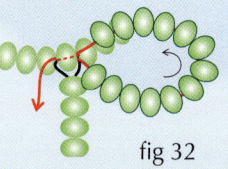
fig 32

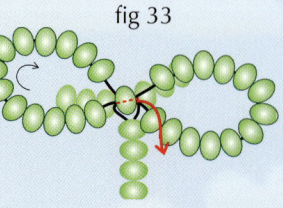
fig 33

Thread on 13B and pass the needle through the B bead again to point in the original direction around the neck of the bauble (fig 33).

Pass the needle through the beads of the foundation row to emerge from the middle B bead between the next two frame attachments. Repeat from step 24 three times to add the remaining three hearts and six more B bead loops to the foundation row.

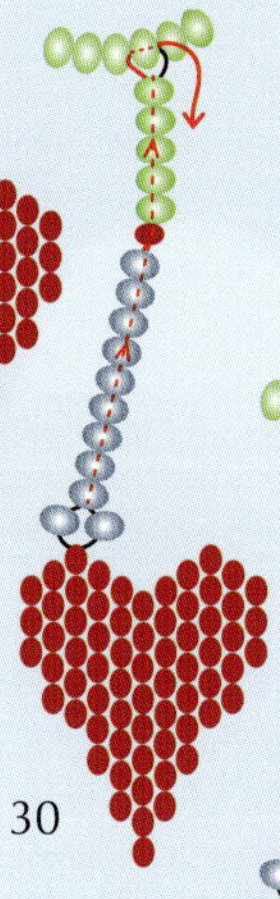

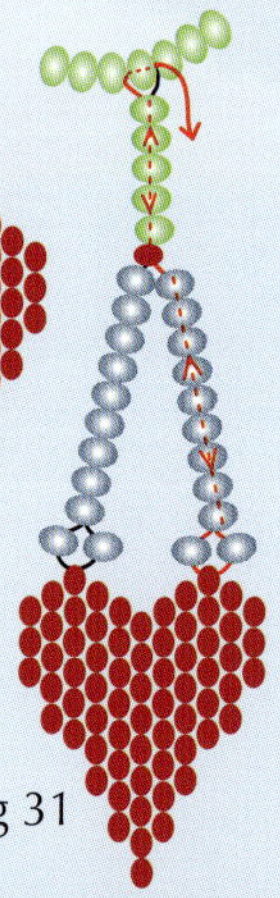

Finish off all remaining thread ends neatly and securely.

Extra Info....
If you adjusted the bead count in step 2 you may find you have an even number of beads between the frame attachment positions.
If so, treat the middle two B beads as a single unit. Pass the needle through both of the beads each time the instruction specifies the single B bead on the foundation row.

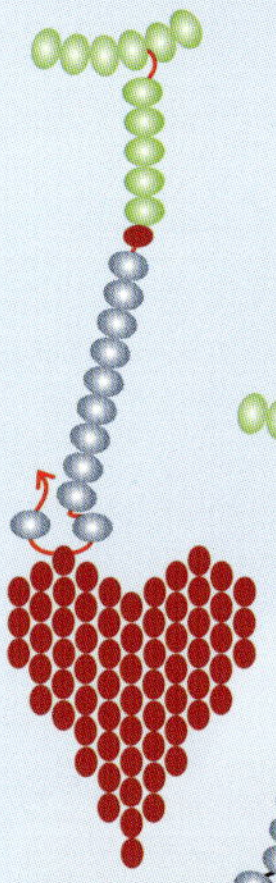

24 Thread on 5B, 1A and 10D. Referring to fig 29 pass the needle through the top A bead on one side of the first heart motif. Thread on 1D (fig 29).

Pass the needle up through the ninth D bead of the 10D and the following beads to emerge at the top of the strand.

Pass through the B bead on the foundation row again (fig 30).

25 Pass the needle down through the 5B and 1A and thread on 10D. Referring to fig 31 make a matching connection on the other side of the heart adding 1D bead and passing up to the top of the strand once more.

Pass the needle through the B bead on the foundation row (fig 31).

fig 29

fig 30

fig 31

27 **The Hanging Loop** - Prepare the needle as in step 2 and thread on 1F and 3B.

Repeat step 10 to make two 13B loops (fig 34).

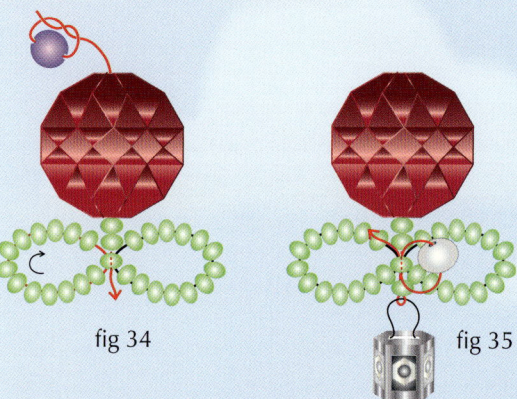
fig 34   fig 35

Thread on 1B and pass the needle through the loop at the top of the bauble. Pass the needle back up the bottom 2B beads.

Add two C bead berries to each side of this B bead as in step 13 (see fig 35). Pass the needle up through the following 2B and 1F.

28 Referring to fig 36 thread on 1B, 1C, 1B, 3A and 51B. Pass the needle back down the first B bead of the 51B and the following 1A.

Thread on 1A and pass through the lowest A bead to pull the two middle A beads alongside one another (fig 36).

The connection to the bauble and the 50B loop both need to be reinforced.

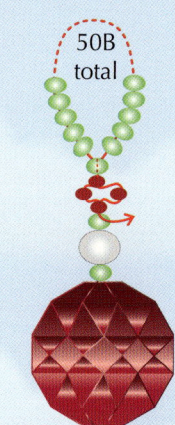
fig 36

Pass the needle down, up and around the main thread pathway twice more to make the connections strong. Finish off all remaining thread ends neatly and securely.

Mistletoe Inspiration

Mistletoe Earrings

These dainty mistletoe sprigs make delightful earrings. Use tiny freshwater pearls for the berries to make them extra special.

You Will Need
Materials

2g of size 15/0 green lined crystal AB seed beads B
1g of size 8/0 ceylon white seed beads C
1g of size 15/0 silver lined gold seed beads G
Two 4mm silver plated jump rings
A pair of silver plated earfittings
A reel of white size D beading thread

29 Prepare the needle with 1.2m of single thread and tie a keeper bead 15cm from the end.

Thread on 1G and 22B.

30 Work steps 10 and 11 to add two loops to the end of the stem.

Pass the needle through the first two beads of the first loop, up the first two beads of the second loop and through the bottom bead of the stem in the opposite direction (fig 37).

31 Work step 13 to add 1C to either side of the bottom bead on the stem.

Pass the needle up through the following eight beads of the main stem. Thread on 5B for the side stem.

32 Repeat steps 30 and 13 to make two loops and add two berries to the end of the stem.

Pass the needle back up the remaining 4B of the stem and the following 5B of the main stem.

33 Thread on 3B for a second side stem.

Repeat step 32 to complete the side stem passing the needle back up through the first 2B of the side stem and the remaining beads of the main stem to emerge from the G bead at the top (fig 38).

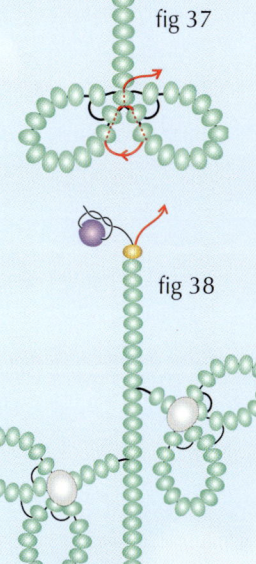
fig 37

fig 38

34 Thread on 11G and pass back up the single G bead at the top of the main stem to make a loop (fig 39). Repeat to make a second loop (fig 40).

35 Thread on 7B. Pass the needle down the first B bead just added and the following G bead on the stem. Pass through the last G bead of the first loop (fig 41).

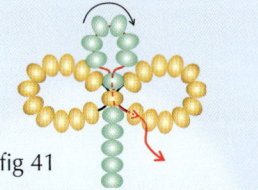
fig 41

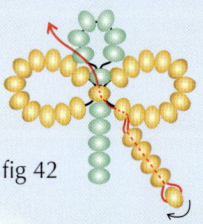
fig 42

Thread on 5G. Leaving aside the last 1G bead to anchor the strand pass the needle back up the top 4G beads of the strand, the 1G of the loop and the G bead on the main stem (fig 42).

Pass the needle through the following B bead and the 6B of the loop. Pass back down through the G bead on the stem and the last 1G of the second loop (fig 43).

Thread on 5G and repeat fig 42 to complete the bow.

Finish off the thread ends neatly and securely.

Attach the earfitting to the top loop with a jump ring and repeat to make the second earring.

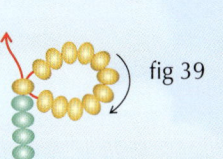
fig 39

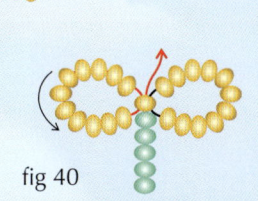
fig 40

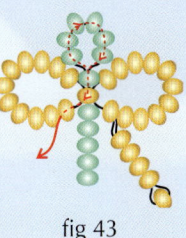
fig 43

Poinsettia Bauble

You Will Need

Materials

One 60mm frosted purple glass bauble
10g of size 10/0 silver lined red seed beads A
8g of size 10/0 silver lined green seed beads B
1g of size 8/0 frost silver lined pale topaz seed beads C
2g of size 10/0 silver lined gold seed beads D
10g of size 10/0 green scarab seed beads E
One 12mm emerald green fire polished faceted bead F
5m of 0.2mm gold-coloured soft wire
A reel of black size D beading thread

Tools

A size 10 beading needle
A pair of scissors to trim the threads
A pair of wire cutters

The bright reds and greens of Poinsettias are associated with Christmas and celebration all over the world. Famously the red petals are not petals at all, but brightly-coloured bracts which need just the right light conditions to become vibrant and showy. They can be tricky to keep in a centrally-heated home, so try these ever-lasting beaded delights instead.

The Decoration is Made in Six Stages
The large red Poinsettia bracts are made.
Then the smaller red bracts are worked.
The green leaves are made with a similar technique.
A series of plain bands is stitched around the bauble.
The Poinsettias and leaves are attached to the bands.
The hanging loop completes the decoration.

Extra Info....
The veins of the bracts and leaves are constructed around a very simple woven wire framework.
The wire gives the beading a stiffer, more arrangeable final appearance. If you want to make the whole project in thread you can, but the blooms will be softer, and will need stiffening afterwards if you want to use them on the underside of the bauble as shown in the main photograph opposite.
Also see the Extra Info box on page 19 - the Frosted Fir Tree is made with a very similar technique.

1 The Large Red Bracts - Cut 50cm of the 0.2mm wire. Thread 5A onto the wire and hold these beads 10cm from the far end. Pass the long end of the wire through the first A bead threaded to bring the beads into a ring (fig 1).

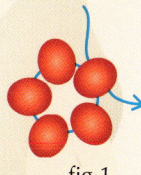
fig 1

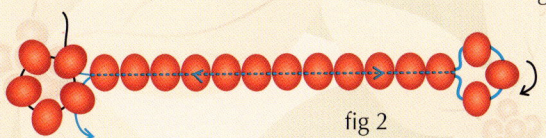
fig 2

2 Thread on 15A. Leaving aside the last 3A beads to anchor the strand, pass the wire back down through the other beads just added and the next A bead around the ring of 5A to make a rod of beads (fig 2).

Do not pull the wire too tightly - you will need to get a needle in and out between the beads so leave about 1mm of play along the length.

Repeat around the ring to make five stems in total (fig 3).

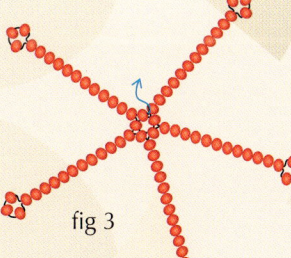
fig 3

3 The two ends of the wire will now be adjacent to one another - twist them together twice close to the ring of 5A. Be careful not to block the holes in the beads of the ring. Do not trim yet.

4 Prepare the needle with 1.5m of single thread and tie a keeper bead 15cm from the end.

Pass the needle up one of the stems of beads to emerge from the tenth A bead of the stem. Pull the thread through so the keeper bead pulls up to the ring end of the stem. The veins of the bract are added using this thread.

5 Thread on 2A. Pass the needle back through the first A bead just threaded to bring the end A bead into an anchor. Pass the needle through the tenth A bead of the stem towards the ring of 5A (fig 4).

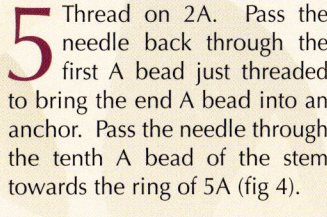
fig 4

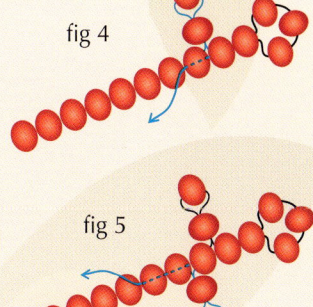
fig 5

6 Thread on 2A. Pass the needle back through the first A bead as before and the following 2A along the stem. Position this new vein on the opposite side of the stem (fig 5).

7 Thread on 3A. Leaving aside the last A bead to anchor the strand pass the needle back through the previous 2A and the next 1A bead along the stem. Position this new vein on the opposite side of the stem (fig 6).

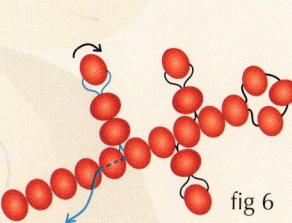
fig 6

8 Referring to fig 7 throughout thread on 3A. Make the vein as before, on the opposite side of the stem, passing back through 2A beads of the stem to be in the correct position for the next vein.

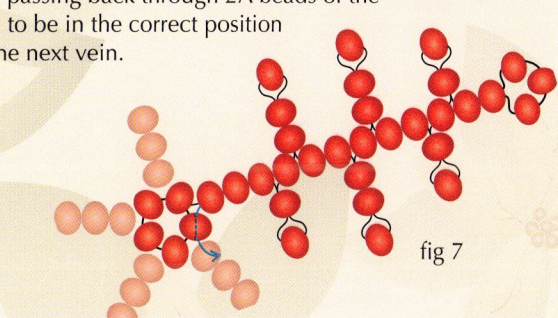
fig 7

Make the new vein with 3A as before, on the opposite side of the stem, passing back through 1A of the stem to be in the correct position for the last vein.

For the last vein thread on 2A. Make the vein as before on the opposite side of the stem. Pass the needle through the remaining 3A of the stem and the following 1A of the ring (fig 7).

Repeat steps 5 to 8 for each of the remaining stems around the central ring.

55

12 The needle should be emerging from one of the 5A beads of the ring. Thread on 1C and 1D. Pass the needle back down the C bead and through the following 1A of the ring to draw the D bead into an anchor (fig 11).

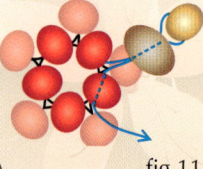

fig 11

Repeat four more times to complete a circle of five tiny buds.

Thread on 1C and 1D. Pass the needle back down the C bead as before and through an A bead on the opposite side of the ring to draw this last bud into the centre of the ring.

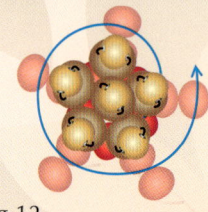

fig 12

13 Wind the thread around the base of the buds to draw them into a tight cluster (fig 12). Pass the needle through one of the A beads of the ring to secure the thread. Remove the needle and leave this thread end loose.

Remove the keeper bead and finish off this shorter thread end neatly and securely through the beads of the adjacent stem.

If possible thread the wire ends through a few beads before trimming neatly. If not possible, make sure the final twist is firm and neat. Trim it to 3mm and tuck into the centre of the flower behind the buds.

Make two more sets of large red bracts to match.

9 The needle should be emerging between the beads of the ring at the base of the first stem.

fig 8

Pass the needle up the first 1A of the first stem.

Thread on 3A and pass the needle through the end A bead of the first 3A vein (fig 8).

10 Referring to fig 9 thread on 3A and pass through the end A bead of the next vein on this side of the stem.

Thread on 2A and pass through the end A bead of the next vein on this side of the stem.

fig 9

Thread on 1A and pass through the 3A anchor beads of the stem (fig 9).

14 The Small Red Bracts - Cut 30cm of 0.2mm wire and make a ring of 5A as in step 1. Thread on 10A.

As in step 2 leave aside the last 3A beads to anchor the strand and pass back through the first 7A and the following 1A of the ring (fig 13).

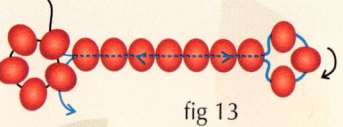

fig 13

Repeat to make five stems in total.

15 Prepare the needle as in step 4 and pass up through the first stem to emerge through the fifth A bead. Fig 14 shows the veins for the bract.

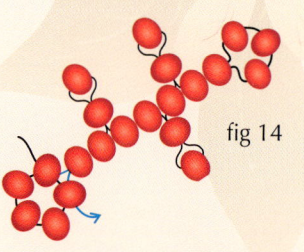

fig 14

Following this diagram work the veins for this stem and the remaining four stems around the ring as before.

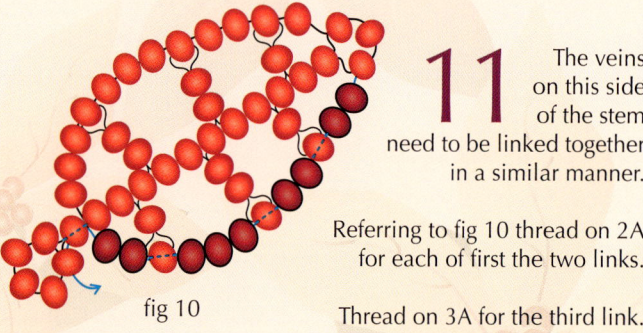

fig 10

11 The veins on this side of the stem need to be linked together in a similar manner.

Referring to fig 10 thread on 2A for each of first two links.

Thread on 3A for the third link.

Thread on 2A and pass down the first A bead of the stem. Pass through the following 1A bead of the ring (fig 10).

Repeat steps 9 to 11 for each of the remaining four stems.

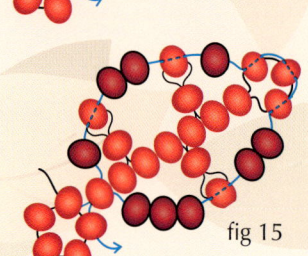

fig 15

16 Referring to fig 15 pass the needle up the first A bead of the first stem and thread on 1A.

Pass through the A bead at the end of the first vein along and thread on 2A for the next gap.

Complete the outline as before following fig 15.

Repeat fig 15 four more times to complete the remaining four bracts.

17 Referring to step 12 space three buds around the ring at the centre of the bracts. Bring them into a cluster as in step 13.

Finish off the short thread end neatly and securely. Finish off the wire ends as before.

Make two more sets of small red bracts to match.

18 **The Green Leaves** - Referring to steps 1 and 2 make a ring of 12B. Thread on 17B and pass back down the first 14B to make a stem. Pass through the following 4B of the ring (fig 16).

fig 16

Repeat at 4B intervals around the ring to make three stems in total.

19 Prepare the needle as in step 4 and pass up through the first stem to emerge through the twelfth B bead.

Referring to fig 17 make the veins of this leaf and the remaining two leaves as before.

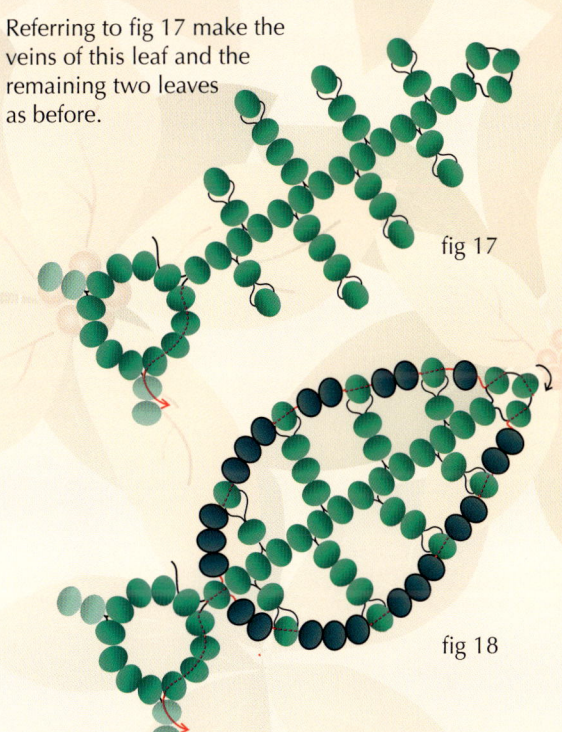
fig 17

fig 18

20 Fig 18 shows the B beads needed to link up the ends of the veins. Pass the needle up through the first B bead of the stem and thread on 3B. Following fig 18 complete the outline as before.

Repeat for the remaining two leaves. Finish off the short thread ends and the wires as before.

Repeat from step 18 four more times to make five sets of the green leaves in total.

21 **The Plain Bands** - Prepare the needle as in step 4 and thread on 28E. Pass the needle through the first E bead in the same direction to bring the beads into a ring.

Drop this ring over the neck of the bauble (fig 19).

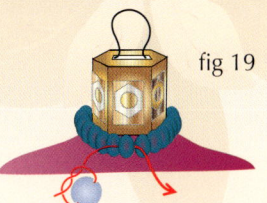
fig 19

The ring needs to fit quite snugly so you may need to adjust the bead count slightly.

If you need to make an adjustment, do so in multiples of 4E, so the final bead count is divisible by four.

22 The bands are made in right-angle weave. The first band starts at the ring of beads around the neck and passes underneath the bauble to attach to the opposite side of the ring.

Thread on 3E. Pass the needle through the E bead on the ring in the same direction as before and the following 2E (fig 20).

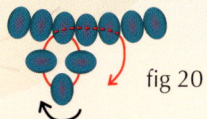
fig 20

Thread on 2E. Referring to fig 21 pass the needle through the adjacent bead of the previous stitch, the E bead on the ring and the 2E just added (fig 21).

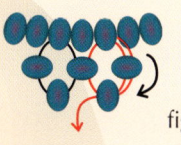
fig 21

This starts the weave - each stitch completes a group of four and moves the needle to the correct position to start the next stitch. The thread will make a series of circular loops so follow the diagrams carefully.

23 Thread on 3E. Pass the needle through the last E bead of the previous stitch and the first E just added (fig 22).

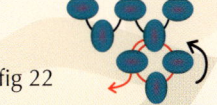
fig 22

Thread on 2E. Pass the needle through the end bead on the adjacent row, the nearest E bead on the side of the previous stitch and the first 1E just added (fig 23).

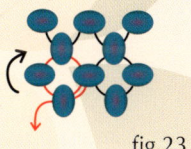
fig 23

Thread on 3E. Pass the needle through the bead at the end of the previous stitch, the 3E just added and the bead at the end of the adjacent row (fig 24).

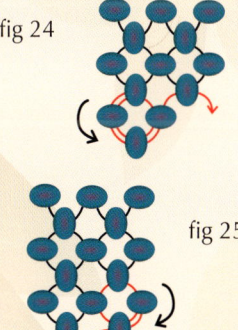
fig 24

fig 25

Thread on 2E. Pass the needle through the adjacent bead of the last stitch, and the following three beads of the new stitch (fig 25).

24 Repeat the four stitches in step 23 until the band is long enough to reach underneath the bauble and up the other side to meet the ring made in step 21.

There is no set number of rows for the band - it will depend on the exact dimensions of your bauble - do not stretch the beading.

The bands need to fit a little more loosely around the bauble. Slip a pencil between the band and the bauble and re-measure the band. Make any additional stitches you need to bring the band up to length with this additional obstacle in the way. The bands will be reinforced and tightened over the bauble in steps 31 and 32.

57

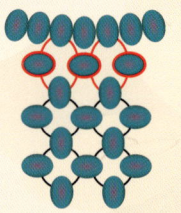

fig 26

25 Fig 26 shows the join between the end of the band and the ring around the neck.

Using the same stitch path add the 3E beads outlined in red, to join the end of the band to the ring exactly opposite the starting position.

26 Locate the three beads on the neck ring halfway between the ends of the band just made.

The first and third E beads of this trio will support the end of the second band - see fig 27 showing the second band connecting to the ring.

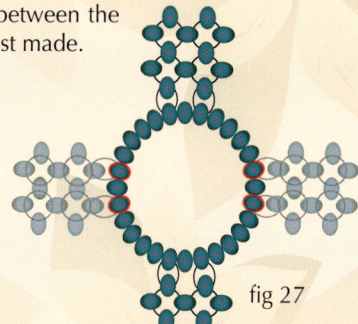

fig 27

Pass the needle through the beads of the ring and start the new band as in step 22.

27 Work sufficient rows as step 23 to reach the edge of the first band as it crosses the bottom of the bauble. You need to join the new band to the edge of the first band here.

Referring to fig 28 locate the two E beads on the first band closest to the middle of this edge and add the beads shown in red to link the two bands together in a T-shape.

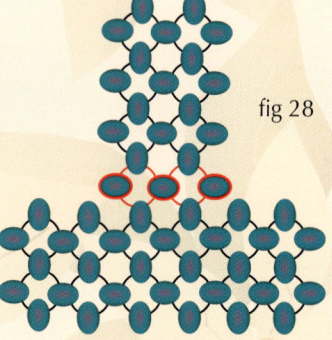

fig 28

28 Work the needle through the beads across the width of the first band and restart the new band creating a cross at the base of the bauble (see fig 29).

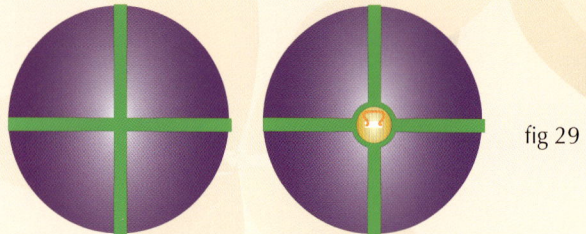

fig 29

Complete the band by linking to the ring around the neck of the bauble exactly opposite the start of this band (see fig 29).

fig 30

29 You have two bands around the bauble that join together at the base and at the ring (fig 29).

You now need to add a band around the circumference of the bauble to join the four sections together (fig 30).

30 Pass the needle through the beads of the first band to emerge halfway down the side of the bauble. As before locate the two beads that will best support the end of the band and start to work out horizontally, in right-angle weave, around the circumference of the bauble.

You will need to keep adjusting your grip on the bauble to check when you need to link up to the next vertical band. Make sure you make the link to the correct two beads on the edge of this band to maintain the horizontal path of the new band. Make the link as in fig 28.

Pass the needle through the beads of the vertical band and restart the horizontal band on the far side. Work around the bauble until you have made all four connections. Remove the needle and leave the thread hanging loose.

31 The bands are now strengthened and tightened around the bauble. Prepare the needle as in step 4 and pass it through the beads of the neck ring to emerge at the top of one of the bands.

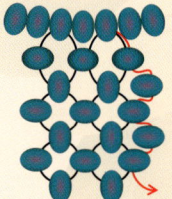

fig 31

Pass the needle through the first E bead down one edge of the band and thread on 1E. Pass through the next bead down this edge of the band and thread on 1E. Pass through the next bead along the edge of the band (fig 31).

Continue down the edge until you reach the corner.

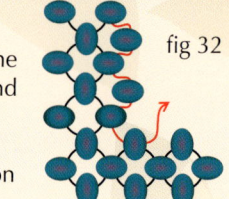

fig 32

Pass through the next bead around the edge of the horizontal band (fig 32) and continue to add the E beads in the gaps.

Work around the remainder of this section turning the second corner as in fig 32.

Pass the needle through to the second section around the top of the bauble and repeat. Repeat for the final two sections at the top of the bauble. The bands should feel a bit tighter around the bauble.

32 Now move onto the four lower sections. You need to control the tension in the thread to complete the tightening of the bands around the bauble. Work these sections as before but you may need to add 1E into the corners around the circumference of the bauble just to ease the fit a little.

If the top four sections seem too tight ease off the keeper bead a little to allow a bit more thread through those beads.

When the bands all fit snugly, finish off all remaining thread ends neatly and securely.

Extra Info....

If you are careful not to scratch the bauble, you can pin the leaves and bracts to the bands and try out different arrangements before you decide on your preferred option.

33 **Attaching the Poinsettias** - The poinsettias and leaves are stitched to the bands with the attached threads. The red bracts sit on top of the leaves, so the leaves need to be attached first.

Use simple stitches to pass between the centres of the motifs and the bands - you may want to add a few additional stitches to hold down the edges of the motifs, but not too many or you will loose the 3D effect of the decoration. Do not finish off any ends until you have everything attached and are happy with the arrangement.

For the design on page 54 -
Place one leaf and a large red poinsettia at the top of a band close to the bauble cap.
Count one vertical band around and place one leaf and a large red poinsettia halfway down.
Count one vertical band around and place one leaf and a large red poinsettia three-quarters of the way down.
Count one band around and place one leaf and a small red poinsettia a third of the way down the band.
Return to the first band and place one leaf and a small red poinsettia two-thirds of the way down the band.
Place the last small red poinsettia at the top of the band on the opposite side of the cap to the first poinsettia.

When you are happy with the positions and the attachments finish off the thread ends neatly and securely.

34 **The Hanging Loop** - Prepare the needle as in step 4. The loop is made from right-angle weave.

To start the strap thread on 4E. Pass the needle through the first two beads to make a ring (fig 33).

Thread on 3E and pass the needle through the last bead of the previous stitch and the first of the 3E just added (fig 34). You have completed the first row (as in fig 23). Repeat figs 24 and 25.

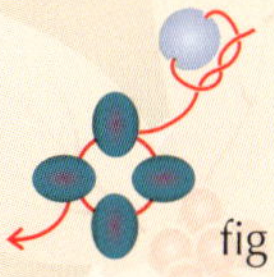

Following the same technique as before (in figs 22 to 25) work 9cm of right-angle weave.

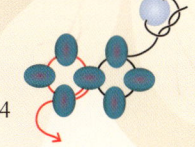

fig 33

fig 34

35 At the end of the band reposition the needle to emerge between the end 2E beads. Thread on 4E. Pass the needle through the first of the 4E and the second E bead at the end of the band (fig 35).

Pass the needle through the following E along the edge and thread on 1D. Pass the needle through the next E bead along the edge (fig 36). Work down the edge to add 1D into each gap.

At the far end of the band make a stitch as in fig 35 and work down the other edge to add 1D into each gap as before.

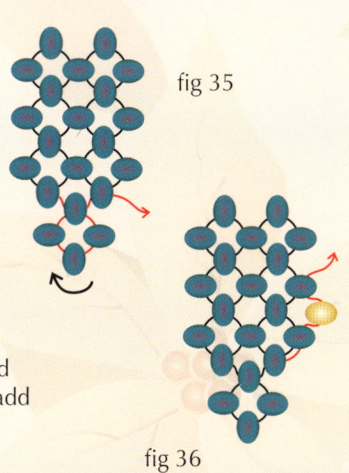

fig 35

fig 36

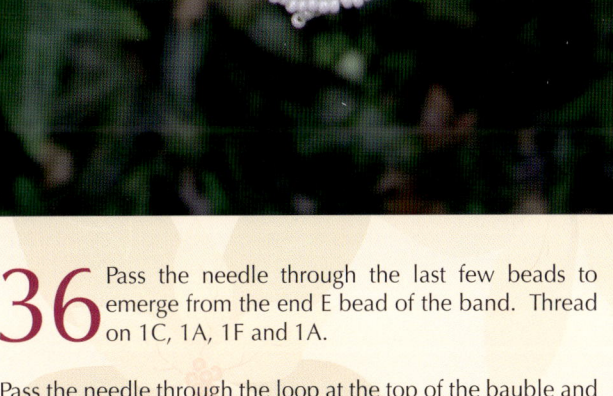

36 Pass the needle through the last few beads to emerge from the end E bead of the band. Thread on 1C, 1A, 1F and 1A.

Pass the needle through the loop at the top of the bauble and back up through the beads just added.

Pass the needle through the E bead at the end of the band (fig 37).

Pass the needle through the beads just added to make the connection strong.

Bring the other end of the band around and link that end E bead to the top loop of the bauble through the 1C, 1A, 1F and 1A beads to complete the loop. Reinforce this connection too and finish off all of the remaining thread ends neatly and securely.

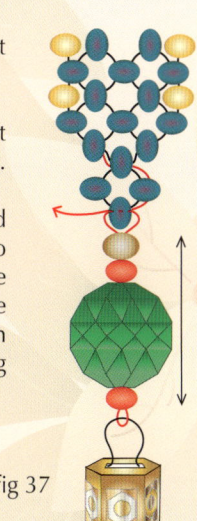

fig 37

Poinsettia Inspiration

Sinaloa Bauble

Named after the Mexican state where Poinsettias grow wild, the Sinaloa Bauble is a simplified interpretation of the Poinsettia Bauble design.

The basic methods for the design are the same as for the Poinsettia design, but as the bands around the bauble are more visible, they are given a contrasting trim.

You Will Need

Materials

One 60mm frosted grey glass bauble
5g of size 10/0 white ceylon seed beads A
4g of size 10/0 silver lined grey seed beads B
1g of size 8/0 frost silver lined grey seed beads C
6g of size 10/0 silver lined crystal seed beads D
8g of size 10/0 frost crystal seed beads beads E
One 12mm crystal AB fire polished faceted bead F
3g of size 10/0 metallic silver seed beads G
1.5m of 0.2mm silver coloured soft wire
A reel of white size D beading thread

37 The Large Bracts - Using the A beads make one set of large bracts as in steps 1 to 13.

38 The Small Bracts - Using the B beads make one set of bracts as in steps 14 to 17.

39 The Leaves - Make one set of leaves as in steps 18 to 20 in the B beads and one set in the G beads.

Extra Info....

If you want a simply stylish bauble design -

Bead the Sinaloa bands over a bauble and add the bow motif from the Garland Bauble design to the hanging loop.
or
Bead the Sinaloa bands over the bauble and add flat-backed sew-on stones to the intersections. Edge the stones with a ring of seed beads for a professional finish.

40   **The Bands** - Work step 21 to add a close-fitting ring of E beads to the neck of the bauble.

41   As for the Poinsettia Bauble, the bands are made in right-angle weave.
The first band starts at the ring of beads around the neck and passes underneath the bauble to attach to the opposite side of the ring.

Thread on 2E and 1D. Pass the needle through the E bead on the ring in the same direction as before and the following 2E (fig 38).

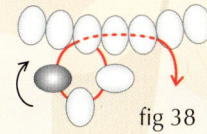

fig 38

Thread on 1D and 1E. Referring to fig 39 pass the needle through the adjacent E bead of the previous stitch, the E bead on the ring and the D and E beads just added (fig 39).

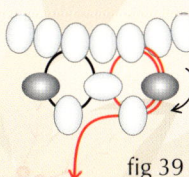

fig 39

This starts the weave - each stitch completes a group of four and moves the needle to the correct position to start the next stitch. The thread will make a series of circular loops, so follow the diagrams carefully.

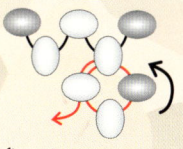

fig 40

42   Thread on 2E and 1D. Pass the needle through the last E bead of the previous stitch and the first E just added (fig 40).

Thread on 1E and 1D. Pass the needle through the end E bead on the adjacent row, the E bead on the side of the previous stitch and the E bead just added (fig 41).

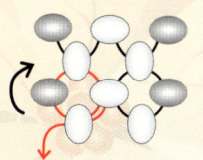

fig 41

Thread on 1D and 2E. Pass the needle through the E bead at the bottom of the previous stitch, the 1D and 2E just added and the E bead at the bottom of the previous row (fig 42).

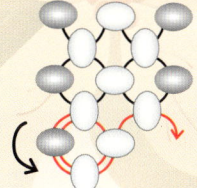

fig 42

Thread on 1D and 1E. Pass the needle through the adjacent E bead of the last stitch, the E bead on the previous row and the following D and E beads just added (fig 43).

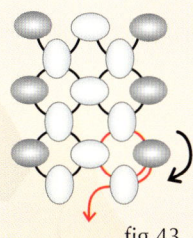

fig 43

Repeat the four stitches in step 42 until the band is long enough to reach underneath the bauble and up the other side to meet the ring made in step 40.

Read through the sizing advice in step 24 and adjust the number of rows you have worked accordingly.

43   Make the join to the other side of the neck ring as in step 25.

Read through step 26 and start the new row with the same bead sequences as step 41.

Work through steps 27 to 30 keeping the D beads on the outer edge of the bands.

44   Using D beads work steps 31 and 32 to strengthen the band edges. This will complete the contrasting trim on the bands.

45   **Attaching the Poinsettias** - Using the technique described in step 33 attach the Poinsettias to the bands.

For this bauble design -
Place the B bead leaf and the large poinsettia at the top of the band close to the bauble cap.
Place the G bead leaf and the small poinsettia at the top of the band on the opposite side of the cap.

46   **The Hanging Loop** - As for the Poinsettia Bauble, the loop is made in right-angle weave. There is a similar adjustment in the bead sequence to create the contrast trim to match the bands already made.

To start the strap thread on 3E and 1D. Pass the needle through the first 2E beads to make a ring (fig 44).

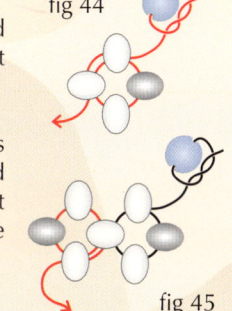

fig 44

Thread on 1E, 1D and 1E and pass the needle through the last E bead of the previous stitch and the first E bead just added (fig 45). You are now in the same position as fig 41.

fig 45

Starting with fig 42 follow the same technique and bead sequences as in step 42 to work 9cm of right-angle weave.

Make the remainder of the hanging loop as in steps 35 and 36.

Belle Époque Bauble

You Will Need

Materials

One 60mm frosted pale blue glass bauble
3g of size 15/0 silver lined capri blue seed beads A
5g of size 15/0 transparent teal AB seed beads B
7g of size 10/0 silver lined capri blue seed beads C
5g of size 10/0 silver lined pale teal seed beads D
2.5g of size 15/0 silver lined crystal seed beads E
Three 6mm capri blue AB fire polished faceted beads F
Twenty-one 4mm teal fire polished faceted beads G
Twenty-five 4mm capri blue fire polished faceted beads H
Thirteen 4mm tanzanite fire polished faceted beads J
Four 6mm tanzanite fire polished faceted beads K
2g of size 6/0 transparent teal AB seed beads L
One 8mm turquoise fire polished faceted bead M
A reel of turquoise size D beading thread

Tools

A size 12 beading needle
A pair of scissors to trim the threads

The lustrous iridescence of a dragonfly's wings flashing above a languid lily pond inspired many of the great designers of the Belle Époque. Although the motif is often seen in jade green and vivid turquoise you can ring the changes with delicate snowy white and crystal or plummy purples with gold and bronze for a very decadent version that would be perfect for the 19th Century fin de siècle mood.

The Decoration is Made in Five Stages

First you will make the three dragonflies.
Secondly, the rosettes that support the fringes are made and linked together with swags.
A fitted foundation row around the neck of the bauble is made next.
Straps are threaded down from the foundation row to support the dragonflies and the rosettes.
The hanging loop completes the decoration.

1 The Dragonflies - Prepare the needle with 1.5m of single thread and tie a keeper bead 15cm from the end.

Thread on 1F. Pass the needle through the F bead a second time to make a strap of thread to one side (fig 1).

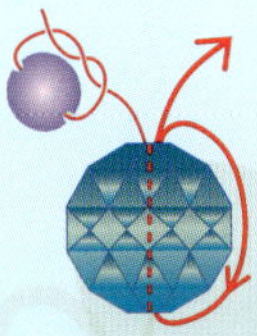

Pass the needle through the F bead again to make a strap to the other side of the F bead (fig 2).

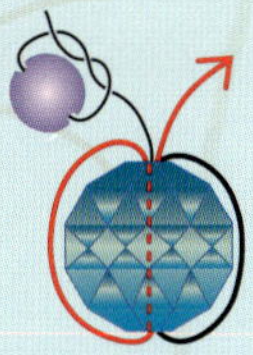

fig 1

fig 2

Repeat both stitches to give you a double strap of thread to each side of the F bead.

2 Thread on 1A. Pass the needle under the two threads to one side of the F bead hole and through the A bead in the opposite direction (fig 3) - this is a brick stitch.

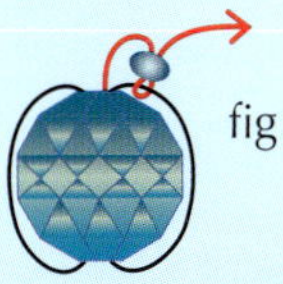

fig 3

Thread on 1A and repeat to add the new bead alongside the first A bead (fig 4).

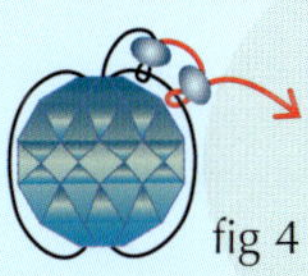

fig 4

3 Thread on 45A. Pass the needle under the two thread strap and through the last A bead threaded in the opposite direction as before (fig 5). This long row forms the outer edge of the first wing.

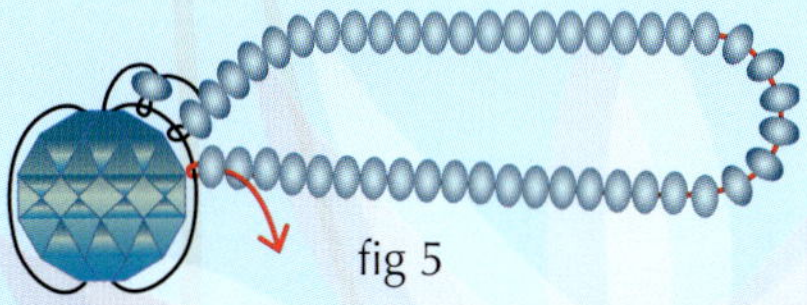

fig 5

4 Pass the needle through the next 1A bead along and thread on 4B. Pass the needle through the third A bead along the wing (fig 6).

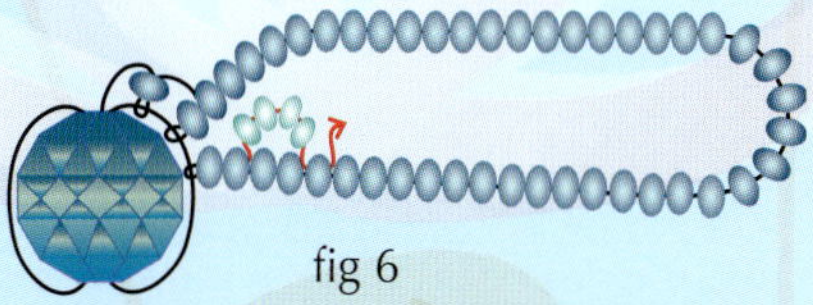

fig 6

Thread on 5B and pass the needle through the fourth A bead along the wing (see fig 7).

Repeat the last stitch twice. Pass through the next 2A beads of the wing (fig 7).

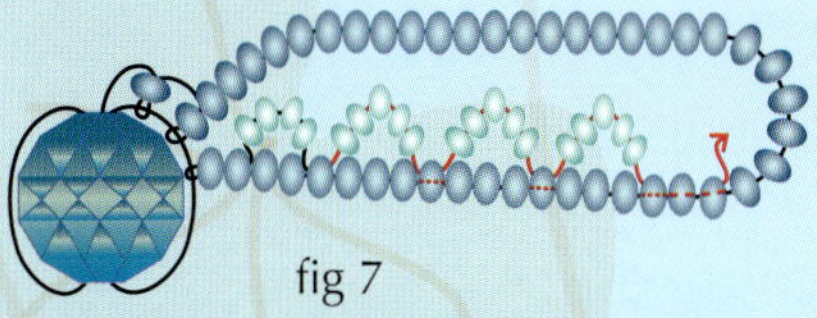

fig 7

5 Referring to fig 8 thread on 1G.

Pass the needle through the seventh A bead around the wing and back through the G bead.

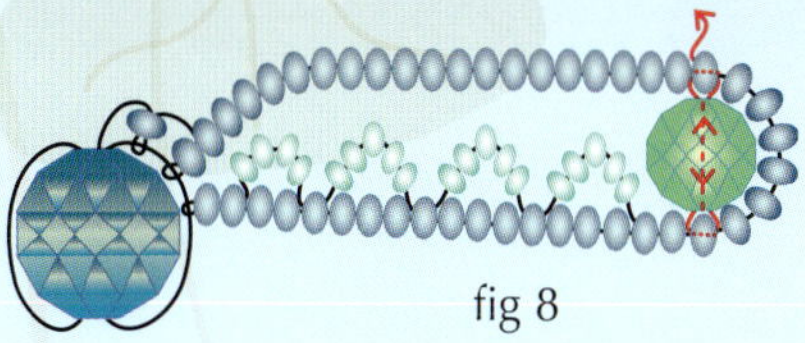

fig 8

Pass the needle through the A bead at bottom of the G bead, back up the G bead and through the seventh A bead around to point towards the F bead (fig 8).

6 Pass the needle through 2A and thread on 2B.

fig 9

Pass the needle through the middle B bead on the last 5B loop and thread on 2B. Pass the needle through the fourth A bead along (fig 9).

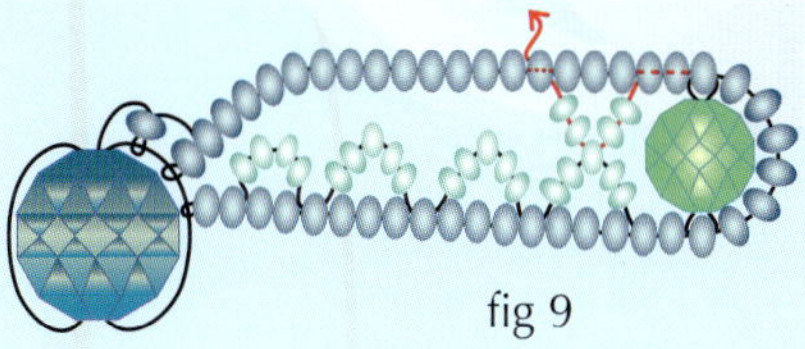

7 Referring to fig 10 thread on 2B and pass through the middle B bead of the next loop along.

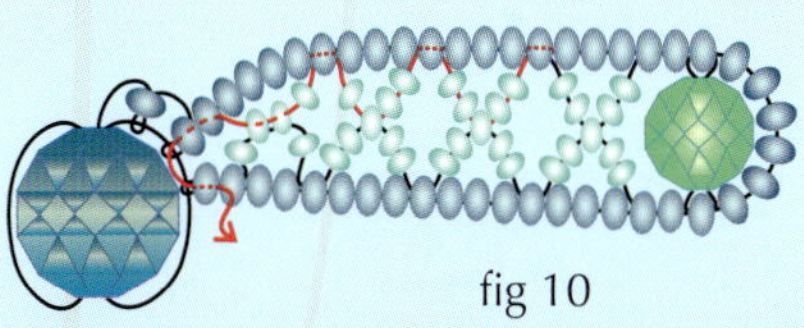

fig 10

Thread on 2B and pass through the fourth A bead along.

Thread on 2B and pass through the middle B bead of the next loop along and thread on 1B.

Pass the needle through the fourth A bead along and thread on 1B. Pass the needle through the middle 2B beads of the next loop.

Pass the needle through the last 2A beads of the top of the wing and out through the next A bead around the F bead (fig 10).

8 Thread on 1A. Pass the needle under the double thread around the F bead and back up the new A bead as before (fig 11).

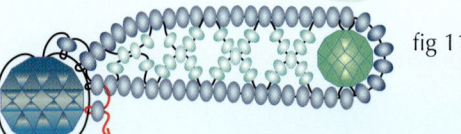

fig 11

Repeat steps 3 to 7 inclusive to make the second wing (fig 12).

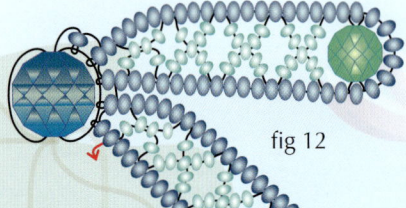

fig 12

fig 13

9 Pass the needle through the A beads around the edge of this wing to emerge 3A from the F bead on the top edge of the wing (fig 13).

The two wings need to be stitched together here to make the beading a little firmer.

10 Referring to fig 14 pass the needle though the fourth A bead of the first wing and back through the A bead on the second wing to make a square stitch. Pass through the next A bead along the lower wing (fig 14).

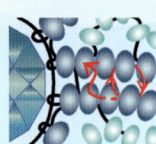

fig 14

Repeat the square stitch twice to link each of the following 2A beads to the corresponding 2A on the first wing (fig 15).

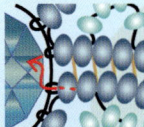

fig 15

11 Referring to fig 16 pass the needle up through the first A bead on the lower edge of the wing and add 1A with a brick stitch to the double thread strap (as figs 4 and 11).

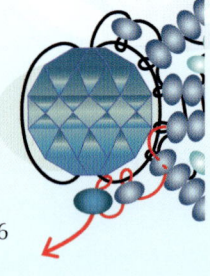

fig 16

12 Thread on 1C and brick stitch the new bead as close as possible to this side of the hole in the F bead (fig 16).

13 Thread on 1H, 1C, 1H, 1C, 1H and 3C.

Leaving aside the last 3C beads to anchor the strand pass the needle back up through the last H bead and the four beads above it.

Pass through the 1C added in step 11 and the F bead (fig 17).

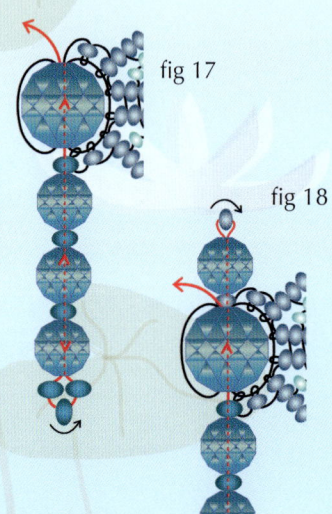

fig 17

fig 18

14 Thread on 1A, 1H and 1A.

Referring to fig 18 leave aside the last A bead to anchor the work and pass the needle down through the H bead just added and the following beads to emerge at the base of the body. Pass the needle through the 3C beads at the base and back up through the body beads to emerge immediately above the F bead (fig 18).

You are now in the correct position to work the wings on the other side of the body.

Repeat steps 2 to 11 inclusive.

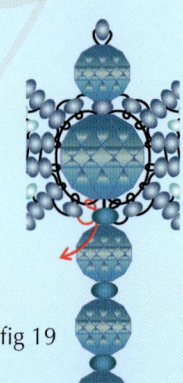

fig 19

15 Referring to fig 19 pass the needle down through the C bead added in step 12, under the double thread as closely as possible to this side of the hole in the F bead and out through the C bead (fig 19). This centres the C bead properly and holds the lower edge of these wings in place more firmly.

Finish off the thread ends neatly and securely without blocking the hole in the top A bead of the head.

Repeat to make two more dragonfly motifs.

16 The Rosettes - Prepare the needle with 2m of single thread and tie a keeper bead 15cm from the end. Thread on 1K and 7C. Pass the needle through the K bead to bring the C beads into a strap to one side (fig 20).

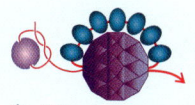
fig 20

Thread on 7C and pass the needle through the K bead again to make a second strap on the opposite side of the larger bead (fig 21).

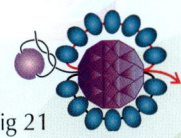
fig 21

Pass the needle through the first 2C beads of the new strap.

17 Thread on 8B, 1C, 3D, 1C, 1L, 1C and 3B. Leaving aside the last 3B beads to anchor the strand, pass the needle back up through the last C bead and the following beads to emerge 1B bead from the top of the strand (fig 22).

Thread on 1B and pass through the C bead at the top of the strand and the following 1C (fig 23). This centres the strand beneath the C bead.

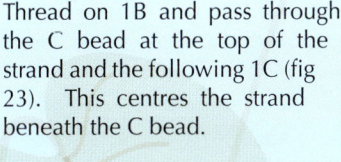
fig 22   fig 23   fig 24

18 Thread on 16B, 1C, 3D, 1C, 1L, 1C and 3B. As before leave aside the last 3B beads to anchor the strand and pass back up through the beads just threaded to emerge 1B bead from the top.

Referring to fig 24 pass the needle through the adjacent B bead at the top of the previous strand, through the C bead at the top of this strand and the following 1C.

19 Thread on 20B, 1C, 3D, 1C, 1L, 1C, 1B, 1J and 4B. Leaving aside the last 3B beads pass the needle up through the B bead below the J bead and the J bead (fig 25).

Thread on 6B. Pass the needle through the 3B beads of the anchor and thread on 6B (fig 26).

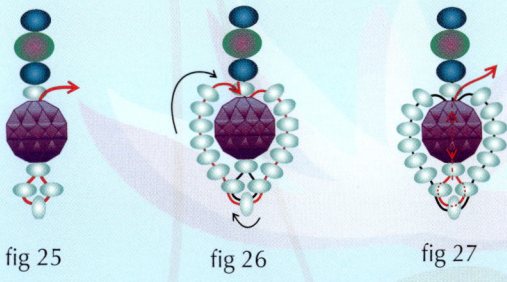
fig 25   fig 26   fig 27

Referring to fig 27 pass the needle down the J and single B bead, through the 3B beads of the anchor and back up to emerge from the top of the J bead.

Pass the needle up through the remaining beads of the strand to emerge 1B from the top. Link this strand to the previous strand as in fig 24 passing through 2C beads at the top to be in the correct position to start the next strand.

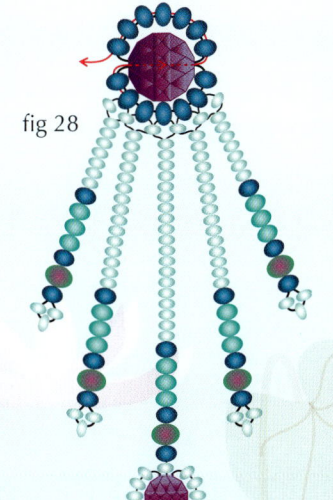
fig 28

20 Referring to fig 28 make one strand as in step 18 and one as in step 17.

Pass the needle through the K bead and the 7C beads of the top strap (fig 28).

21 Thread on 20C, 1H, 6C, 1H, 6C, 1H, 27C and 1K. Pass the needle through the last 7C beads in the same direction as before to bring them into a strap around the K bead (fig 29). This K bead is the central bead of the next rosette.

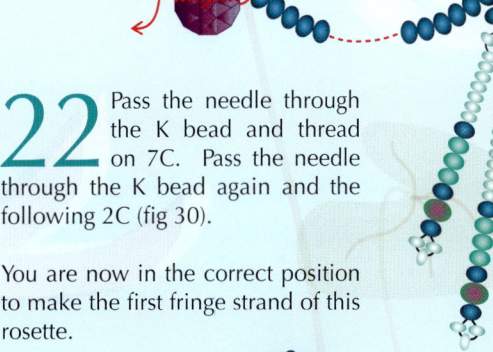
fig 29

22 Pass the needle through the K bead and thread on 7C. Pass the needle through the K bead again and the following 2C (fig 30).

You are now in the correct position to make the first fringe strand of this rosette.

fig 30

Repeat steps 17 to 22 inclusive.

Repeat steps 17 to 20 inclusive.

23 Thread on 20C, 1H, 6C, 1H, 6C, 1H and 20C. Pass the needle through the first 6C beads of the top strap around the first K bead (fig 31). This will bring the swags and rosettes into a circle.

24 Thread on 1D. Pass the needle through the last C bead passed through in the same direction and the new D bead to make a square stitch (fig 32).

25 Repeat to add 1D to the next C bead with a square stitch (fig 33).

Thread on 2D. Pass the needle through the next 1C bead and back through the 2D (fig 34).

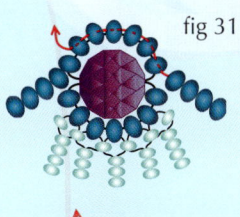
fig 31

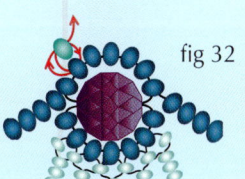
fig 32

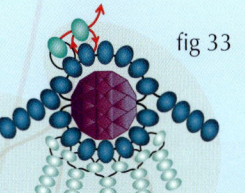
fig 33

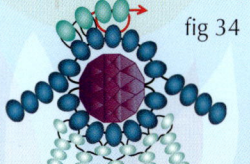
fig 34

65

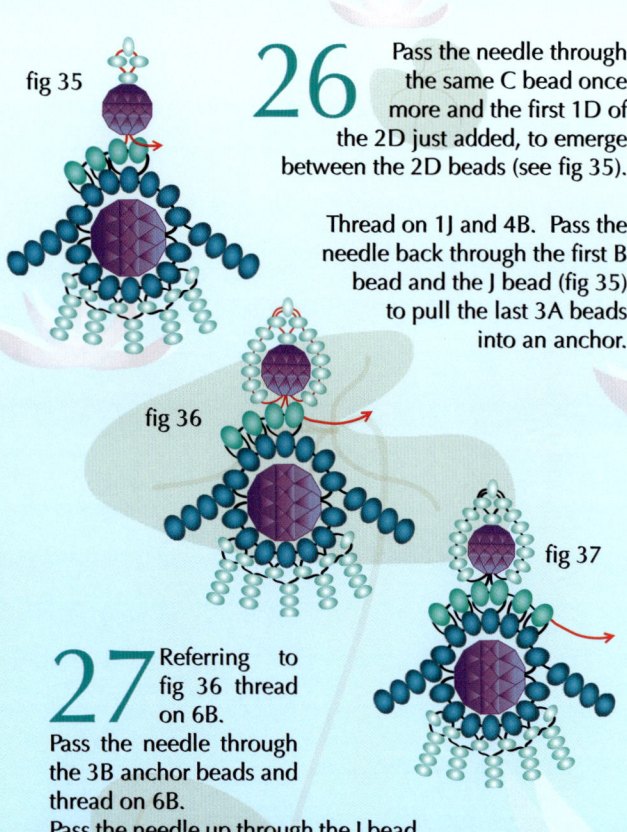

fig 35

fig 36

fig 37

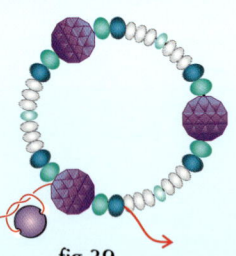

fig 39

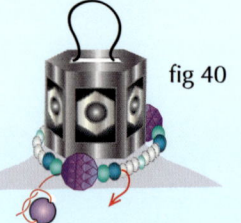

fig 40

fig 41

26 Pass the needle through the same C bead once more and the first 1D of the 2D just added, to emerge between the 2D beads (see fig 35).

Thread on 1J and 4B. Pass the needle back through the first B bead and the J bead (fig 35) to pull the last 3A beads into an anchor.

27 Referring to fig 36 thread on 6B.
Pass the needle through the 3B anchor beads and thread on 6B.
Pass the needle up through the J bead to pull the B beads into a frame around the J bead as before.
Pass the needle through the following 1B, the 3B beads of the anchor and back down to emerge at the bottom of the J bead.

Pass the needle through the second D bead to centralise the motif (fig 36).

28 Square stitch 1D to each of the following 2C beads - you are now in the correct position to start to string the next swag (fig 37).

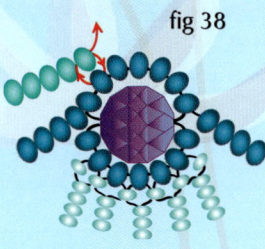

fig 38

29 Thread on 18D, 1G, 5D, 1G, 5D, 1G and 19D.

Locate the next rosette around the work. Pass the needle through the second C bead of the top strap on this rosette, bringing the needle through to point towards the first C bead of the strap.

Pass the needle through the last D bead threaded to complete a square stitch (fig 38).

30 Repeat steps 25 to 29 inclusive.

Repeat steps 25 to 28 inclusive. Thread on 18D, 1G, 5D, 1G, 5D, 1G and 18D. Pass the needle through the first D bead added in step 24 to close up the circle of swags. Finish off this and any remaining thread ends neatly and securely.

31 The Foundation Row - Prepare the needle with 1.5m of single thread and tie a keeper bead 15cm from the end. Thread on 1J, 1D, 1C, 3E, 1B, 3E, 1C and 1D. Repeat this sequence twice.

32 Pass the needle through the first 1J, 1D and 1C to bring the beads into a circle (fig 39).

Drop this ring over the top of your bauble - it needs to fit snugly around the base of the neck (fig 40).

If it is too tight, adjust the E bead count accordingly, to give you three equidistant C/D/J/D/C sequences with the single B bead halfway between each set.

Make sure the needle is emerging from the C bead as shown in fig 40.

33 Attaching the Dragonflies & Rosettes - Thread on 17E. Pass the needle through the A bead at the top of a dragonfly motif and thread on 17E.

Referring to fig 41 pass the needle through 1C, 1D, 1J, 1D and 1C on the foundation ring to suspend the dragonfly motif from a loop of beads.

Pass the needle through the beads of the foundation row to emerge from the last bead of the next C/D/J/D/C sequence.

Repeat step 33 twice.

Pass the needle through the foundation row to emerge from the next B bead.

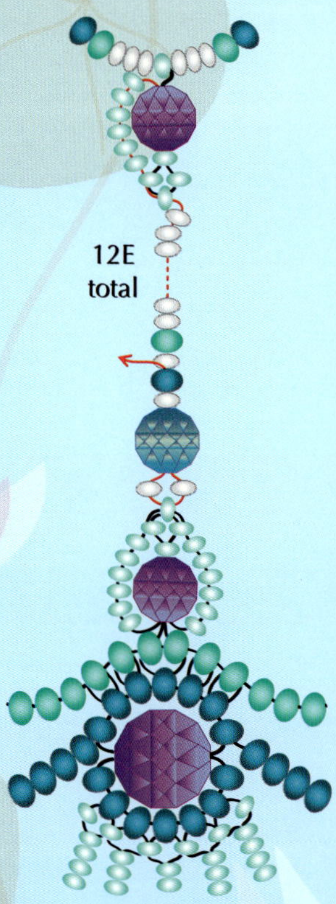

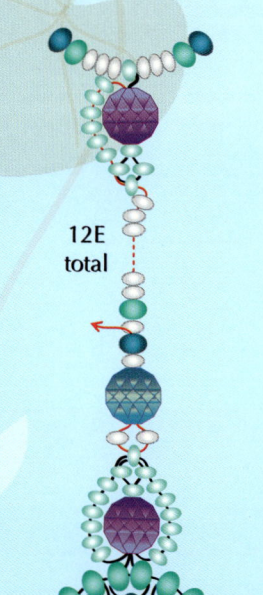

12E total

fig 43

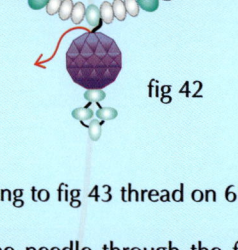

fig 42

34 Thread on 1J and 4B. Pass the needle back up through the first B bead and the J bead to pull the last 3B beads into an anchor (fig 42).

Referring to fig 43 thread on 6B.

Pass the needle through the first 2B beads of the anchor and thread on 12E, 1D, 1E, 1C, 1E, 1H and 1E.

Pass the needle through the B bead at the tip of the first rosette and thread on 1E.

Pass the needle up through the H bead and the following 1E and 1C (fig 42).

You now need to make a link to the top wings of the dragonflies on either side.

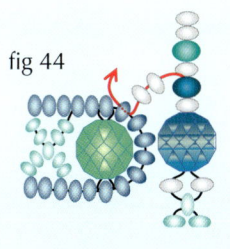
fig 44

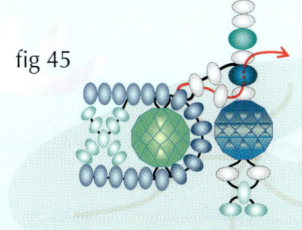
fig 45

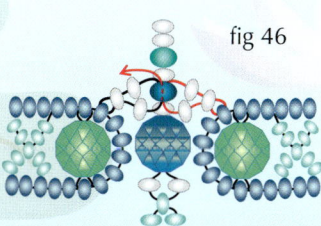
fig 46

35 Thread on 2E. Pass the needle through the top A bead of the curve around the end of the top wing of the adjacent dragonfly (fig 44).

Pass the needle back through the last E bead and thread on 1E. Pass the needle through the C bead towards the top of the bauble (fig 45).

Thread on 2E. Pass the needle through the corresponding A bead on the end of the top wing of the other adjacent dragonfly (see fig 46) and back through the last E bead. Thread on 1E and pass the needle up though the C bead (fig 46).

Pass the needle up through the following 1E, 1D and 11E.

36 Referring to fig 47 thread on 1E and pass though the B bead at the tip of the anchor made in step 34 in the same direction as before. Pass through the following 1B of the anchor and thread on 6B.

As before pass the needle down through the J bead, through the B beads of the anchor and back out of the top of the J bead. Pass the needle through the B bead on the foundation row in the same direction as before (see fig 47).

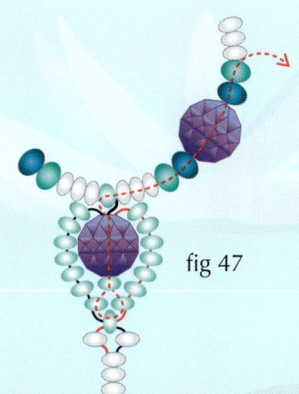
fig 47

Pass the needle through the foundation row to emerge from the next B bead (fig 47).

Repeat steps 34 to 36 inclusive twice more. Finish off the thread ends neatly and securely.

37 The Hanging Loop - Repeat step 16 to the end of fig 21. Pass the needle through the 7C of the first strap and thread on 1C. Pass the needle through the 7C of the second strap and thread on 1C. Pass the needle through the first C bead of the first strap to pull the new beads into the gaps above the holes in the F bead (fig 48).

Pass the needle through the following 7C.

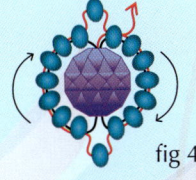
fig 48

38 Thread on 1M and 1C. Pass the needle through the loop at the top of the bauble and back up through the C and M beads. Pass the needle through the C bead at the bottom of the F bead in the same direction as before to centre the link (fig 49).

Pass the needle up and down this link twice more to strengthen. Pass the needle through the C beads around the F bead to emerge from the fifth C bead after the top of the link to the bauble.

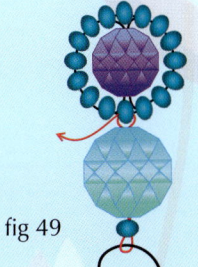
fig 49

39 Referring to fig 50 and steps 24 - 25 square stitch 1D to this C bead and the next 1C. Square stitch 2D to the next 1C and 1D to the C bead at the top of the F bead. Make a 2D stitch and finish with two 1D stitches (fig 50).

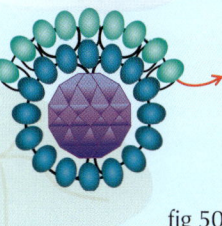
fig 50

Pass the needle back through the C beads and along the new D beads to emerge from the central D bead. Thread on 1J and 4B. Pass the needle back down the first 1B and the J bead as before (fig 51).

Thread on 6B and pass through the 3B anchor. Thread 6B and pass up through the J bead and the following B beads to emerge from the B bead at the tip of the anchor (fig 52).

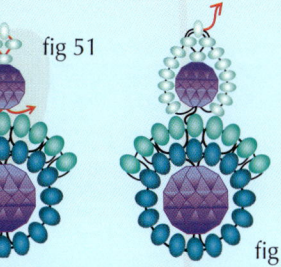
fig 51

fig 52

40 Thread on 1E, 1H, 2E, 1C and 50D. Pass the needle back down the C bead to draw up the loop (see fig 53). Pass through the following 2E and 1H. Thread on 1E and pass through the B bead at the tip of the anchor in the same direction as before (fig 53).

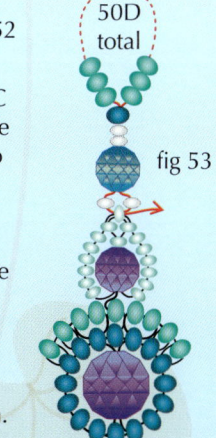
50D total

fig 53

Pass the needle through the connection to the loop, and the loop itself, twice more to strenghten.

Pass the needle through the B beads at the tip of the J bead and down through the J bead. Pass through the D bead at the base of this motif in the same direction as before. Reinforce this link too.

Finish off the thread end neatly and securely. Remove any remaining keeper beads and finish off these ends similarly.

67

Christmas Pudding Bauble

You Will Need

Materials

For the gold bauble -

One 40mm frosted gold glass bauble
8g of size 10/0 silver lined brown seed beads A
3g of size 8/0 chalk black seed beads B
Eighteen 4mm black fire polished faceted beads C
4g of size 10/0 white lined crystal seed beads D
4g of size 10/0 silver lined emerald seed beads E
Three 6mm red fire polished faceted beads F
One 8mm black fire polished faceted bead G
A reel each of black and white size D beading thread

For the black bauble substitute -

One 40mm frosted black glass bauble
3g of size 8/0 silver lined bronze seed beads B

Tools

A size 10 beading needle
A pair of scissors to trim the threads

One of the first signs that Christmas is approaching is an intoxicatingly festive aroma - spicy, sweet and slightly boozy - of a plum pudding being mixed with a wooden spoon in that creamy-coloured bowl that is saved for 'proper old-fashioned' cookery. This is a no-calorie version of the traditional British, show-stopping and waistline-expanding pudding served at the end of the festive meal.

The Decoration is Made in Five Stages
The bauble is covered with a fitted net of black and brown beads to form the plum pudding layer.
A separate white swagged section is assembled.
The top of the white swags are decorated with leaf motifs and red berries.
This completed section of swags, berries and leaves then drops over the plum pudding and is stitched into place.
The hanging loop is added to finish the design.

Extra Info....
The beaded net for the bauble needs to fit quite snugly. Although a bauble can be manufactured to a high standard the finished dimensions can vary a little. In addition, different batches of beads, and indeed beads within a batch, can also vary very slightly in size.

Simple bead count adjustments, if needed, are made in the final stages as the net comes together around the neck of the bauble - guidance is given where necessary.

3 Row 1 - Thread on 5A and 6B. Pass the needle through the first B bead again in the same direction to draw the 6B beads into a ring (fig 2).

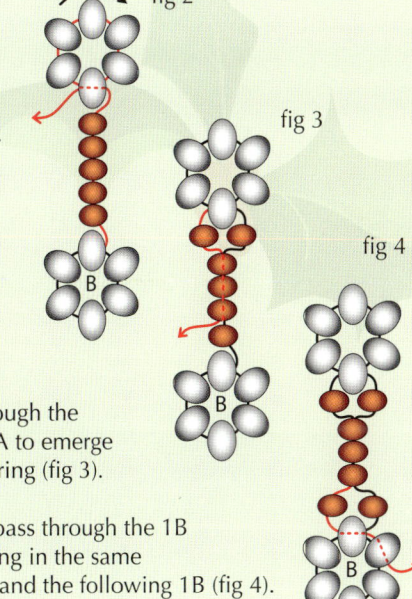

Pass the needle through the beads of the ring once more to make the shape a little firmer.

Make sure the needle is emerging from the first 1B of the ring as fig 2.

Thread on 1A.

Pass the needle through the middle 3A of the 5A to emerge 1A above the base ring (fig 3).

Thread on 1A and pass through the 1B bead on the base ring in the same direction as before and the following 1B (fig 4).

1 **The Plum Pudding** - The pudding net starts at the base of the bauble and works up, in a series of concentric rows, to the neck of the bauble.

Prepare the needle with 1.5m of single black thread. Tie a keeper bead 15cm from the end.

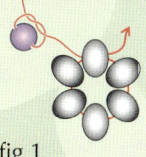

2 Thread on 6B. Pass the needle through the first B in the same direction as before to draw the beads into a circle (fig 1).
Pass the needle through the following 6B beads to strengthen the ring.

fig 1

This ring will sit at the base of the bauble and will be referred to as the 'base ring'.

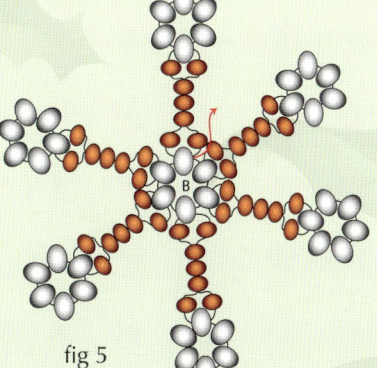

fig 5

4 Repeat step 3 five more times to complete a six-spoked star with a ring of 6B at the end of each spoke (fig 5).

These six 6B rings will be called the 'Row 1 Rings' or R1R.

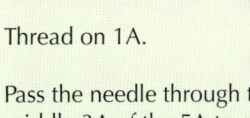

The base of the black bauble shows the ring of 6B beads very clearly.

Extra Info....
Although the beaded net is not difficult to make, it can be hard to keep your place in the pattern. Tie a scrap of bright thread to the base ring so it's easier to identify.

5 Fig 6 shows a simplified plan for beadwork showing a vertical section of the concentric rows. At the bottom you can see the base ring marked B.

Each one of the base ring B beads links through a strap to another B bead ring - this is the row you have just worked (R1R) - the diagram shows just two of these R1R rings. You can see that the straps from the base ring (shown in brown) link onto the B beads marked 1 on the R1R rings.

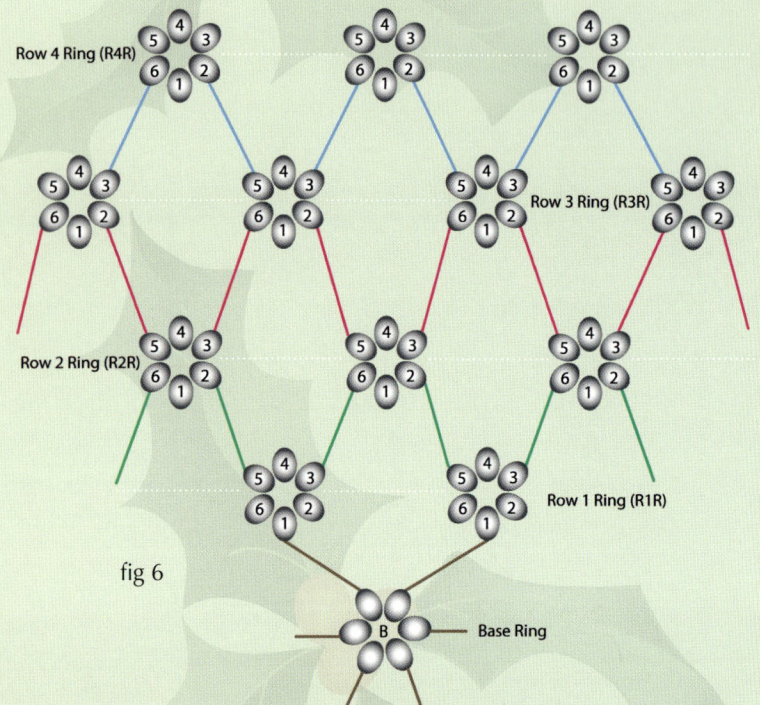

fig 6

Now look at the straps between rows R1R and R2R (shown in green). The straps here go from the B beads marked 5 and 3 on the R1R rings to the beads marked 2 and 6 on the R2R rings.

This same arrangement is used on the links between the R2R and R3R rings (shown in pink) and the R3R and R4R rings (shown in blue).

This arrangement of straps makes an evenly spaced diagonal lattice pattern - note that on the R2R, R3R and R4R rings the beads marked 1 and 4 at the top and bottom of the ring are not used in the link pattern.

You will find it useful to refer back to this diagram.

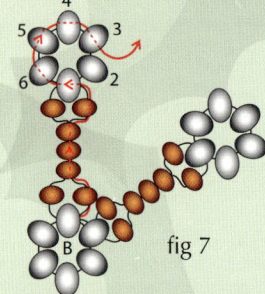

6 At the moment the needle is emerging from a B bead on the base ring - you need to pass it through the beads of the adjacent strap to emerge through the bead marked 3 of the R1R at the end of that strap (fig 7).

Note how the thread passes through the beads following the path of the previous thread without skipping across the corner where the R1R joins the strap. You must do this each time you reposition the needle through a strap - if you cut the corner the work will pull out of shape. It does not matter which side of the number 3 bead the needle is emerging from as long as it is the number 3 bead.

You are now in the correct position to make the first strap shown in green in fig 6.

7 Row 2 - Thread on 5A and 6B. Pass the needle through the first B bead again, in the same direction, to draw the 6B beads into a ring - this is your first R2R ring (fig 8).

Pass the needle through the beads of the ring once more to make it a little firmer - make sure the needle is emerging from the first B bead of the ring as fig 8.

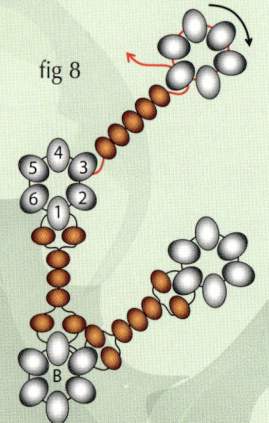

fig 8

8 Thread on 1A.

Pass the needle through the middle 3A of the new 5A (as fig 3) to emerge 1A above the R1R.

Thread on 1A and pass through the same B bead on the R1R (marked 3 in fig 9) in the same direction as before (see fig 9).

You have just completed the first green link as shown on fig 6 - note that this first link connects bead 3 on the R1R to bead 6 on the new R2R (see fig 9).

Reposition the needle up through the A beads of the strap just made and around the B beads of the R2R to emerge through bead 2 on this ring (fig 9).

Following fig 10 make a similar link from bead 2 on the new R2R ring to the bead marked 5 on the next R1R ring around.

You have now completed the second link shown in green on fig 6.

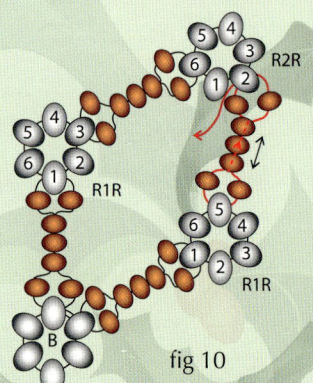

fig 10

9 To reposition the needle for the start of the third green link follow fig 11.

Pass the needle down through the beads of the strap just completed and around the B beads of the following R1R to emerge from bead 3 on fig 6 and fig 11.

Repeat from step 7 to step 9 inclusive to create a new strap, a new R2R ring and to link that new R2R ring to the next R1R ring around the work.

Repeat until you have completed a full circuit of the design adding six new R2R rings in total (see fig 12).

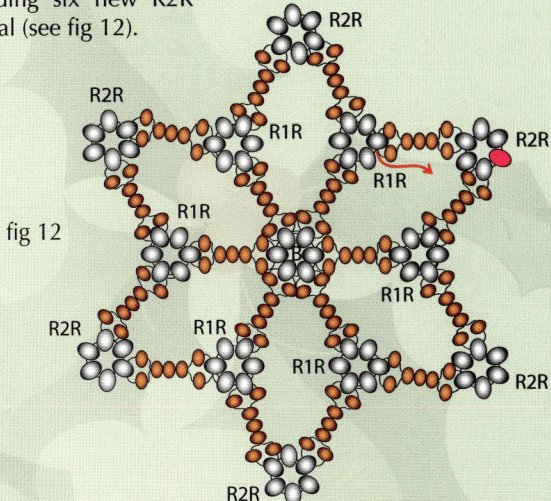

fig 11

10 Referring back to fig 6 you will see you have made the R2R row and the green links - you must now make the pink links and the R3R row. These pink links reach out from the beads 3 and 5 on the R2R row and they join onto the new row R3R at beads 6 and 2 respectively - exactly the same as the row just worked.

Reposition the needle to emerge through bead 3 on the closest R2R ring (marked pink on fig 12) before you start the new row.

Follow the bead sequence in steps 6 to 9 inclusive to create a new strap, a new ring (this ring will be a R3R ring) and a second strap to the next R2R around the design.

Repeat five more times to complete the third row - you will then have six R3R rings (fig 13).

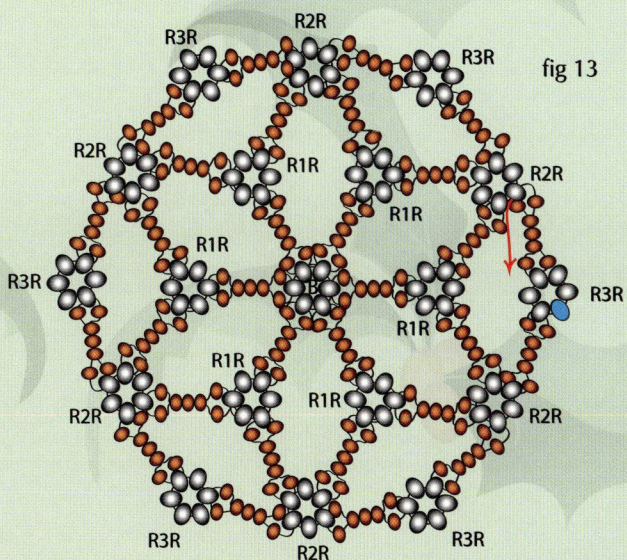

fig 12

fig 13

11 Fig 13 shows the lattice laid out flat but you will have noticed that it is forming a cupped shape.

To check on your progress pop the bauble inside the lattice - it will be very far from fitted at this stage but the work is starting to enclose the bauble. Remove the bauble for the moment.

You have to work another row in a similar fashion.

Refer to fig 6. You can see that row 4 connects in the same manner to the third row as the third row connected to the second row.

Reposition the needle to emerge through the bead marked 3 on the closest R3R ring (marked blue in fig 13) and work a further row exactly the same as the last row to create six new rings (R4R) held on straps between the R3R rings just worked.

Once the row is complete pop the bauble back into the lattice and position the base ring at the bottom of the bauble.

To close up the top of the lattice around the bauble you will need to work one more row as before. This last row of beading will be almost completely concealed by the white swags when they are added to the top of the design so it needs to be quite tight and smooth.

12 Reposition the needle as before to emerge from bead 3 on the closest R4R of the row just worked.

*Thread on the 5A beads for the strap and a further 6A beads for the ring. Using A beads instead of B beads for the ring makes the texture a little smoother and allows you to bring the beading closer together at the top of the bauble. Pass the needle through the first of the 6A beads just added to form the ring.

Complete the first 5A strap, the ring and 5A strap to the next R4R around the lattice as before - then stop. You just need to pause to check the beading for size.

Reposition the lattice so the base ring corresponds with the bottom of the bauble. Check that the top of the 5A ring just completed either just touches the neck of the bauble or falls no more than 3mm short of it. If that is the case work the rest of the row as before substituting 6A beads for the 6B beads on each occasion.

If the A bead ring is very short of the bauble neck unpick back to * and work the same pattern substituting the 5A strap for a 6A or 7A strap. Re-check for size before completing the remainder of the row with this new count for the bead strap.

Similarly if the ring is creeping up the neck of the bauble, the lattice is a little too big. Unpick to * and work the row with a strap count of 4A or 3A - whichever gives you a better fit.

13 Pass the needle through the beads of the last row to emerge through the A bead at the top of the closest A bead ring (fig 14). This bead and the corresponding A beads on the other five A bead rings need to be linked together to make the lattice fit snugly.

fig 14

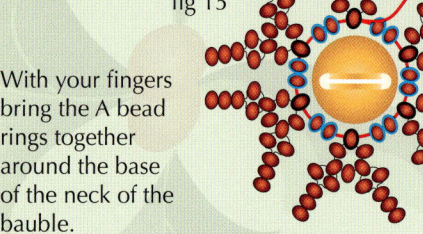

fig 15

With your fingers bring the A bead rings together around the base of the neck of the bauble.

Fig 15 shows a top view of the bauble - here it has been neccessary to add 2A beads in-between the top A beads of the rings to complete a neat circle around the base of the bauble neck - you may find that 2A is perfect - you may need 1A or 3A. Experiment a little until you achieve a neat ring with no thread showing.

Pass the needle through the beads of this final collar once more to make it firm. You now add a simple embellishment to the lattice.

14 The embellishment adds C beads, on A bead supports, into the spaces in the lattice pattern.

You will need to reposition the needle several times - work the needle through the beads of the lattice as before - do not cut any corners and follow the path of the previous thread even if it means going right around a circle to get to the bead you need to emerge from.

Fig 16 shows a simplified diagram of the position of the C beads.

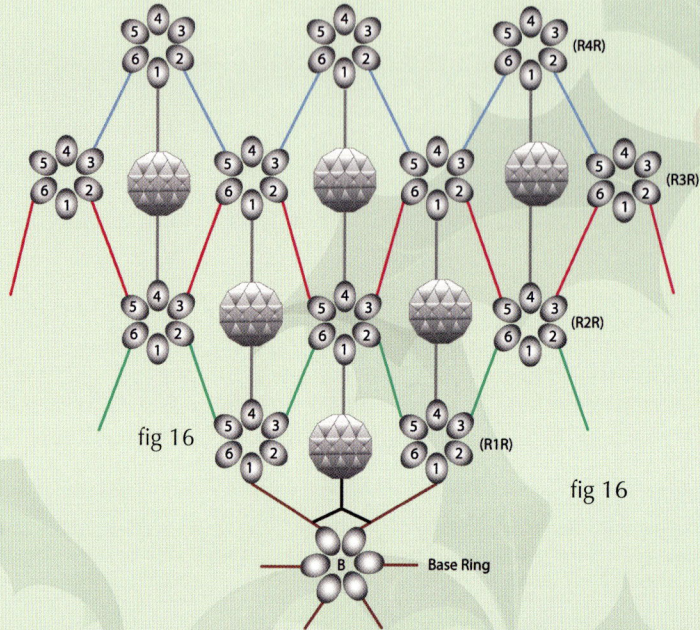

fig 16

fig 16

On the top row of embellishment you will see that the C bead is in the centre of the space suspended between the number 1 bead at the base of the R4R ring and bead number 4 of the R2R ring immediately below it.

The second row of embellishment fits into the lattice in the same way between the R3R and R1R rows.

The lowest row of embellishment is a little different as the space is more restricted here.

Reposition the needle through the beads of the lattice to emerge from bead number 1 of the closest R4R.

15 Thread on 3A, 1C and 3A. Pass the needle through bead number 4 on the R2R at the bottom of this space in the lattice (fig 17).

Thread on 1A. Pass the needle through the middle 1A of the last 3A added to bring the needle out pointing towards the C bead.

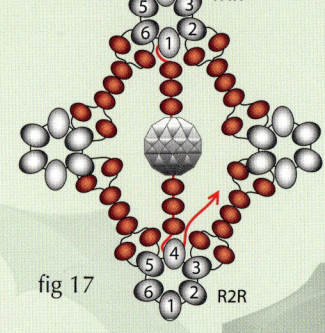

fig 17

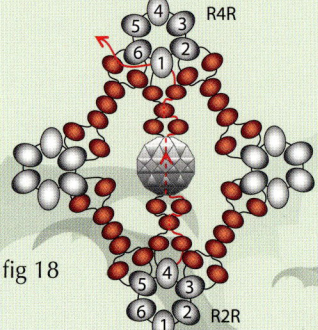

fig 18

Thread on 1A and pass up through the C bead. Thread on 1A and pass through the middle 1A of the 3A above the C bead and thread on 1A. Pass through bead number 1 on the R4R in the same direction as before (fig18).

72

16 Pass the needle through the first 3A beads added above the C bead and thread on 4A.

Pass the needle through the first 3A beads added below the C bead to draw the new 4A into a strap to the side of the C bead.

Pass the needle through bead number 4 on the R2R in the same direction as before (fig 19).

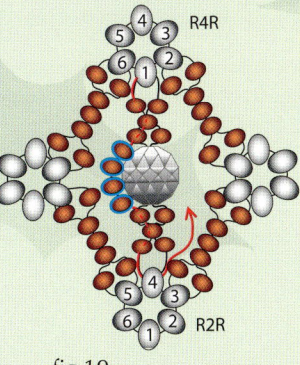

fig 19

Repeat the last stitch to add 4A to the other edge of the C bead (fig 20).

Pass the needle down through the beads of this embellishment to emerge from the bead marked 1 on the R2R ring.

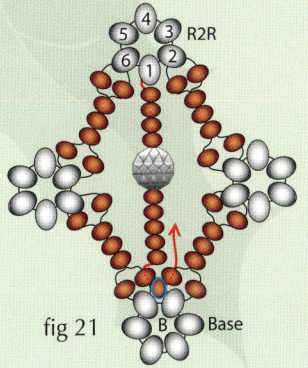

fig 20

This is the correct position to add the slimmer embellishment of the lowest row (see fig 16).

17 Following fig 21 thread on 4A, 1C and 5A. Pass the needle through one of the A beads immediately above the B bead of the base ring.

Thread on 1A and pass the needle up through the other A bead above the B bead on the base ring (fig 21).

fig 21

Following fig 22 add 1A in this position, 1A both below and above the C bead and 1A just below bead 1 of the R2R ring.

This completes the slimmer embellishment.

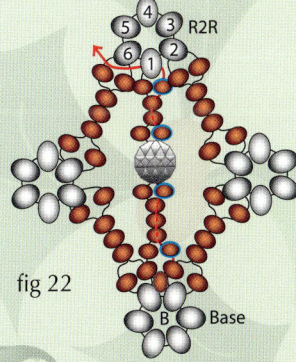

fig 22

18 You now have the two types of embellishments needed to complete the sequence.

Repositioning the needle through the beads of the lattice as you go, add the slimmer embellishments to the lowest row of spaces and two rows of the more elaborate type to the middle and upper rows as shown in fig 16.

Do not add any embellishment to the very top row of spaces on the lattice as they will not show once the white swags are added.

Once all of the embellishments are completed remove any keeper beads and finish off all of the thread ends neatly and securely.

19 **The White Swags** - Prepare the needle with 1.5m of single white thread and tie a keeper bead 15cm from the end.

Thread on 30D. Pass the needle through the first D bead in the same direction as before to draw the beads up into a ring (as fig 1).

Check this ring will fit over the top of the bauble and sit around the base of the neck. You may need to adjust the bead count.

The pattern requires a ring bead count that is divisible by six, so if 30D is too small try 36D or 42D. If you adjust the D bead number you will need to take that into account as you proceed with the pattern to create six equally spaced swags.

The following bead counts around the ring assume a total count of 30D. If you have made a count adjustment you will need to make an allowance for the extra beads within each of the six swag sections. The adjustment for 36D is shown in red brackets for guidance.

Extra Info....
The lattice covering is so pretty it makes a very good bauble design without the addition of the white swags, leaves and berries.
Try making a turquoise and blue lattice over a gold bauble, or black and gold beads over a red bauble for simply stunning results.

20 Pass the needle through the beads of the ring once more to make it a little more firm.

Thread on 41D. Count back 3D around the ring of 30D. Pass the needle through these 3D towards the top of the 41D and the following 5D (6D) around the ring (fig 23).

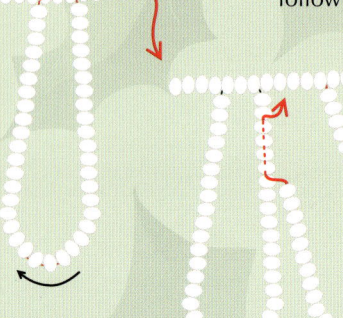

fig 23

fig 24

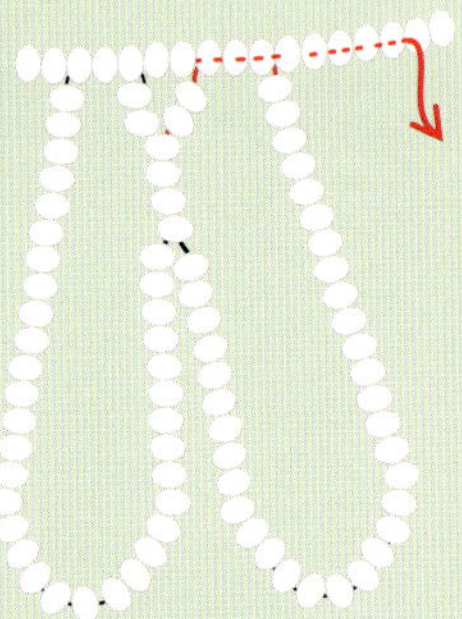

fig 25

*Thread on 35D. Pass the needle through the 6th, 5th, 4th and 3rd D beads of the last swag (fig 24). Thread on 2D and pass the needle through the 3D before the start of this swag and the following 5D (6D) of the ring (fig 25).

Repeat from the * three more times to give you five swags in total. If you are using the 36D bead ring you should have 3D beads between the swags not 2D as shown.

The last swag needs to link the fifth swag to the first swag.

Thread on 2D. Pass the needle through the 39th, 38th, 37th and 36th D beads of the first swag and thread on 29D.

fig 26

Pass the needle up through the 6th, 5th, 4th and 3rd D beads of the fifth swag and thread on 2D.

Pass the needle through the third D bead (4th) around the ring (fig 26).

fig 27

21 Pass the needle through the next 2D beads of the ring and the first 2D beads of the swag.

Thread on 25D.

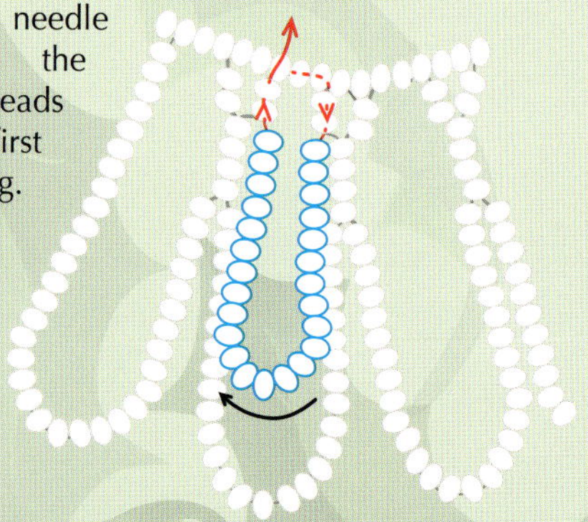

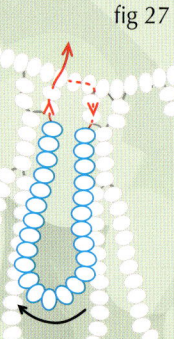

Pass the needle up through the 2D beads at the other side of the this large swag to complete a medium-sized swag inside the large swag (fig 27).

22 Pass the needle through the following 1D of the ring and thread on 15D. Pass the needle through the same 1D bead on the ring to draw up a small swag inside the other two (fig 28).

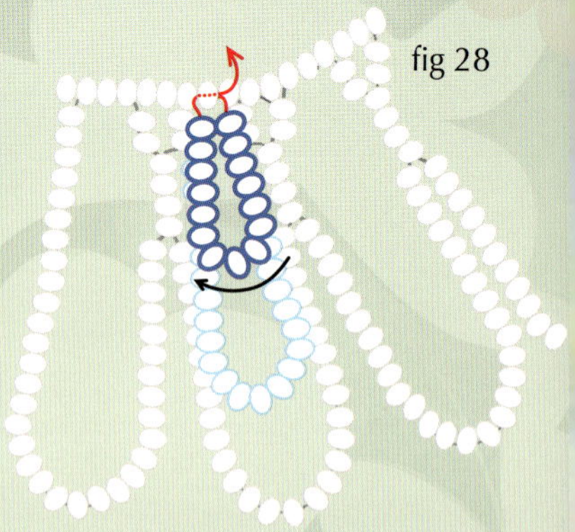

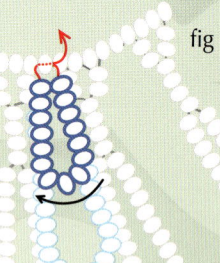

fig 28

Pass the needle through the following 5D (6D) beads of the ring.

Repeat steps 21 and 22 to add a medium and a small swag to each of the large swags.

Leave the needle attached and emerging from one of the D beads of the top ring.

23 The Leaves & Berries - There are three pairs of leaves and three berries to be made, in situ, on the top ring of D beads. The three pairs of leaves need to be equally spaced around the ring - each pair with its associated berry will occupy three adjacent D beads on the ring - try to avoid any D beads that may have become very full of thread already.

If neccessary reposition the needle for the first leaf at your preferred position on the D bead ring.

24 Each leaf has a main stem and four leaf ribs which are then linked together to make the distinctive holly leaf shape. You will need to pull the thread quite firmly to make the stem and ribs taut.

Thread on 15E.

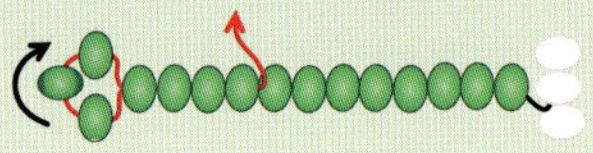

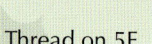

fig 29

Leaving aside the last 3E beads threaded to anchor the strand pass the needle back through the next 4E (fig 29).

Thread on 5E.

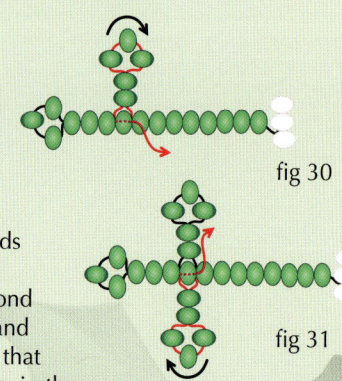

fig 30

Leaving aside the last 3E beads to anchor the strand pass the needle back through the second and first E beads just added and the E bead on the main stem that the needle had emerged from, in the same direction as before (fig 30).

fig 31

Thread on 5E and make a similar leaf rib to the other side of the main stem (fig 31).

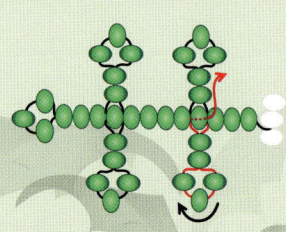

fig 32

Pass the needle through the following 5E beads of the main stem and repeat the leaf ribs to either side of this E bead (fig 32).

25 Pass the needle through the following 2E beads of the stem to emerge between the first and second E beads at the base of the leaf.

Thread on 3E.

Pass the needle through the 3E beads at the end of the last leaf rib made (fig 33).

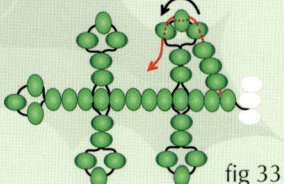
fig 33

Thread on 5E and pass the needle through the 3E beads at the tip of the next rib along.

Thread on 2E and pass the needle through the 3E beads at the tip of the leaf stem (fig 34).

Thread on 2E and pass through the 3E at the tip of the following leaf rib and thread on 5E before you pass through the 3E at the tip of the last leaf rib. Thread on 3E. Pass the needle through the first E bead of the leaf stem to emerge adjacent to the D bead ring.

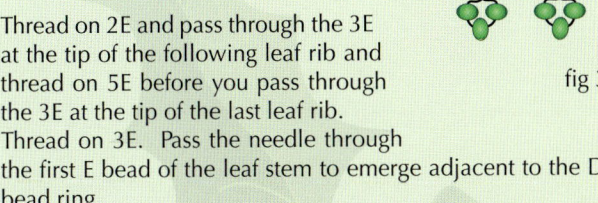
fig 34

Pull the thread quite tightly to crinkle the leaf into a twisted holly shape. Pass the needle through the D bead on the ring at the base of the leaf.

26 To make a berry thread on 4E, 1F and 4E. Pass the needle through the next D of the ring to draw the berry into place.

Pass the needle through the next D bead of the ring and thread on 15E to start the second leaf of the pair. Complete this leaf as before.

Pass the needle through the D beads of the ring to the next position you have allocated for the leaves and berries. Complete the second set of leaves and a berry here. Make the third set in the remaining gap on the D bead ring.

For a different effect use PVA glue to cover the bauble in mixed brown beads & add the stitched swags, leaves and berries.

27 **Attaching the Swags** - Drop the swagged section with the attached leaves and berries over the top of the bauble.

Arrange the swags as you want them to sit. Use the swag thread to make a few small stitches between the D bead ring and the top row of A beads on the plum pudding layer to keep the two sections together. Finish off all of the thread ends neatly and securely.

28 **The Hanging Loop** - Prepare the needle with 1m of double thread. Approximately 10cm from the cut ends tie the thread onto the wire loop at the top of the bauble with a secure double knot.

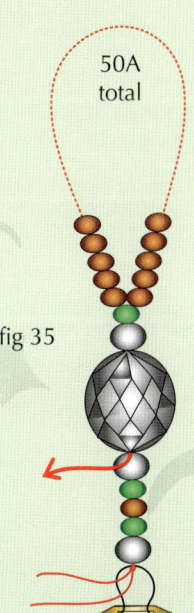

Thread on 1B, 1E, 1A, 1E, 1B, 1G, 1B, 1E and 50A.

Pass the needle back through the last E bead threaded and the following 1B and 1G to draw the 50A up into a loop (fig 35).

Pass the needle through the following beads to emerge at the wire loop.

Pass the needle through the wire loop and back up through the bead sequence to emerge just below the loop of 50A.

Pass the needle through the 50A to strengthen the loop and back through the bead sequence below it to once again emerge at the wire loop.

Tie the needle end of the thread to the loose thread ends here with a secure double knot. Pass the needle up through the beads above the loop to conceal the ends neatly before trimming.

Attach the needle to the remaining two thread ends and neaten in a similar fashion before trimming.

Vintage Bauble

You Will Need

Materials

One 60mm frosted silver glass bauble
8g of size 10/0 silver lined rose pink seed beads A
4g of size 10/0 silver lined lilac seed beads B
4g of size 10/0 silver lined crystal seed beads C
2.5g of size 2 silver lined crystal bugle beads D
8g of size 10/0 white ceylon seed beads E
Fourteen 6mm crystal AB fire polished faceted beads F
Twenty-seven 4mm crystal AB fire polished faceted beads G
1g of size 8/0 silver lined pink seed beads H
A reel of white size D beading thread

Tools

A size 10 beading needle
A pair of scissors to trim the threads

As pretty as a picture in frosted white and rose pink this looks lovely hanging from a silvery branch. Swap the colours for chocolate and cream for an indulgent display or frosted blue and white for a frosty winter theme. The flower bud motifs make wonderful earrings too.

The Decoration is Made in Six Stages
The six large rosettes are the first motifs to be made.
Three smaller rosettes are made next.
Followed by six leaf motifs.
The top ring for the neck of the bauble is made.
The swags and drop flower buds that connect the rosettes together are made.
The hanging loop completes the decoration.

4 The needle will be emerging from the A bead of the ring immediately before the edge of the first petal.

Pass the needle through the adjacent 1A of the first petal and thread on 5A. Pass the needle through the first A bead of the seventh petal and the following 3A of the ring (fig 7).

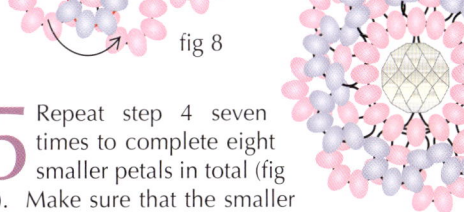
fig 7

1 **The Large Rosettes** - Prepare the needle with 1.5m of single thread and tie a keeper bead 15cm from the end.

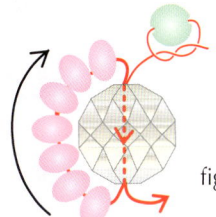

Thread on 1F and 7A. Pass the needle through the F bead in the same direction to bring the 7A beads into a strap around the side of the F bead (fig 1).

fig 1

fig 2

Thread on 7A. Pass the needle through the F bead to bring the new 7A beads into a strap at the other side of the F bead (fig 2).

Thread on 5B. Pass the needle through the previous 2A beads of the ring and the following 2A to form the first petal of the second layer (fig 8).

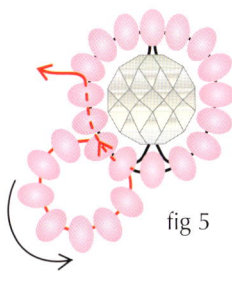
fig 8

fig 9

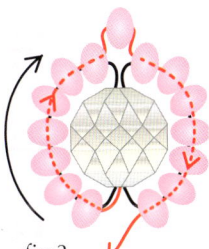

2 Pass the needle through the 7A beads of the first strap and thread on 1A.

Pass the needle through the following 7A of the second strap to pull the new A bead into the gap above the hole in the F bead (fig 3).

fig 3

Thread on 1A. Pass the needle through the first 2A of the first strap (fig 4) to pull the new A bead into the gap at this end of the F bead and complete a ring of 16A around the F bead.

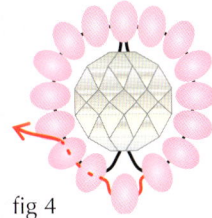
fig 4

5 Repeat step 4 seven times to complete eight smaller petals in total (fig 9). Make sure that the smaller petals all sit to the front of the rosette - they will overlap each other slightly.

Remove the needle leaving the thread end hanging loose - do not knot the thread. Set this rosette aside for the moment.

Make another five large rosettes to match.

Extra Info....
Leaving the thread ends unfinished prevents the holes in the beads from becoming blocked with knots or excessive volumes of thread. The loose thread ends will be finished securely when the motifs are complete and all of the necessary connections within the design are made.

3 Thread on 7A.
Pass the needle through the 2A beads of the ring and the following 2A to make the first petal (fig 5).

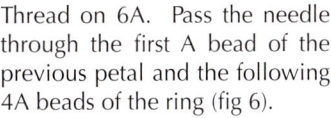
fig 5

Thread on 6A. Pass the needle through the first A bead of the previous petal and the following 4A beads of the ring (fig 6).

Repeat this stitch five more times to complete seven petals. The last petal will need to link the seventh petal to the first petal.

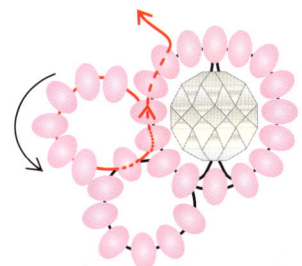
fig 6

77

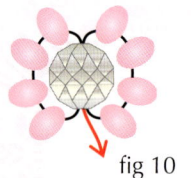
fig 10

6 **The Small Rosettes** - Prepare the needle as in step 1 using just 1m of single thread.

Thread on 1G and 4A. Pass the needle through the G bead to pull the A beads into a strap to the side. Thread on 4A and repeat to make a second strap to the other side of the G bead (fig 10).

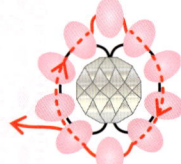
fig 11

As before add 1A bead above the hole at each end of the G bead (fig 11).

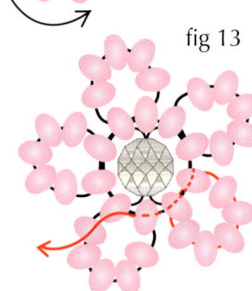
fig 12

7 Thread on 5A. Pass the needle through the previous 2A on the ring and the following 2A to make the first petal (fig 12).

Repeat to make three more petals.

Make the fifth petal with 5A but only pass the needle through 3A beads on the ring (fig 13) to emerge between the 2A beads at the base of the first petal.

fig 13

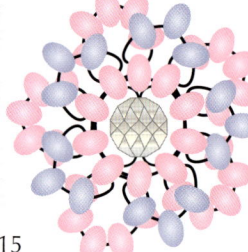
fig 14

8 Thread on 3B. Pass the needle through the previous 2A on the ring and the following 2A beads (fig 14).

Repeat to make five B bead petals in total - as before make sure they all come to the front of the rosette (fig 15).

Remove the needle leaving the thread end hanging loose - do not knot the thread.

Set this rosette aside for the moment.

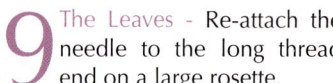
fig 15

Make another two small rosettes to match.

9 **The Leaves** - Re-attach the needle to the long thread end on a large rosette.

Make sure the thread is emerging from an A bead on the central ring.

Thread on 10C, 1D and 4C. Leaving aside the last 3C beads to anchor the strand pass the needle back up through the C bead below the D bead and the following 1D and 9C beads (fig 16).

Note - for clarity the following diagrams will just show the leaf beads and 1A bead on the rosette.

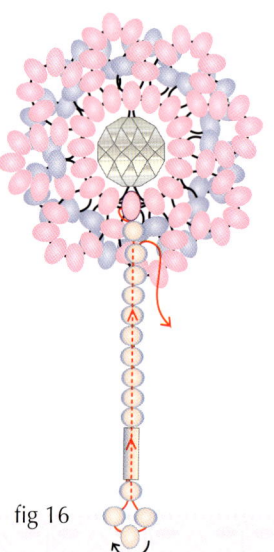
fig 16

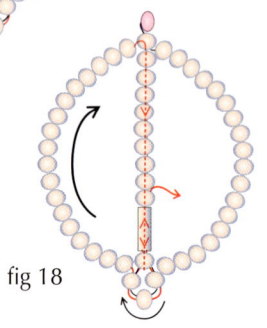
fig 17

10 Thread on 18C. Pass the needle through the 3C beads of the anchor (fig 17).

Thread on 18C. Pass the needle down through the 9C above the D bead, the D bead and the following 1C, through the 3C of the anchor and back up the central stem to emerge from the first C bead above the D bead (fig 18).

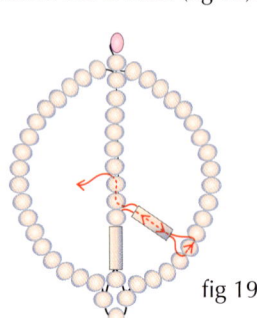

fig 18   fig 19

11 Thread on 1D. Referring to fig 19 pass the needle through the fifth C bead on the right hand strap and back up the D bead. Pass the needle up through the following 2C on the central stem.

Referring to fig 20 thread on 1D and 1C. Pass the needle through the sixth C bead on the left hand strap and back up the 1C and 1D beads just added. Pass the needle up through the following 1C on the central stem.

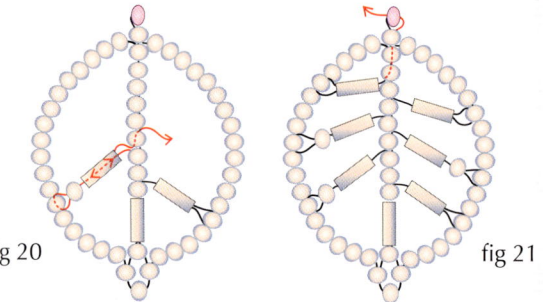
fig 20   fig 21

12 Fig 21 shows the remaining four arms that you need to add to the central stem.

For the next arm thread on 1D and 1C. Make a link to the eighth C bead on the right hand strap and pass up through 1C on the main stem.

For the fourth arm make a similar link to the tenth C bead on the left hand strap and pass up through 1C on the main stem.

Make a 1D link to the twelfth C bead on the right passing up through 1C on the main stem and a final 1D arm to the fourteenth C bead to the left.

Pass up through the remaining C beads of the stem and the A bead on the rosette in the same direction as before to centre the leaf below the rosette (fig 22).

Pass back down the stem beads of the leaf to emerge through the middle C bead of the anchor at the tip of the leaf.

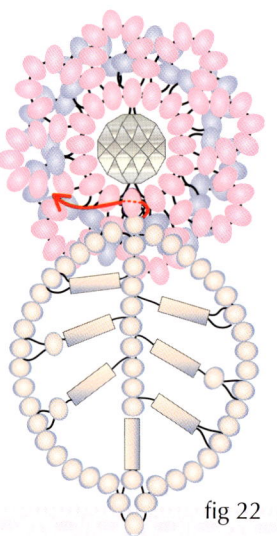
fig 22

14 Prepare the needle with a new 1.5m single thread and attach a keeper bead 15cm from the end.

Thread on 10C, 1D and 4C to start a new leaf motif (see fig 24). Pass the needle back up through the stem as before leaving a 3C anchor to emerge 9C above the D bead (fig 24).

Make the remainder of the leaf as before. When you have made the last 1D link pass the needle up to the very top of the central stem.

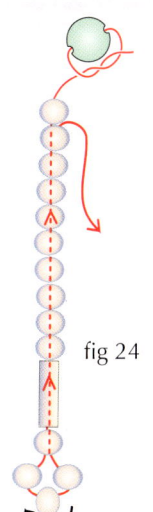

fig 24

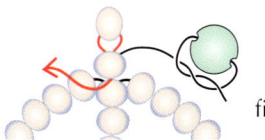

fig 25

Thread on 1C and pass down through the first C bead of the stem to pull the new C bead to sit across the top of the stem (fig 25).

Pass the needle down the main stem, the D bead and the beads of the anchor to emerge through the central C bead of the anchor.

15 Pick up one of the large rosettes not attached to a leaf. Pass the needle through the A bead at the tip of one of the petals (see fig 26). Pass the needle though the C bead at the tip of the anchor again to centralise the rosette underneath the leaf tip (fig 26).

Repeat the stitch to strengthen the link.

Finish off the thread end neatly and securely between the beads of the leaf.

Remove the keeper bead on the leaf and finish off this end in a similar manner taking care not to block the hole in the C bead added in fig 25.

Repeat steps 14 and 15 to make two more leaf motifs with a large rosette linked to the tip .

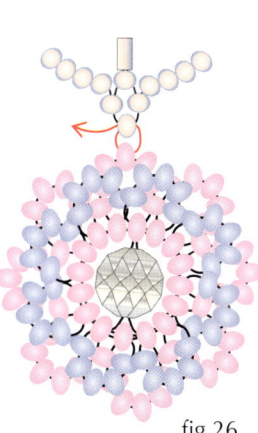

fig 26

13 Pick up the first small rosette and flip it over so you can see the back of the work.

Thread on 8E. Referring to fig 23, pass the needle through one of the A beads of the ring around the G bead centre.

Thread on 3E and pass the needle up through the next 4E beads and thread on 1E.

Pass the needle through the C bead at the tip of the leaf to centre the small rosette underneath the leaf (fig 23).

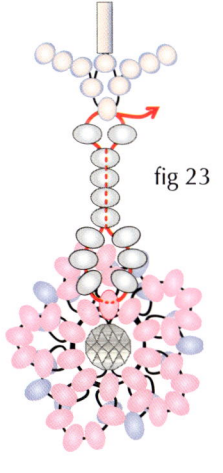

fig 23

Finish off the thread end neatly and securely without blocking the holes in the A bead rings around the centres of the two rosettes. Remove the keeper beads from both rosettes and finish off these ends similarly.

Repeat steps 9 to 13 inclusive twice to make a total of three leaf and rosette groups.

16 The Top Ring for the Bauble Neck - You will have -

Three *long* links with a large rosette, a leaf and a small rosette in a line.
Three *short* links with a leaf and a large rosette.
These are joined together with a single row of E beads to make a band around the neck of the bauble.

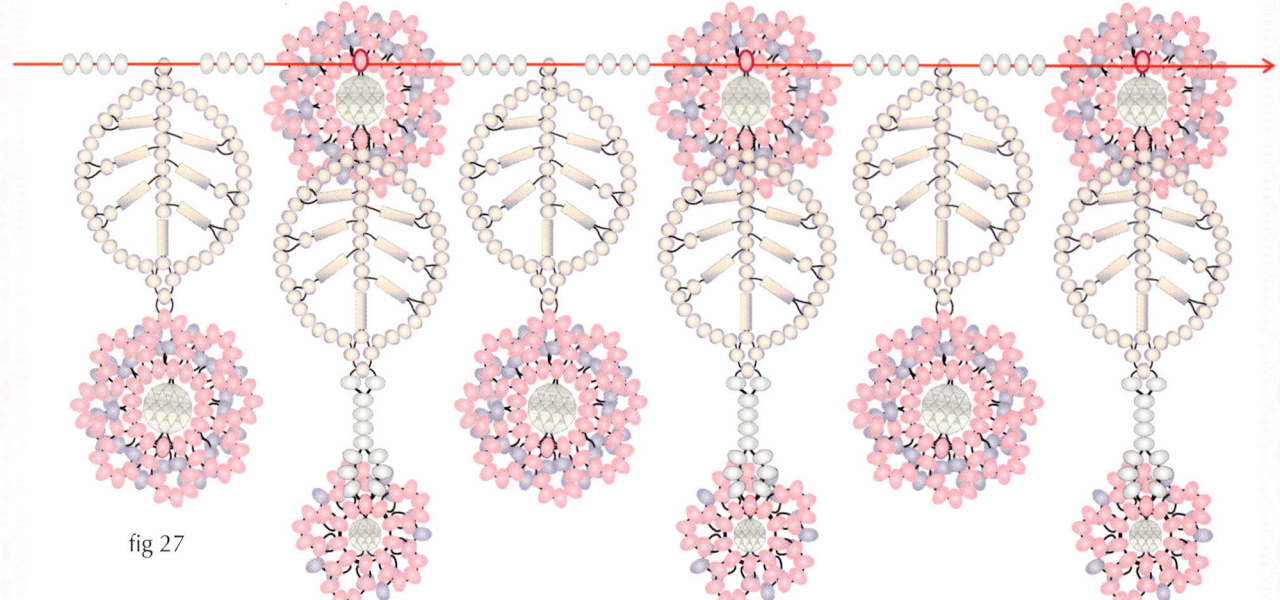

fig 27

17
Prepare the needle with 75cm of single thread and tie a keeper bead 15cm from the end. Referring to fig 27 thread on 4E and pass through the top C bead of a leaf motif at the top of a short link. Thread on 4E.

Flip over the first long link and locate the A bead on the ring at the back of the large rosette immediately opposite the attachment to the leaf motif. Pass the needle through this A bead. Repeat until the six links and E beads are in the sequence as shown above. Make sure that the large rosettes are all facing the same way before proceeding.

Drape the row around the neck of the bauble and pass the needle through the first 4E beads to draw it up close. The row needs to fit quite snugly around the base of the neck. If necessary adjust the E bead count between the motifs until they are equally spaced around the neck of the bauble. Pass the needle through the first bead of the row to complete the ring. Pass the needle through the beads of the ring several times to strengthen it. Finish off both ends of the thread neatly and securely.

18 The Swags and Drop Flowers -
The swags and drop flowers attach to the back of the large and small rosettes. Fig 28 shows the back of the two sizes of rosette motifs.

The connections for the swags and drop flowers need to be made through the A beads on the central rings of the rosettes. It is important that you pick the A beads directly opposite the connections to the leaf motifs above the rosettes. These beads are marked in bright pink on fig 28. Note that on the large rosette there are two A beads marked - on the small rosette just one A bead. On the large rosette you will need to pass through both of the marked beads to make the connection.

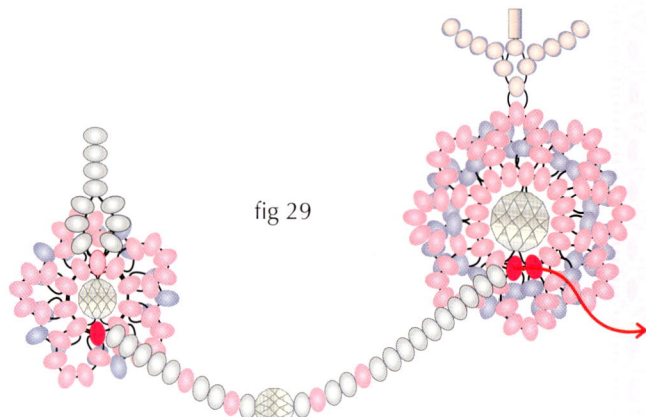

fig 29

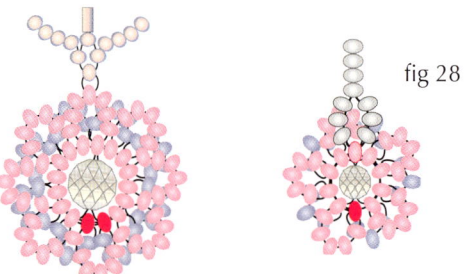

fig 28

Either attach the needle to an existing long thread end, or start a new thread, but bring the needle through the work to emerge from the bead marked in bright pink (fig 29) on the first small rosette.

19
Thread on 5E, 1A, 2E, 1A, 1E, 1G, 1E, 1A, 2E, 1A and 10E. Pass the needle through the 2A beads marked on fig 28 at the back of the next large rosette around the bauble. Make sure the needle passes through the 2A beads in the correct direction (fig 29).

Thread on 1E.

Pass the needle through the 2A beads on the back of the rosette again to bring the new E bead parallel to the 2A (fig 30).

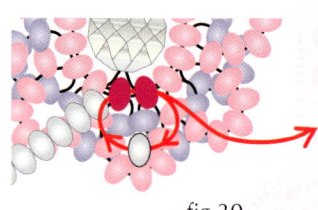

fig 30

20 Thread on 10E, 1A, 2E, 1A, 1E, 1G, 1E, 1A, 2E, 1A and 5E. Pass through the single A bead (marked in bright pink on fig 28) on the back of the next small rosette around the bauble.

Thread on 1E and pass through the single A bead on the back of the rosette again to bring the new E bead parallel to this A bead (as fig 30).

Repeat steps 19 and 20 around the bauble to make six swags in total. The last swag will link up to the first small rosette. Don't forget to add the single E bead to the A bead on the back of this rosette to finish off the row.

21 Pass the needle through the new single E bead just added at the back of the first rosette.

The needle will be pointing in the opposite direction around the bauble. You are now in the correct position to start the second row of swags and add the flower drops. This second row of swags will be made in the direction that the needle is pointing now.

Thread on 8E, 1A, 2E, 1A, 1E, 1G, 1E, 1A, 1E, 1G, 1E, 1A, 2E, 1A and 12E. Pass the needle through the single E bead added to the back of the last large rosette around the bauble - remember you are going in the opposite direction around the bauble.

You now need to add the first flower drop.

22 Thread on 20E, 1B, 1E, 1A, 1B, 1A, 2E, 1A, 1E, 1D, 1E, 1B, 1E, 1G, 1H, 1F, 1B and 3E.

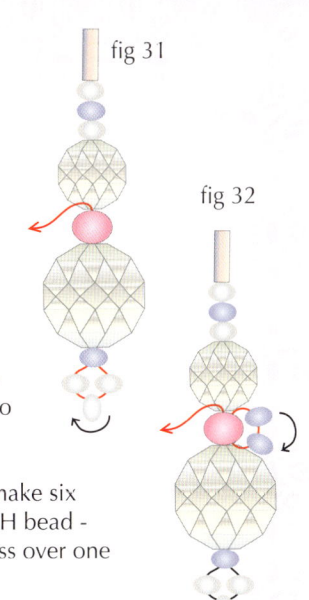

*Leaving aside the last 3E beads to form the anchor pass the needle back up the B, F and H beads (fig 31).

Thread on 2A. Pass the needle up through the H bead again to bring the 2A into a small strap to the side of the H bead (fig 32).

Repeat this stitch five times to make six small straps in total around the H bead - make sure the straps do not cross over one another.

23 The needle will be emerging from the H bead.

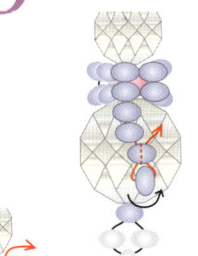

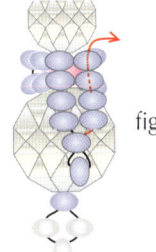

Pass the needle down through the 2A beads of the closest strap and thread on 4A.

Leaving aside the last 1A bead to anchor the strand pass the needle back up through the third A bead just added (fig 33).

Thread on 2A. Pass the needle up through the 2A beads of the next strap around the H bead (fig 34) to complete the first petal of the bud.

Pass the needle down through the 2A beads of the next strap around the H bead and repeat to make a second petal.

Repeat to complete a third petal. The needle will emerge from the top of the last 2A strap around the H bead.

24 Pass the needle up through the G bead and the following beads of the main strand to emerge just below the single E bead at the back of the rosette.

Pass the needle through this 1E in the same direction as before to centralise the strand below the rosette (fig 35).

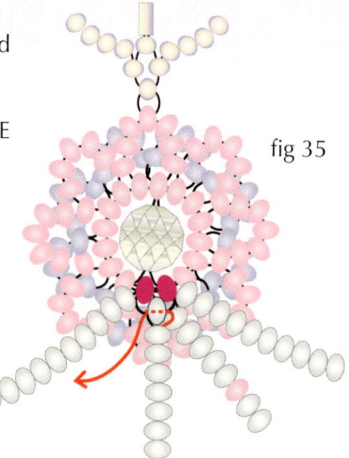
fig 35

25 For the next swag thread on 12E, 1A, 2E, 1A, 1E, 1G, 1E, 1A, 1E, 1G, 1E, 1A, 2E, 1A and 8E.

Pass the needle through the single E bead at the back of the next small rosette around the bauble.

You need to add a slightly shorter flower bud strand from this position.

26 Thread on 3E, 1B, 1E, 1A, 1B, 1A, 2E, 1A, 1E, 1D, 1E, 1B, 1E, 1G, 1H, 1F, 1B and 3E.

Repeat from * in step 22 to complete the anchor, the flower bud and the strand to bring the needle to emerge from the single E bead at the back of the small rosette.

27 Repeat the swag and flower drop sequence twice more to complete the second layer of swags. You will need to add a long flower drop strand from each of the large rosettes and a short flower drop strand from each of the smaller rosettes. Do not forget to add the last flower drop strand from the small rosette at the start of this swag row.

Finish off all of the remaining thread ends neatly and securely.

28 The Hanging Loop - Repeat steps 1 to 5 to make a large rosette. Pass the needle through the beads of the A bead ring at the centre of the rosette to emerge from the A bead at one end of the hole in the central F bead.

From this position make a leaf following figs 17 to fig 21. Making the connection through this A bead on the rosette ring will line up the stem of the leaf with the hole in the F bead.

When the leaf is complete the needle will be emerging from the same A bead on the ring at the centre of the rosette on the back of the flower.

29 When the finished decoration is displayed both the back and the front of this rosette will be on show. To match the back of the rosette to the front add eight 5B bead petals (as in figs 14 and 15) to the A bead ring at the back of the rosette.

30 Pass the needle through the A beads of the ring so the needle can pass straight through the F bead from the leaf end of the F bead to emerge at the other end (fig 36).

Pass the needle through the A bead on the ring at this end of the F bead bringing the needle through to emerge between the A bead layer of petals and the B bead layer at the back of the rosette.

Thread on 4C. Pass the needle through the metal loop at the top of the bauble.

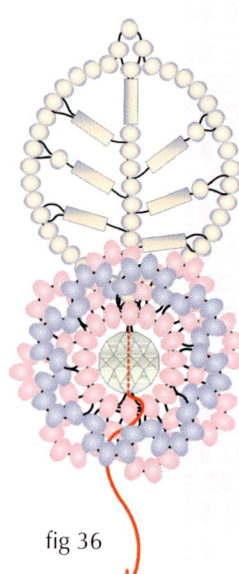
fig 36

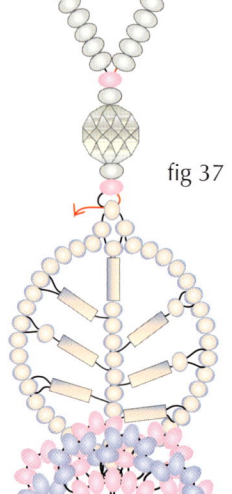
fig 37

31 Pass the needle back up through the 4C beads and through the same A bead on the ring at the centre of the rosette.

Pass the needle down through the 4C beads again, through the bauble loop and back up the 4C beads to strengthen the link. Repeat once.

Pass back up through the F bead and the C and D beads of the main stem of the leaf to emerge from the C bead at the top of the leaf tip. Thread on 1A, 1E, 1F, 1E and 1A.

Thread on 6E and 1B. Repeat this sequence four times. Thread on 6E. Pass the needle back down the last A bead threaded to form the loop and through the following four beads to emerge at the top of leaf. Pass the needle through the C bead at the tip of the leaf to centralise the beading above the leaf (fig 37).

Pass the needle through the connection to the loop and the loop at least one more time to strengthen before finishing off all of the remaining thread ends neatly and securely.

Colour Inspirations

Perfect for a wedding day, a 'thank you Mum' or a christening gift, you can take the vintage pastel palette and create fabulous momentos for very special occasions.

Here you can see the Mistletoe Kisses Bauble with eau-de-nil mistletoe leaves and pearly berries surrounding a heart made from Delica bead colour DB1341.

The Garland Bauble is made with four bows and swags (see page 90) with the same eau-de-nil seed beads for the leaf motifs but with mauve berries and lilac bows.

Garland Bauble

You Will Need

Materials

One 60mm frosted gold glass bauble
10g of size 10/0 silver lined purple seed beads A
8g of size 10/0 transparent teal AB seed beads B
4g of size 10/0 silver lined gold seed beads C
4g of size 8/0 silver lined red seed beads D
1.5g of size 3 transparent purple AB bugle beads E
Seven 4mm purple AB fire polished faceted beads F
Four 6mm purple AB fire polished faceted beads G
A reel of purple size D beading thread

Tools

A size 10 beading needle
A pair of scissors to trim the threads

Garlands of winter greenery have been brought into the home around the time of the winter solstice by many generations of diverse cultures. The Druids hold the holly tree to be sacred and the Celts believed that the boughs would bring protection during the hard days around the turn of the year. The tradition endures, even if our need is to reconnect with nature, not to ask it for solace.

The Decoration is Made in Six Stages

First you make the bows for the bauble.
The tassel strands are added below the bows.
The bows are linked together with the swags.
A foundation row around the neck of the bauble is made.
The foundation row is linked to the bows to bring the decoration together over the bauble.
The hanging loop is added to the top of the bauble.

1 The Bows - Prepare the needle with 1.8m of single thread and tie a keeper bead 15cm from the end.

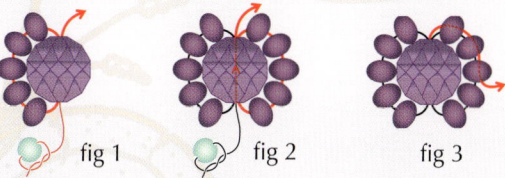

fig 1   fig 2   fig 3

Thread on 1F and 5A. Pass the needle through the F bead in the same direction as before to bring the A beads into a strap to one side (fig 1). Thread on 5A and repeat to make a second strap on the opposite side of the F bead (fig 2).

Pass the needle through the first 3A beads of the second strap (fig 3). The last 2A beads passed through will support the bow loop on this side of the F bead.

2 Row one - Thread on 1A. Pass the needle through the previous A bead in the same direction as before and the new A bead to bring the two beads parallel (fig 4). This is a square stitch.

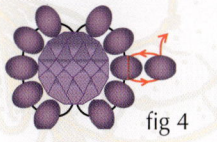 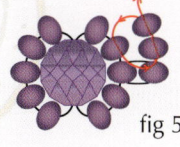 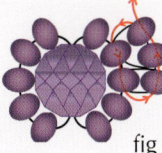

fig 4   fig 5   fig 6

Thread on 2A. Pass the needle through the next A bead of the previous row, in the same direction as before, and through the 2A beads just added (fig 5) (3A total).
Pass the needle through the 2A beads on the previous row and the 3A beads of the new row to reinforce the work (fig 6).

3 Start row two with 1A and square stitch it to the last A bead of the previous row (fig 7).

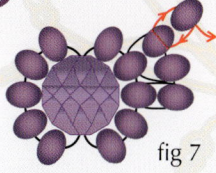 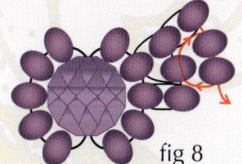

fig 7   fig 8

Thread on 2A. Pass the needle through the next A bead of the previous row and through the new 2A (fig 8).
Thread on 1A and square stitch to the last A bead of the previous row (4A total).

Reinforce the previous row and the new row as in fig 6.

Extra Info....
The bows are made in square stitch. If you are not familiar with this stitch you may find it useful to refer to page 11 - Square Stitch Basics.

fig 9   fig 10

4 Start row three with two single A bead stitches (see fig 9). Thread on 2A. Pass the needle through the next A bead of the previous row and the 2A beads just added (fig 9). Finish the row with a single A bead and reinforce as before (5A total) (fig 10).

5 Start row four with a single A bead stitch.
Thread on 2A and make the next stitch as in fig 8.
Make a single A bead stitch.
Thread on 2A and make this stitch as in fig 8.
Finish the row with a single A bead stitch (7A total) (fig 11).
Reinforce as before.

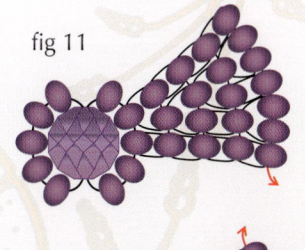

fig 11

6 Start row five with three single A bead stitches.
Thread on 2A and make the next stitch as in fig 8.

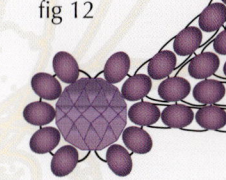

fig 12

Finish the row with three single A bead stitches (8A total) (fig 12). Reinforce as before.

You now start to decrease to make the remainder of the bow loop.

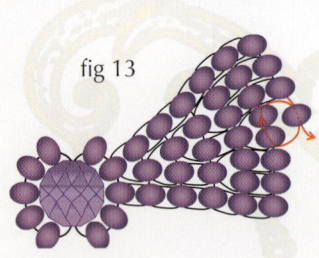

fig 13

7 Start row six with three single A bead stitches. Thread on 1A. Pass the needle through the next 2A beads on the previous row and through the new 1A (fig 13) to make a decrease.
Finish the row with three single A bead stitches (7A total) and reinforce as before.

As you pull the reinforcing thread through the beads the new row will pull to the front of the previous row. Allow this to happen naturally - row five is the end of the fold in the bow loop - this new row and the following rows work back towards the F bead.

8 Row seven - Make one single A bead stitch and one decrease stitch as in fig 13.
Make one single A bead stitch and another decrease stitch as in fig 13.
Finish the row with a single A bead stitch (5A total) and reinforce the row.

Row eight - Make two single A bead stitches and one decrease stitch as in fig 13. Make a single A bead stitch to finish the row (4A total) and reinforce as before.

Row nine - Make a single A bead stitch and one decrease stitch as in fig 13. Make a single A bead stitch to finish the row (3A total) and reinforce as before.
This row now needs to link to the 2A beads on the strap around the F bead.

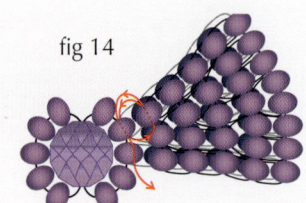

fig 14

fig 15

9 Referring to fig 14 make a square stitch between the last bead of the row and the second A bead of the strap around the F bead.
Pass the needle through the second and third A beads of the strap (fig 14).

Make a similar square stitch between this A bead on the strap and the last A bead of the previous row. Pass the needle through to emerge from the fourth A bead of the strap (fig 15). This bead will support the tail of the bow on this side of the F bead.

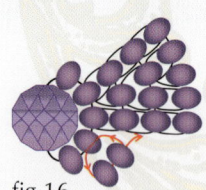

fig 16

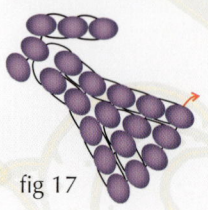

fig 17

10 Row one - Thread on 2A. Pass the needle through the A bead on the strap and the new 2A (fig 16).

Referring to fig 17 throughout and remembering to reinforce each row:

Row two - Square stitch two single A beads to each of the beads of row one.

Row three - Make a single A bead stitch and a two bead stitch as in fig 8 (3A total).

Row four - Make a single A bead stitch and a two bead stitch as in fig 8. Finish the row with a single A bead stitch (4A total).

Row five - Make two single A bead stitches, a two bead stitch as in fig 8 and a single A bead stitch to complete the row (5A total) (fig 17).

11 Make two single A bead stitches (fig 18). Thread on 1A and pass through the 2A beads just added to make a point (see fig 19). Pass the needle through the stitch again and through the last 3A beads of row five (fig 19).

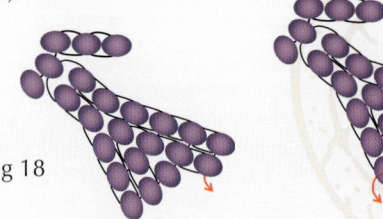

fig 18 fig 19

12 Referring to fig 20 repeat step 11 on this end of the row. Make sure you pass to the far end of row five and work the needle down through the rows to emerge at the bottom of the strap around the F bead.

Pass the needle up through the F bead (fig 20).

fig 20

Repeat from fig 3 to make a bow loop and tail on the other side of the F bead (see fig 21).

When the bow is complete leave the thread end loose and remove the needle. Repeat from step 1 to make two more identical bows.

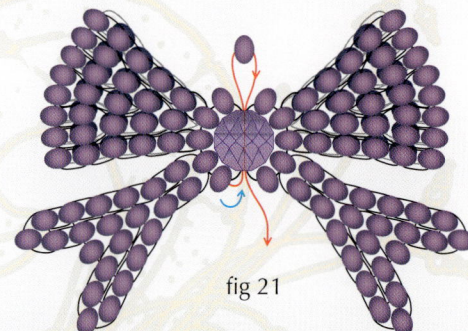

fig 21

13 The Tassel Strands - Pick up the first bow - the needle should be emerging from the top of the F bead.
Thread on 1A and pass the needle down through the F bead (fig 21).
This single A bead will enable you to turn the needle at the top of each tassel strand.

14 Thread on 1A, 30B, 1C, 1B, 1E, 1B, 4C and 3D. Pass the needle through the first D bead in the same direction as before to draw the 3D beads into a small ring (fig 22).

15 Thread on 4B. Pass the needle through the first 3B beads in the same direction as before to create a ring of 4B (fig 23). Thread on 3B and pass the needle through the end bead of the last stitch in the same direction to create a second ring of 4B (fig 24).

Referring to fig 25 pass the needle through the beads of this ring once more, the 2B following and the next D bead around the ring to complete a holly leaf motif (fig 25).

16 Following figs 23 and 24 create two more B bead rings. Pass the needle through the following 2B of the end ring to emerge at the tip of the motif (fig 26).

Thread on 2C, 1B, 1D, 1G, 1C and 3B.

Leaving aside the last 3B beads to anchor the strand, pass the needle back up through the bottom C bead and the five beads above it.

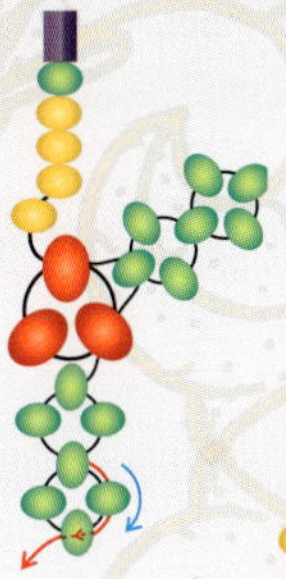

Pass the needle through the B bead at the tip of the leaf in the same direction as before to centralise the strand (fig 27).

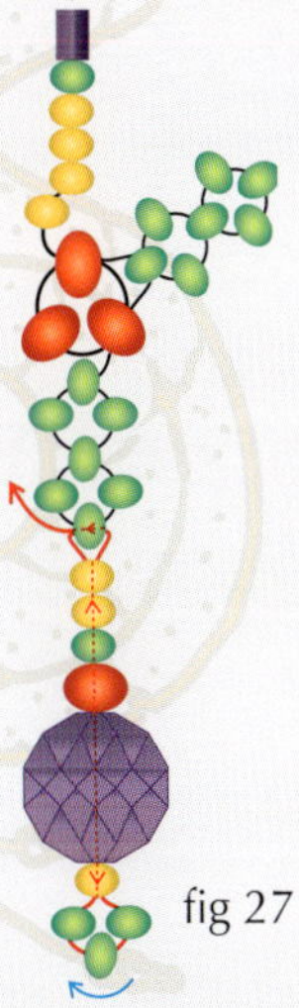

Referring to fig 28 pass the needle back through the B beads of the leaf and out through the next D bead around the ring (fig 28).

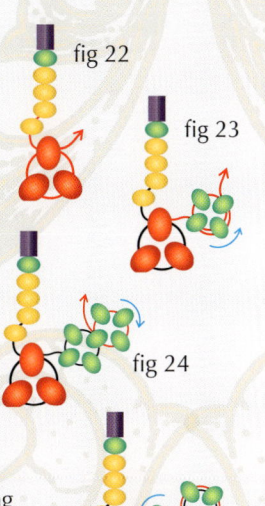

fig 22

fig 23

fig 24

fig 25

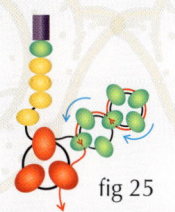

Repeat step 15 to add a third holly leaf motif here.

Thread on 1C and pass up through the second C bead of the strand (fig 29).

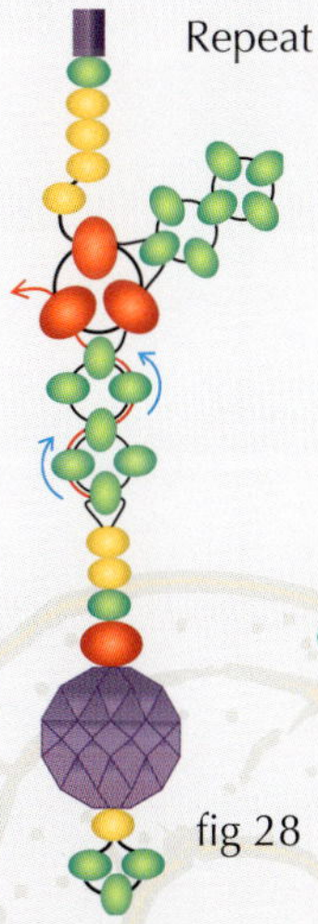

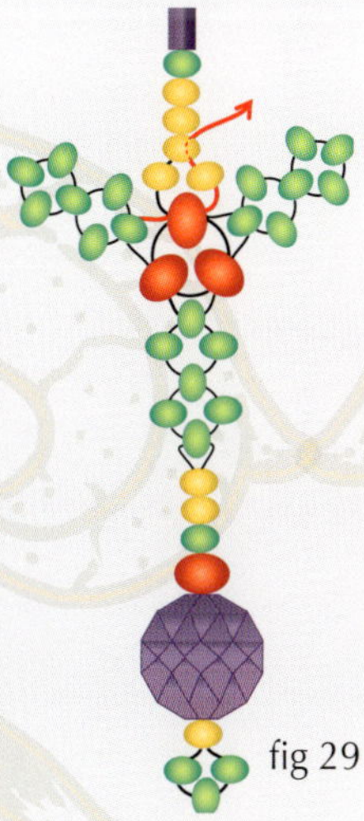

17 Pass the needle up through the remaining beads of the strand, through the F bead and the A bead added in step 13.

Pass the needle down the F bead and the following 1A to be in the correct position to make the next strand (fig 30).

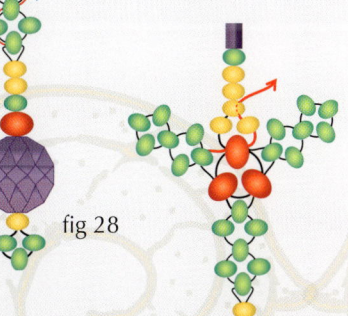

fig 26

fig 27

fig 28

fig 29

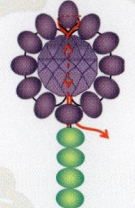

fig 30

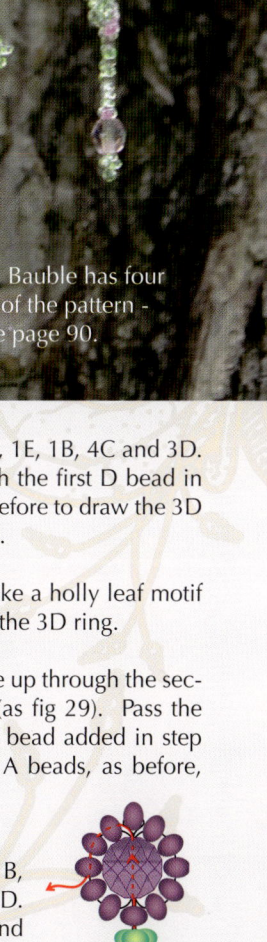

The Beau Bauble has four repeats of the pattern - see page 90.

18 Thread on 20B, 1C, 1B, 1E, 1B, 4C and 3D. Pass the needle through the first D bead in the same direction as before to draw the 3D beads into a small ring (as fig 22).

Repeat step 15 three times to make a holly leaf motif in each of the three gaps around the 3D ring.

Thread on 1C and pass the needle up through the second C bead of the main strand (as fig 29). Pass the needle to the top, through the A bead added in step 13 and back through the F and A beads, as before, ready to make the next strand.

19 Thread on 8B, 1C, 1B, 1E, 1B, 4C and 3D. Complete the third strand as in step 18 but when the needle emerges from the top of the F bead pass the needle through the first 3A beads of the strap around the F bead (fig 31).

fig 31

Leave the thread end hanging loose and remove the needle. Set this bow aside and repeat from step 13 with the remaining two bows.

20 **The Swags** - Select the bow with the longest tail of thread from step 19 and reattach the needle. Thread on 13B, 1C, 1B and 3D. Pass the needle through the last B bead in the same direction to draw the last four beads into a ring (fig 32).

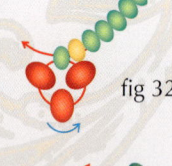
fig 32

21 Thread on 3B. Pass through the B bead of the ring again to draw up the first ring of a leaf motif. Pass through the following 2B (fig 33).

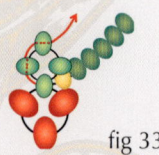
fig 33

Thread on 3B and complete the leaf as before (figs 24 and 25) passing the needle through the B bead on the ring and the following 1D.

Following figs 23-25 make a holly leaf in this new gap between the D beads (fig 34) and one in the following gap. Pass the needle through the B bead at the top of the ring (fig 35).

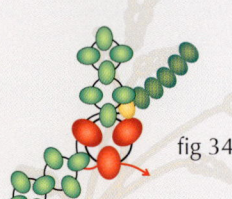
fig 34

22 Thread on 1C, 9B, 1C, 1B and 3D. Pass the needle through the last B bead in the same direction to draw the last four beads into a ring (as fig 32).

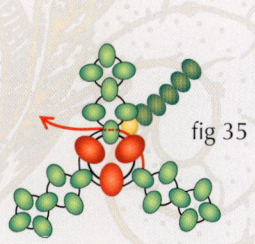
fig 35

Repeat step 21 to complete a second cluster of three leaves.

Repeat step 22 and step 21 to make another swag and cluster.

Thread on 1C and 13B. Pick up a new bow and referring to fig 36, pass the needle up through the 3A beads of the strap towards the top of the bow, the A bead at the top and the following 3A (fig 36) to emerge alongside the thread end from step 19.

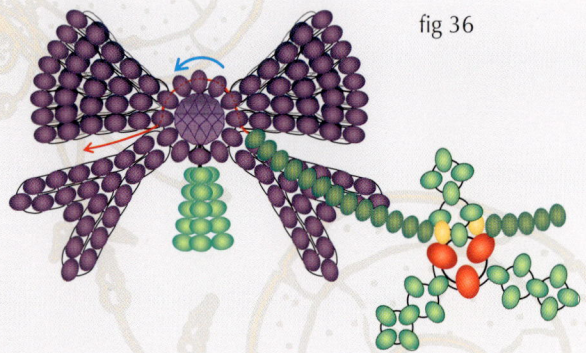
fig 36

23 Decide which of the thread ends emerging from this A bead is the longest and use it to repeat from step 20 to complete the next swag.

Repeat from step 20 one more time to link the third bow to the first bow.

Finish off all remaining thread ends neatly and securely taking care not to block the holes in the A beads at the top of the bows.

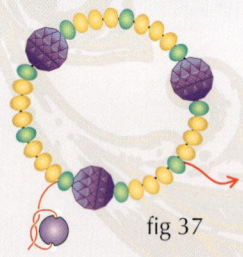
fig 37

24 **The Foundation Row** - Prepare the needle as in step 1 and thread on three repeats of 1B, 1F, 1B, 3C, 1B and 3C.

Pass the needle through the first seven beads to bring the work up into a ring (fig 37).

Drop the ring over the neck of the bauble - it needs to fit quite snugly.

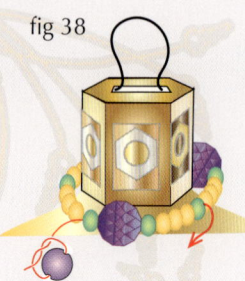
fig 38

If it does not fit well adjust the C bead counts equally around the ring until you have the three single B beads evenly distributed around the neck (fig 38).

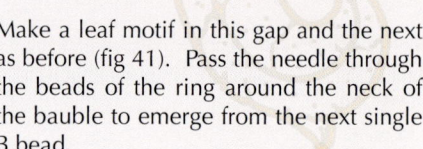
fig 39

25 Check that the needle is emerging from a single B bead as fig 38 and thread on 3D. Pass the needle through the B bead to draw into a small ring (fig 39). Using this B bead as the base of a new holly leaf make the leaf motif and pass the needle through the following D bead of the ring (fig 40).

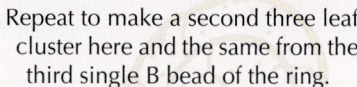
fig 40

Make a leaf motif in this gap and the next as before (fig 41). Pass the needle through the beads of the ring around the neck of the bauble to emerge from the next single B bead.

Repeat to make a second three leaf cluster here and the same from the third single B bead of the ring.

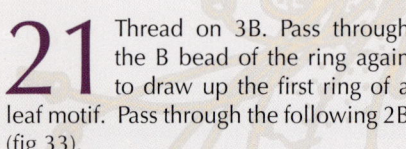

fig 41

88

26 **Making the Links -** Pass the needle through the beads of the neck ring to emerge from the first single B bead again.

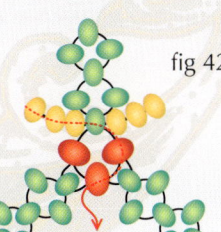
fig 42

Pass the needle through the following 2D beads (fig 42).

27 Thread on 13C. Pass through the A bead at the top of the F bead on the first bow and thread on 1C. Pass up through the second C bead from the bottom of the strand (fig 43).

fig 43

Pass through the following 10C and thread on 1C. Pass the needle through the D bead on the ring in the same direction as before and the following 1D and 1B (fig 44).

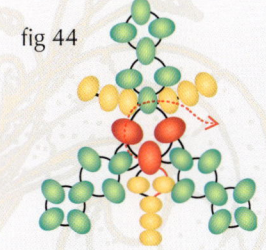
fig 44

Repeat to add a suspension strap between each of the remaining leaf clusters on the neck ring and the remaining two bows.

Finish off all remaining thread ends neatly and securely.

28 **The Hanging Loop -** Repeat steps 1 to 12 inclusive to make one new bow.

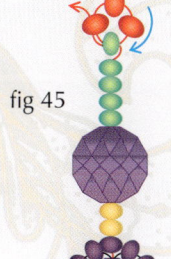
fig 45

29 The needle should be emerging from the top of the F bead.

Thread on 1A, 2C, 1G, 5B and 3D.

Pass the needle through the last B bead and the following 1D of the sequence to bring the top four beads into a ring (fig 45).

Repeat step 15 to make a leaf motif here.

30 The needle should be emerging from the next D bead around the ring.

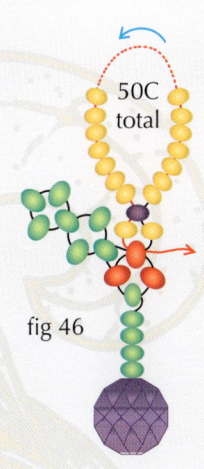
fig 46

Referring to fig 46 thread on 1C, 1A and 50C. Pass the needle back down the A bead in the opposite direction to draw up the loop and thread on 1C.

Pass through the D bead on the ring in the same direction as before (fig 46).

The loop needs to be reinforced. Pass the needle up and down this bead sequence at least three more times.

Finish with the needle emerging from the D bead on the ring as fig 46.

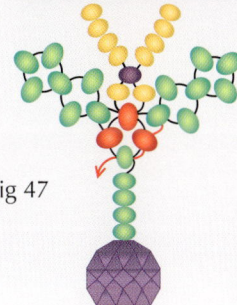
fig 47

31 Make the second leaf motif in this gap and pass the needle through the following 1D and 1B (fig 47).

32 Referring to fig 48 thread on 1B and pass through the second B bead along.

Thread on 1B and pass through the B bead adjacent to the G bead. Pull the thread firmly to create a leaf motif.

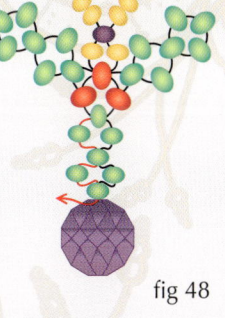
fig 48

33 Pass the needle through the G bead and the five beads below it to emerge at the bottom of the bow. Thread on 1A and pass the needle through the loop at the top of the bauble. Pass the needle back up through the last A bead threaded and the F bead at the centre of the bow.

The connection to the bauble also needs to be reinforced. Pass the needle through the A beads of one of the straps around the F bead and back through the connection to the bauble. Repeat at least once more and finish off all the thread ends neatly and securely.

Garland Inspirations

Beau Bauble

The Garland Bauble design spaces out three bows and three sets of swags around a 60mm bauble. If you like the bow motif why not try out four repeats around the same size bauble.

There are just a few additions to the recipe and a few simple adaptations to the holly swags and the foundation row.

You Will Need

Materials

One 60mm pale blue glass bauble
14g of size 10/0 silver lined crystal seed beads A
10g of size 10/0 frost silver lined blue AB seed beads B
5g of size 10/0 transparent crystal AB seed beads C
6g of size 8/0 frost silver lined blue AB seed beads D
2g of size 3 transparent purple AB bugle beads E
Nine 4mm purple AB fire polished faceted beads F
Five 6mm purple AB fire polished faceted beads G
A reel of white size D beading thread

34 Work through steps 1 to 12 four times to make the four bows to sit around the bauble.

Add tassel strands to each of the four bows as in steps 13 to 19.

35 The Swags - As the gap between the bows is smaller than on the Garland Bauble design the swags need to be a little shorter with two holly sprigs instead of three.

Work through steps 20 and 21.

Thread on 1C, 9B, 1C, 1B and 3D. Pass the needle through the last B bead in the same direction to draw the last four beads into a ring (as fig 32).

Repeat step 21 to complete a second cluster of three leaves.

Thread on 1C and 13B. Pick up a new bow and referring to fig 36, pass the needle up through the 3A beads of the strap towards the top of the bow, the A bead at the top and the following 3A (fig 36) to emerge alongside the thread end from step 19.

Using the longest thread end on each bow, repeat step 35 to link the four bows together.
Finish off all of the thread ends neatly and securely.

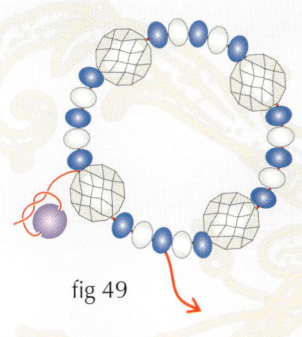

fig 49

36 The Foundation Row - Prepare the needle as in step 1 and thread on four repeats of 1F, 1B, 1C, 1B, 1C and 1B.

Pass the needle through the first four beads to bring them into a ring (fig 49).

Drop the ring over the neck of the bauble - it needs to fit quite snugly.

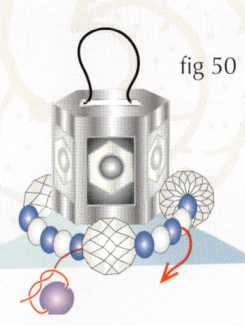

fig 50

If it does not fit well adjust the C bead counts equally around the ring until you have the four central single B beads between the C beads evenly distributed around the neck (fig 50).

37 You now have four central single B beads around the neck of the bauble to use as the bases for holly sprigs. These four sprigs will in turn support the four bows.

Work through steps 25 to 27 to make the holly sprigs and the connections to the bows.

Work through steps 28 to 33 to complete the hanging loop.

A festive tassel using bright red seed beads for the bow and holly sprigs around the top of a tassel.

Use the bow motif to add attractive hanging loops to crystals for the tree.

Or for a quick and stylish gift, stitch a bow onto a hair pin or a brooch back.

Sherwood Bauble

You Will Need

Materials

One 60mm frosted gold glass bauble
7g of size 10/0 silver lined brown seed beads A
4g of size 10/0 scarab green seed beads B
5g of size 10/0 silver lined bronze seed beads C
5g of size 10/0 silver lined gold seed beads D
1.5g of size 3 silver lined brown bugle beads E
Thirty-six 6mm topaz fire polished faceted beads F
Twenty-two 4mm red fire polished faceted beads G
Eight 4mm topaz fire polished faceted beads H
Eight 6mm red fire polished facteted beads J
Five 8mm topaz fire polished faceted beads K
A reel of gold size D beading thread

Tools

A size 10 beading needle
A pair of scissors to trim the threads

There are just a few days every year when the trees are all in their best autumn colours, the chill in the air raises a wispy mist and the sun is low on the horizon, when even the most sceptical of folk start to believe in legends. Make this design in golds, greens and reds for that autumn glow or in white, crystal and pale blue for a touch of frost on a winter's morning.

The Decoration is Made in Seven Stages

Four medium sized leaves are made first.
A ring of seed beads is fitted around the neck of the bauble and links made to the medium leaves.
Four sets of three small leaves are made between the medium leaves.
Large leaves are made and attached to a separate seed bead ring around the neck of the bauble.
Berry clusters are added around the neck.
The two layers of beading over the bauble are stitched together.
The hanging loop is made and attached to the top of the bauble.

1 **The Medium Leaves** - Prepare the needle with 1.5m of single thread and tie a keeper bead 15cm from the end.

Thread on 1F, 19A and 3B. Leaving aside the last 3B beads to anchor the strand, pass the needle back up through the last A bead (fig 1).

Thread on 1B. Pass the needle through the 3B beads of the picot (fig 2).

Thread on 1B.

Following fig 3 pass the needle down through the last A bead of the strand, the 3B beads of the picot and the new B bead just added (fig 3).

2 Thread on 2B, 1C and 1A.

Following fig 4, pass the needle down the bottom 3A beads of the main strand, up through the B bead above the picot and the following 2B.

Thread on 2B, 1C and 2A.

Following fig 5, pass the needle down the fifth and fourth A beads of the main strand, the A and C beads of the previous stitch and up the 2B beads just added.

3 Thread on 2B and 4C.

Following fig 6, pass the needle down the seventh and sixth A beads of the main strand, the 2A and 1C beads of the previous stitch and up the 2B beads just added.

fig 6

This is the method for making the leaves - add two beads for the outer edge (on this leaf 2B) and the beads for the vein of the leaf. Pass down through two beads on the main string, through the beads of the previous vein and up through the two beads just added for the outer edge of the leaf.

4 Using the method shown in steps 2 and 3, and following fig 7 make the remaining veins on this side of the leaf

For the fourth vein thread on 2B, 1C and 4A.
For the fifth vein thread on 2B and 6C.
For the sixth vein thread on 2B, 1C and 5A.

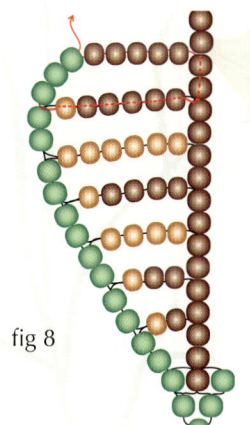
fig 7

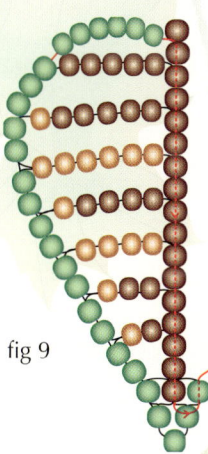
fig 8   fig 9

5 The top of the leaf is rounded off to complete this side of the leaf. Following fig 8 thread on 3B and 5A. Make the stitch as before - the needle needs to pass up through the 3B beads just added instead of the 2B on previous stitches.

Thread on 6B. Following fig 9 pass the needle down through the sixteenth A bead of the stem and the following 15A. Pass the needle up through the B bead above the picot on the other side of the main strand.

Repeat from fig 4 to fig 8 inclusive to make a mirror image set of leaf veins to this side of the main strand.

8 You have four medium leaves to suspend from the ring - with a count of 32D the ring will divide into four sets of 8D - if necessary make a similar calculation for your D bead count.

Thread on 9D, 1C, 2D and 1A. Pass the needle through the middle C bead of the picot at the top of the first medium leaf (see fig 13). Thread on 1A, 2D, 1C and 9D.

Pass the needle through the eighth C bead (or your calculated bead count) around the ring (fig 13).

fig 13

Repeat to make three more loops supporting the remaining three medium leaf motifs.

Pass the needle down through the first 5D beads of the first loop made (fig 14).

A new loop will need to be created between this D bead and the corresponding D bead on the adjacent loop to support the small leaf motifs.

fig 14

6 Thread on 6B to shape the top of the leaf as before. Following fig 10 pass the needle down through the sixteenth A bead of the stem and the following 15A.

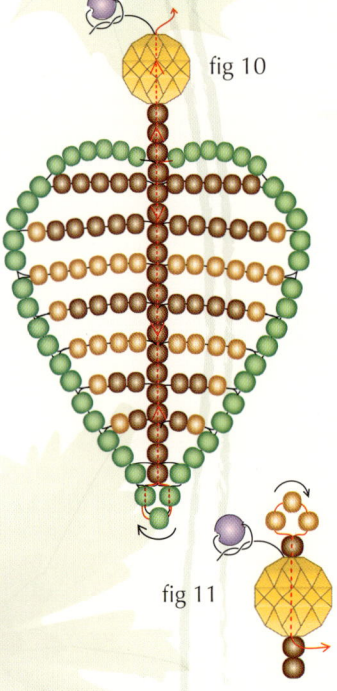

fig 10

Pass the needle through the 3A beads of the picot and back up the A beads of the main strand to emerge from the F bead at the very top of the work.

Thread on 1A and 3C. Pass the needle down through the A bead just added and the following F bead to draw the 3C beads into a picot on the top of the work (fig 11).

Finish off both of the thread ends neatly and securely. Set the leaf aside for the moment.

fig 11

Make three more medium leaves to match.

9 The Small Leaves - Thread on 45D, 1C, 1D, 1E, 1D, 1C, 1A, 1G, 1A, 1C, 1A, 1F, 1A, 1C, 8A and 3B.

Pass the needle back up the last A bead threaded to pull the 3B beads into a picot (fig 15) - this is the tip of the small leaf.

With reference to figs 3 to 6 work the first three veins as before (fig 16).

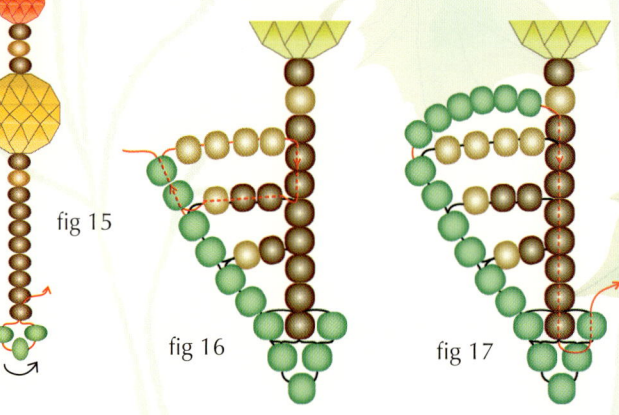

fig 16   fig 17

7 The Fitted Ring and Linking the Medium Leaves - Prepare the needle with 1.5m of single thread and tie a keeper bead 15cm from the end.

Thread on 32D. Drape the beads around the neck of the bauble - they need to make a snug ring around the base of the neck. If the ring is loose remove 4D; if it is too tight add 4D. Adjust the bead count in multiples of 4D beads until the fit is satisfactory. The following instructions will assume a bead count of 32D - you will need to bear in mind any adjustments you may have made to the bead count.

Pass the needle through the first D bead to draw up the ring (fig 12).

Pass the needle through the beads of the ring a second time to make it firmer.

fig 15

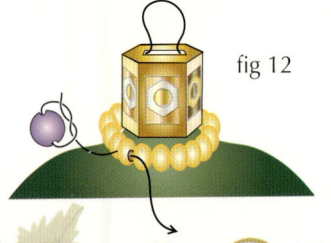

fig 12

Thread on 6B. Pass the needle down the last 8A beads on the main strand and up through the B bead above the picot on the other side of the main strand ready to begin the other side of the leaf (fig 17).

Work this side of the leaf to be a mirror image of the first side.

On completion of the leaf pass the needle down through the A beads of the main strand and the first 2B beads of the picot to emerge from the very bottom B bead of the leaf.

12 Thread on 30D, 1C, 1D, 1E, 1D, 1C, 1A, 1G, 1A, 1C, 1A, 1F, 1A, 1D, 8C and 3A.

Pass the needle back up through the last C bead threaded to pull the 3A beads into a picot for the bottom of the new leaf.

You will notice that the bead colours have changed below the F bead on this strand to make the new leaf with a different colour combination.

fig 20

Referring to fig 20 complete the new leaf motif following the method in step 9 but swapping -

A beads for C beads
B beads for A beads
C beads for D beads.

Once the leaf motif is complete add an F bead to the tip of the leaf as in fig 18 (see fig 20). Pass the needle back up through the beads of the main strand to emerge at the top of the strand.

10 Referring to fig 18 thread on 1C, 1A, 1F, 1A and 3C.

Pass the needle back up through the last A bead and the following 1F and 1A.

Thread on 1C and pass through the B bead at the tip of the leaf picot in the same direction as before to centralise the F bead below the leaf motif (fig 18).

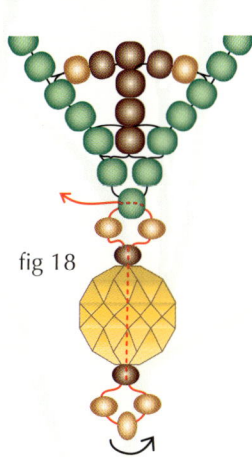

fig 18

11 Pass the needle through the following 1B bead of the picot and the 8A beads of the main strand.

Pass back up through the beads of the main strand above the leaf motif to emerge 30D above the top C bead of the sequence.

Thread on 15D.

Referring to fig 19 locate the fifth D bead down the adjacent loop from step 8.

Pass the needle up through this fifth D bead and the following 4D, 1D on the ring around the neck of the bauble, 5D at the top of the next loop and the first 1D of the loop supporting the leaf just made (fig 19).

The next leaf motif will hang from this position.

fig 21

13 Referring to fig 21, reposition the needle through the D beads of the loops and the ring around the neck of the bauble, to emerge through the corresponding D bead on the other side of the first small leaf.

This is the correct position to add the third leaf strand.

14 Thread on 15D, 1C, 1D, 1E, 1D, 1C, 1A, 1G, 1A, 1C, 1A, 1F, 1A, 1D and 11C.

Pass the needle back up through the eighth C bead of the last 11C threaded to pull the last 3C beads into a picot for the bottom of the new leaf. You will notice that the bead colours have changed below the F bead once again to make the new leaf with a different colour combination.

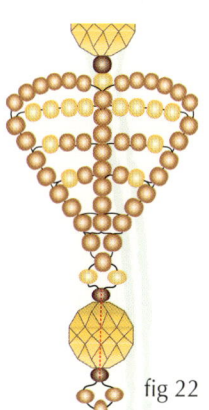

fig 22

Referring to fig 22 complete the new leaf motif following the method in step 9 but swapping -

A and B beads for C beads
C beads for D beads.

Once the leaf is complete, add an F bead to the tip of the leaf as in fig 18 (fig 22) but note that D beads have been used between the picot tip of the leaf and the A bead above the F bead to ensure a colour contrast.

Pass the needle back up through the beads of the main strand to emerge at the top of the strand.

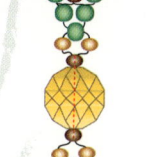

fig 19

15 Pass the needle through the D beads above the current position to emerge at the ring around the neck of the bauble.

Pass through the D beads of the ring to emerge from the D bead immediately before the start of the next loop.

Pass the needle down through the first 5D of that loop (fig 23).

The needle is now in the correct position to start the next set of three small leaves.

fig 23

16 Repeat from steps 9 to 15 three more times to complete three more sets of small leaves.

Remove any remaining keeper beads and finish off any remaining thread ends neatly and securely.

17 **The Large Leaves** - These are made in a very similar manner to the medium leaves.

Prepare the needle with 1.5m of single thread and tie a keeper bead 15cm from the end.

Thread on 22A and 3B and repeat figs 1 to 7 to make the first six veins of the leaf.

For the seventh vein thread on 2B and 8C. Make the stitch as before.

For the the eighth vein thread on 2B, 1C and 8A. Make the stitch as before.

For the ninth vein thread on 4B and 6C. Pass the needle down the next 2A beads of the main strand, through the 8A and 1C beads of the previous vein and the 4B beads just added (fig 24).

Thread on 7B.

Pass the needle down through the next 1A bead on the main strand and the following 19A.

Pass the needle up through the B bead above the picot on the other side of the main strand ready to begin the other half of the leaf (fig 25).

Make this half of the leaf a mirror image of the first half.

fig 24

fig 25

18 Pass the needle down the main strand of the leaf, through the 3B beads of the picot and up around the edge B beads of the leaf to make the motif firmer (fig 26).

Repeat along the other edge of the leaf.

Pass the needle up to the top of the main strand to emerge alongside the keeper bead.

fig 26

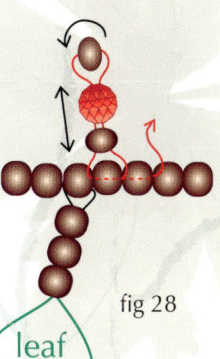

22 Pass the needle through the A beads of the ring to emerge from the first A bead after the first leaf.

Thread on 1A, 1G and 1A. Pass the needle back through the G bead and the following A bead.

Pass the needle through the A bead on the ring and the following 1A (fig 28) - this will complete the first berry and move the needle onto the next berry location.

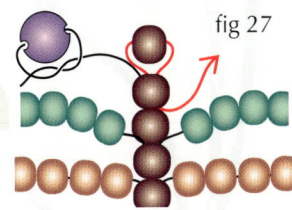

19 Thread on 1A. Pass the needle back down the top A bead of the main strand (fig 27) to pull the new A bead horizontally across the top of this bead.

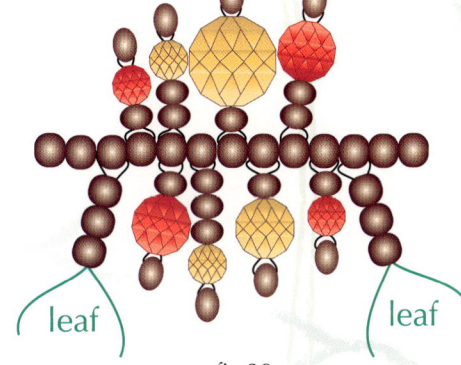

Fig 29 shows the full berry cluster between the first two leaves.

Pass the needle through the following ten beads of the main strand and finish off the thread end neatly and securely. Remove the keeper bead and finish off this thread end in a similar manner.

Repeat steps 17, 18 and 19 three more times to make four large leaves in total.

20 Prepare the needle with 1.5m of single thread and a keeper bead. You now need to make a ring of A beads to fit the neck of the bauble once more. This ring needs to incorporate the four single A beads at the tops of the large leaves just prepared.

If your D bead count in step 7 was 32D you will need to thread 7A between each of the four single leaf-top A beads to give you the required total count of 32. You may need to adjust your bead count according to the exact diameter of the neck of your bauble.

Thread on the required repeat to give you four equally-spaced large leaves along the thread.

Drape the row around the bauble and pass the needle through the first bead of the sequence to form the ring (as fig 12). Pass the needle through the beads of the ring once more to make it a little firmer.

You now add the beaded berry clusters to this ring.

21 The Berry Clusters - First set aside 1K and 2G for the hanging loop. Now divide the remaining faceted beads into four identical piles.

Each pile should contain 1F, 2G, 2H, 2J and 1K. Each pile will make a berry cluster between two adjacent large leaves.

The following instructions refer to a bead count of 7A between the large leaves - you may need to adjust it slightly to accommodate a different bead count between the large leaves.

You have just completed the first berry on the left - you will see that the next A bead along the ring carries two berries.

Thread on 2A, 1H and 1A. Pass the needle back through the 1H and 2A beads and through the A bead on the ring once more.

Thread on 1A, 1J and 1A. Pass the needle back through the J bead, the following A bead just added, the A bead on the ring and the following A bead of the ring to be in the correct position to begin the berry from this next A bead around the ring (see fig 29).

Following fig 29 for guidance make the remaining berries of the cluster between the first two leaves.

Pass the needle through the A beads of the ring to emerge from the first A bead after the second leaf and repeat to make a berry cluster between this leaf and the third leaf.

Repeat twice to complete four sets of clusters in total.

23 Linking the Layers - Before you finish off this thread you need to make a few stitches to link the A bead ring holding the berry clusters and the large leaves to the D bead ring below it on the bauble neck.

Position the top A bead ring so that the tip of the large leaves line up with the longest small leaf strands - this will position the medium leaves in the gaps between the large leaves.

Make a few stitches between the two rings just to hold this arrangement in place.

24 Make sure that the medium leaves are falling into the gaps between the large leaves and if necessary attach a new thread to the top of the first large leaf.

Pass the needle through the edge beads of the first large leaf to emerge through the first B bead above the eighth leaf vein (see fig 30). Thread on 2C.

Pass the needle through the middle C bead of the picot above the adjacent medium leaf in the opposite direction and through the last C bead added in the same direction (fig 30) to bring the holes in the these 2C beads parallel.

Thread on 1C and pass up through the B bead above the eighth vein on the next large leaf around the ring.

Reposition the needle on the far side of this leaf and repeat the link in fig 30.

Repeat twice to complete the beading over the bauble.

Remove any remaining keeper beads and finish off all of the thread ends neatly and securely.

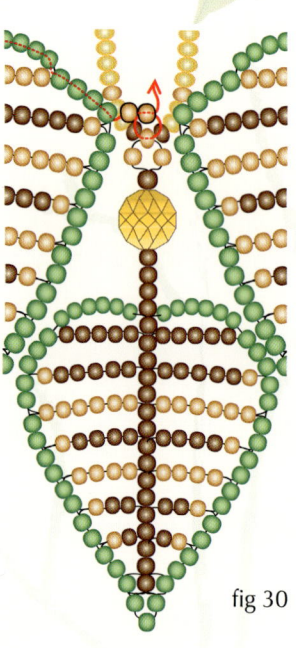

fig 30

25 The Hanging Loop - First you need make a medium leaf which connects to the bauble. The tip of this medium leaf links to a small leaf which, in turn, links to the loop itself.

Prepare the needle with 1.5m of single thread and tie a keeper bead 15cm from the end. Thread on 1K, 17A and 3B.

Work steps 1 to 5 to make a medium leaf. Finish the leaf in a similar fashion to fig 10 with the needle emerging alongside the keeper bead.

Thread on 1A. Pass the needle through the loop at the top of the bauble. Pass the needle back through the 1A just added, the following 1K, 17A and the first 2B beads of the picot to emerge at the tip of the leaf.

Thread on 1C, 1G, 1C, 8A and 3B. The 3B beads form the picot at the tip of the small leaf.

With reference to step 9 and figs 16 and 17 complete the small leaf motif. Finish with the needle emerging from the B bead at the tip of the leaf.

Thread on 1C, 1G, 1C, 1B and 50C. Pass the needle back down the B bead to draw up the loop.

fig 31

26 Pass the needle back through the following 1C and 1G. Thread on 1C. Pass the needle through the B bead at the tip of the small leaf picot in the same direction as previously to centralise the loop above the top of the leaf (see fig 31).

Pass the needle down through the following 1B, 8A, 1C and 1G.

Thread on 1C. Pass the needle through the B bead at the tip of the medium leaf in the same direction as previously to centralise the work (fig 31).

Pass the needle down through the beads of the main strand to emerge at the top of the bauble loop. Pass the needle through the loop and back up through the work to emerge at the bottom of the 50C loop.

Pass the needle through the beads of the loop twice to make it strong and finish off the thread end neatly and securely.

Remove the keeper bead. Attach the needle to this end and pass through the A bead adjacent to the metal bauble loop, through the bauble loop and back up through the A bead to strengthen that join as well.

Finish off the thread end neatly and securely.

Ariel Tassel

You Will Need

Materials

5g of size 10/0 silver lined crystal seed beads A
4g of size 2 transparent crystal bugle beads B
10g of size 10/0 frost transparent crystal seed beads C
Twenty-five 4mm crystal fire polished faceted beads D
Two 12mm crystal fire polished faceted beads E
One 10mm crystal fire polished faceted bead F
A reel of white size D beading thread

Tools

A size 10 beading needle
A pair of scissors to trim the threads
Clear nail varnish to stiffen the wings

finished size of ornament - h. 13cm x w. 11cm

As heralds of joy and celebration all over the world, angels feature in literature, traditional devotional texts, glorious paintings from the early Renaissance and all kinds of folklore. Ariel is also the match-making winged sprite in Shakespeare's The Tempest so perhaps this could be a token for a bride. Made in frosty white and silver or gold this tassel makes a fantastic festive decoration for the tree.

The Decoration is Made in Four Stages
Two separate wings are made first and attached to the body bead.
The tasselled skirt is made as a separate unit.
The skirt, body and head are brought together and the hanging loop added to the top.
The wings are stiffened to complete the design.

Extra Info....
A double thread is used to make the wings - the remainder of the design is made with a single thickness of thread.

If you make a mistake whilst using the double thread you will need to unpick the work. Pull gently on the thread to bring the the needle backwards through the work until you have undone the beading sufficiently.
Do not pass the needle back through the work point first: you will snag the threads and make a very nasty knot.

1 **The Wings** - Prepare the needle with 1.5m of double thread and tie a keeper bead 15cm from the end.

Thread on 52A, 2B and 4A.

Pass the needle through the 36th A bead from the keeper bead. Turn the needle and pass it back through the last 3A threaded (fig 1).

Thread on 1A, 1B and 3A. Pass the needle through the 29th A bead from the keeper bead. Turn the needle and pass it back through the last 2A threaded (fig 2).

Thread on 1A, 1B and 2A. Pass the needle through the 22nd A bead from the keeper bead. Turn the needle and pass it back through the last A bead threaded (fig 3).

Thread on 1A and 1B. Pass the needle through the 16th A bead from the keeper bead. Turn the needle and pass it back through the two beads just added (fig 4).

Following fig 5 pass the needle through the A and B beads of this first rib of the wing to emerge from the first B bead of the line. This will pull the B beads and the 2A between them into a line.

The following ribs all link to the previous rib through the A bead bridges made in figs 1, 2 and 3 and to the top line of the wing with a B bead bridge as in fig 4.

2 The second rib - thread on 5A, 2B and 4A. Pass the needle through the first of the 2A beads between the B beads on the adjacent rib. Turn the needle and pass back through the last 3A threaded (fig 6).

3 The remainder of this rib is made as before linking to the previous rib through the first of the 2A beads between the bugles of the previous rib. Follow fig 7 to complete the rib. At the top of the rib you will see that the top B bead links onto the 14th A bead from the keeper bead. Bring the needle through to emerge from the bottom of the first B bead of the rib to finish (fig 7).

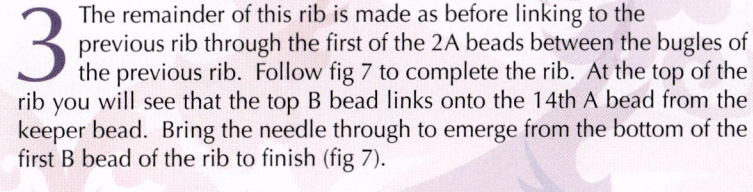

fig 6

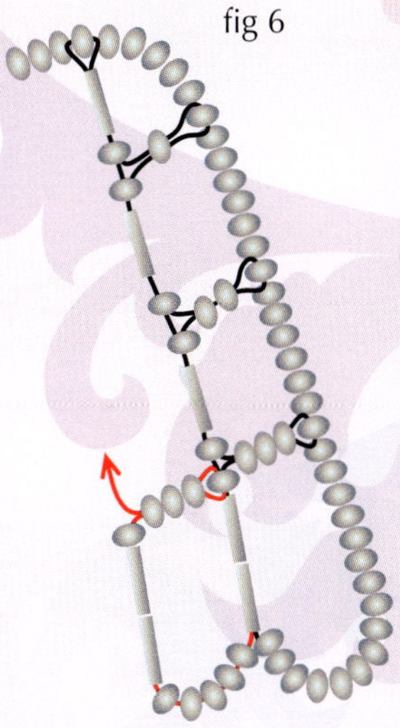

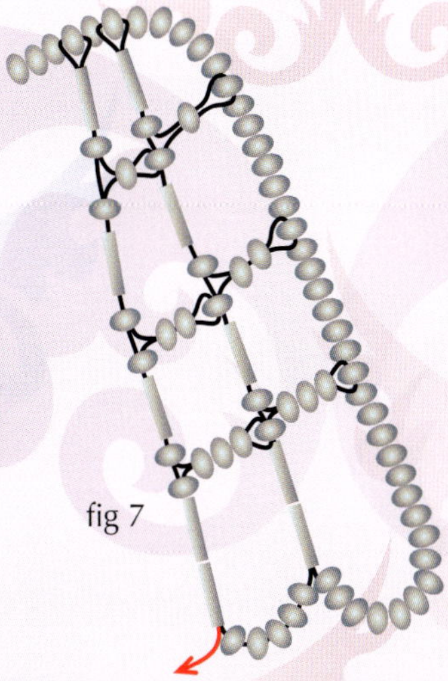

fig 7

4 The third rib - start with 4A, 2B and 4A. Make the first connection back to the previous rib as in fig 6. Work the remainder of the rib as for the previous rib connecting the top of the rib to the 12th A bead from the keeper bead and emerging from the bottom of the first B bead to complete the rib (see fig 8).

5 The fourth rib - start with 7A, 1B and 4A. Make the first connection to the previous rib as in fig 6. Make the remainder of the rib as for the previous one connecting the top of the rib to the 10th A bead from the keeper bead. To complete the rib bring the needle down to emerge from the A bead below the first B bead of the rib. By using only 1B bead for the first stitch of this rib you have started to reduce the length of the ribs and thus shape the wing (see fig 8).

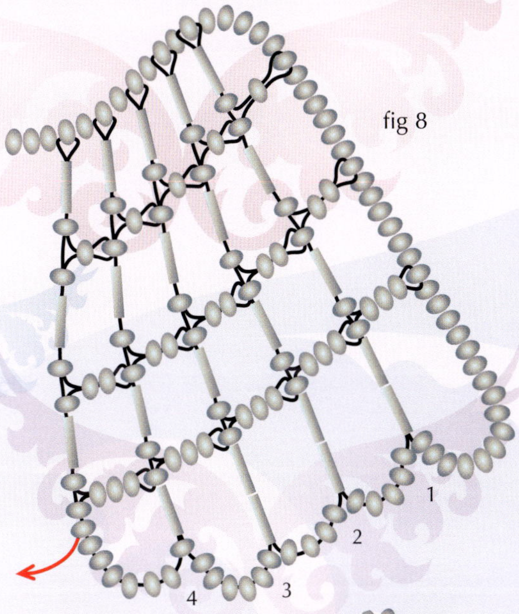

6 The fifth rib - this rib omits the bottom B bead. Thread on 11A. Make the link to the previous rib as before bringing the needle back through the last 3A threaded. Make the remainder of the rib as previously, linking the top to the 8th A bead from the keeper bead. Complete the rib by bringing the needle through to emerge from the third A bead below the first B bead of the rib (fig 8).

fig 8

7 The sixth rib - referring to fig 9 thread on 5A, 1B and 3A. Make the first link to the A bead immediately above the first B bead of the previous rib. Pass the needle back through the last 2A threaded above the new B bead to match the other links on this line across the width of the wing. Thread on 1A, 1B and 2A and make the next link of the rib as before. Thread on 1A and 1B and link the top of the rib to the 6th A bead from the keeper bead. Complete the rib by passing the needle back through the line to emerge from the first A bead below the first B bead of the rib.

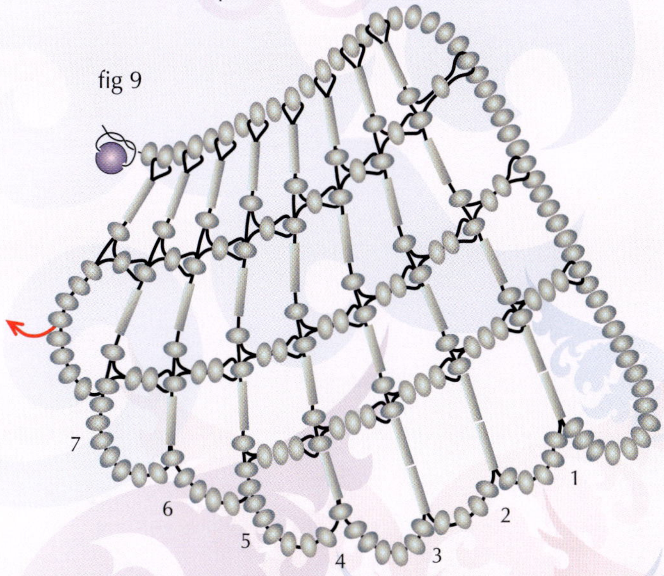

8 The seventh rib - this row reduces the B bead count once more. Referring to fig 9 thread on 10A. Make the link to the previous rib as before bringing the needle back through the last 2A beads to match the other links on this line across the width of the wing. Complete the rib as before making a link to the 4th A bead from the keeper bead at the top and bringing the needle down through the beads to emerge from the second A bead below the first B bead.

fig 9

9 The eighth rib - thread on 9A. Make a link to the previous rib as in fig 9. Thread on 1A and 1B and make the top link to the 2nd A bead from the keeper bead. Pass the needle back down to emerge from the fifth A bead below the B bead (fig 9).

Thread on 3A and put aside this wing for now.

Make a second wing to match.

10 Take the first wing and pass the thread from the lower edge of the wing up through the hole in one of the E beads.

Remove the keeper bead on the top edge and pass this end down through the hole in the E bead (fig 10).

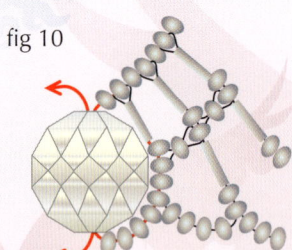

fig 10

11 Pick up the second wing and repeat so that the wings lie symmetrically to either side of the E bead and pull up tight to the E bead. If they do not fit snugly around the E bead remove the wings from the E bead and adjust the count of 3A added at the end of step 9 until they fit tightly (fig 11).

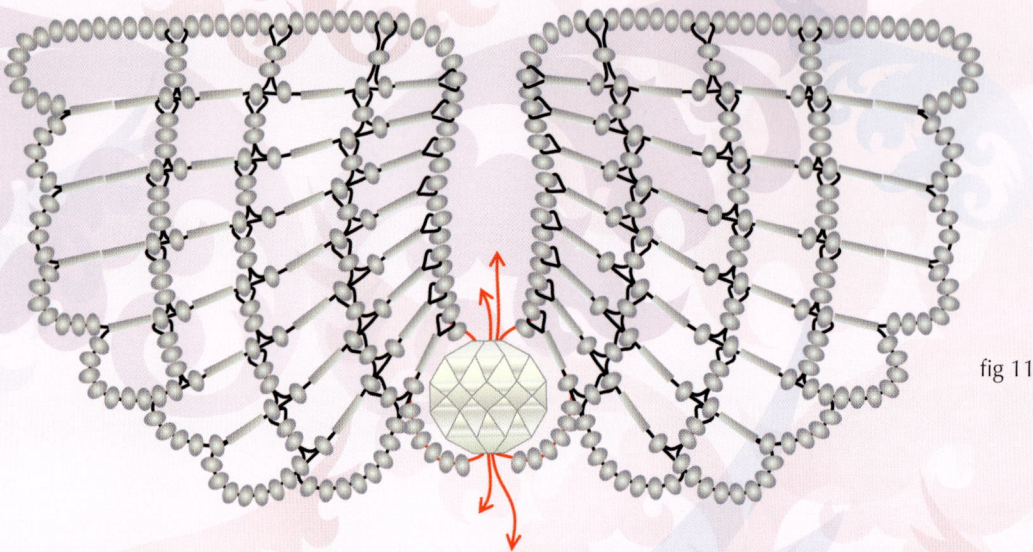

fig 11

12 Working with one wing at a time pass the thread through the beads of the eighth rib and back through the hole in the E bead.

Pass the needle along the beads of the top edge of the wing and up and down the ribs to stiffen the beadwork.

Work until you run out of thread or the holes become too full of thread to allow the needle to pass. Finish off the thread ends for this wing within the beads of this wing - be careful not to block the hole in the E bead.

Repeat for the other wing and set aside for the moment.

13 The Tassel - The skirt tassel needs to be very full to compensate for the width of the wings. To achieve this the tassel is made in two layers around an E bead. One half of the tassel will hang conventionally from the bottom of the E bead - the second longer layer will come out of the top of the E bead and fall down over it filling out the width of the tassel and concealing the E bead underneath its strands.

14 Prepare the needle with 1.5m of single thread and tie a keeper bead 15cm from the end. Thread on 1E, 42C, 1D, 1C and 3A. Turn the needle and leaving aside the last 3A threaded to anchor the strand pass the needle back up through the last C bead, the following D bead and the remaining beads to emerge at the far side of the E bead (fig 12).

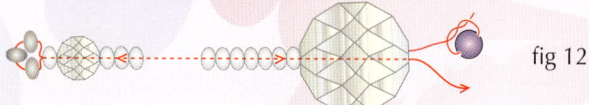

fig 12

Thread on 31C, 1D, 1C and 3A. As before turn the needle and leaving the last 3A beads to anchor the strand pass back up through all of the other beads to emerge at the far side of the E bead (fig 13).

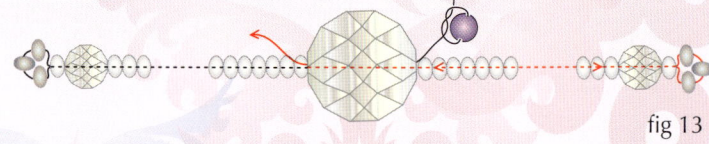

fig 13

Tension the thread in the strands so that they fall softly from either side of the E bead but so that the thread does not show between the beads of the strands.

You are now on the correct side of the E bead to make a second 42C bead strand. Make as before. On completing that strand you will be at the far side of the E bead to make the second 31C strand.

Extra Info....
For the subtle golden tinge on the gold angel swap the thread colour to gold and the A bead to silver lined gold. Keep the other beads the same. The gold thread shows through the seed beads and faceted beads of the skirt and the bugle beads on the wings.

19 The tassel is quite heavy and at present there is only one thickness of thread holding all of the elements together.

Pass the needle up and down through the E and F beads as many times as you can to strengthen the tassel - at the bottom of the tassel turn the needle through one of the top C beads of the 31C bead strands and at the top pass the needle through the beads of the hanging loop.

Finish off this thread end and any other remaining thread ends neatly and securely.

15 Work backwards and forwards through the E bead until you have nine of each length strand.

You cannot keep going through the E bead as it will become blocked with thread, but the number of longer strands will need to increase, to ensure that the E bead is fully covered when it is hung.

16 Bring the needle through to the 42C bead side of the E bead and make a tassel strand as before but do not pass back through the E bead.

Instead turn the needle and pass it through the top C bead of one of the adjacent tassel strands bringing the needle through to point towards the bottom of the strand. This has turned the direction of the thread without passing through the E bead.

Make a tassel strand as before turning the needle through the top C bead of another strand already in situ. Repeat three more times to make fifteen 42C bead strands in total.

At the top of the fifteenth strand pass the needle through the E bead and make one more 31C strand. Pass the needle back through to the 42C strand side of the E bead.

20 Stiffening the Wings - The wings of the angel now need to be stiffened. Working in a well ventilated space lay the angel out flat on a piece of polythene. Paint a very thin coat of clear nail varnish onto the wings. The nail varnish will trickle between the beads and stiffen the threads. Leave to dry completely. Flip the angel over and repeat.

Repeat at least once more on each side. It is better to build up three or four thin coats than two thick coats so take your time. Do not get the varnish onto the C beads as it will spoil the matt finish on these beads.

Ariel Inspiration

Angellic Earrings

Perfect stocking fillers for all ages and a great gift if you have a friend who sings in a choir.

Use cupped flower beads for the skirt, a curved bead for the wings and a 4mm bead for the head.

Thread them onto a headpin, make a loop and an add an earfitting.

17 Assembling the Angel - Hang the E bead of the tassel from the end of the needle thread. Spread the 42C bead strands out around the top of the E bead so that they fall over the edge all the way around - the ends of these strands should now fall to approximately the same length as the 31C strands.

18 Thread on 1A and pass the needle up through the E bead at the centre of the wings. Thread on 1A, the F bead, 1A, 1C and 1A. Thread on 50A beads for the hanging loop. Turn the needle and pass it back through the A bead just above the C bead and the C bead.

Thread on 2C. Pass the needle down through the C bead on the main string once more to bring the two new beads up close (fig 14).

Repeat to add seven more stitches of 2C to complete the halo of the angel.

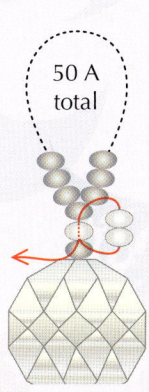

fig 14

103

Christmas Earrings

Three designs for a bit of festive fun

Holly Wreath Earrings

Very Christmassy and easy to make, these would make a super stocking filler. There are tiny bells in the centre of these earrings but you could substitute them with a suitable charm.

You Will Need

Materials

2g of size 10/0 silver lined brown seed beads A
1g of size 8/0 silver lined red seed beads B
1.5g of DB148 silver lined green Delica beads C
Two 10mm Liberty Bell charms or similar
Two 4mm gold plated jump rings
A pair of gold plated earfittings
A reel of green size D beading thread

Tools

A size 10 beading needle
A pair of scissors to trim the threads
A pair of fine pliers to attach the earfittings
A small amount of clear-drying nail varnish

Each Earring is Made in Four Stages

A tight ring of seed beads is made first.
The holly leaves are made at the top of the ring.
The bell is suspended in the centre.
The jump ring is added and connected to the earfitting.

1 The Ring - Prepare the needle with 1.5m of single thread and tie a keeper bead 15cm from the end.

Thread on 1B, 6A, 1B, 6A, 1B, 6A, 1B, 6A, 1B and 6A.

2 Remove the keeper bead. Pull quite hard on both ends of the thread to pull the beads into a firm circle. Tie the tail end of the thread to the needle end pulling the knot down between the beads to conceal. Repeat the knot.

Pass the needle through the adjacent B bead.

3 The Holly Leaves - Thread on 4C.

Leaving aside the last C bead threaded to make an anchor, pass the needle through the third of the 4C in the opposite direction (fig 2).

fig 1

Pass the needle through the first B bead in the same direction as before, to bring the beads into a ring (fig 1).

Pass the needle through all of the beads of the ring twice.

Finish with the needle emerging alongside the keeper bead.

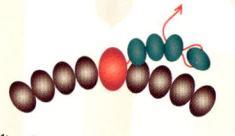
fig 2

Thread on 4C. Pass the needle back through the third of the 4C just added as before to bring the fourth C bead up into an anchor (fig 3).

fig 3

4 Thread on 3C. Turn the needle and pass it back through the second C bead of the 3C just added as before (fig 4).

Thread on 3C and pass the needle back through the second of the 3C just added (fig 5).

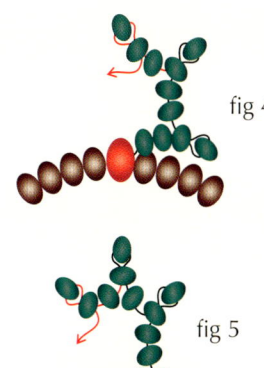

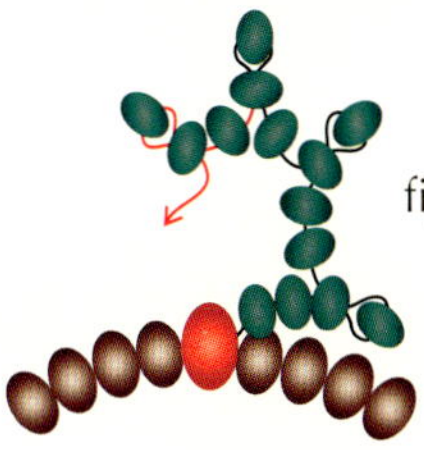

fig 4

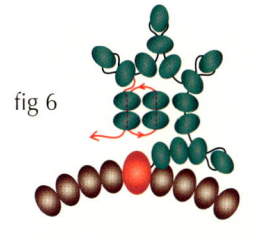

fig 5

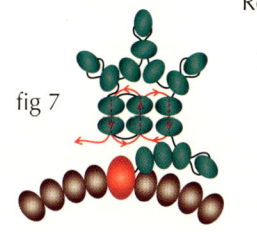

fig 6

5 Thread on 4C.

Referring to fig 6 pass the needle through the first 2C of the 4C just added in the same direction as before to bring the last 2C beads parallel to the first 2C (fig 6).

6 Flatten out the leaf in your fingers so that the points all turn to the outside of the motif.

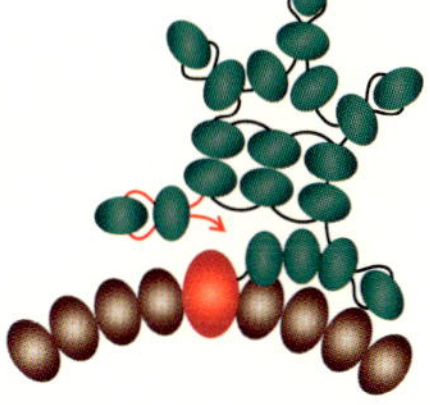

Referring to fig 7 locate the 2C beads between the first two leaf points. Pass the needle up through the last 2C of the previous stitch and down through the 2C beads between the first two points.

Pass the needle up the last 2C beads of the previous stitch once more and down through the first 2C of that stitch (fig 7).

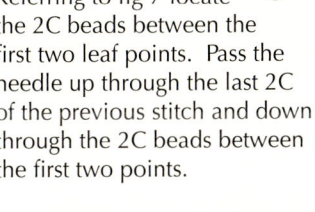

fig 7

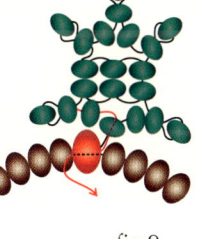

fig 8

fig 9

Thread on 2C. Turn the needle and pass it back through the first bead of the 2C just added (fig 8).

7 Thread on 1C. Pass the needle through the first C bead of the leaf in the opposite direction to complete the leaf (fig 9).

8 Pass the needle back through the B bead and make a second leaf on this side of the B bead following steps 3 to 7.

On completion of the second leaf, pass the needle through the B bead again and the following 6A beads to emerge just before the next B bead around.

9 Lay the holly leaves along the edge of the circular wreath.

Pass the needle through the very end C bead of the adjacent leaf. Pass the needle through the following B bead of the wreath (fig 10).

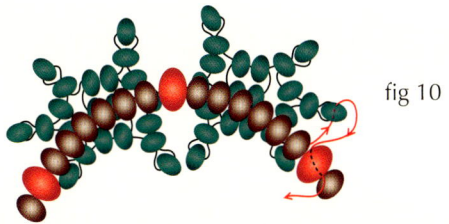

fig 10

Pass the needle through the following 21 beads to emerge just after the third B bead along. Pass the needle through the end C bead on the leaf that lies on this side of the wreath and the following 1A.

Pass the needle through the next six beads to emerge from the B bead between the leaves.

10 The Bell - Pass the needle through the loop at the top of the bell and through the B bead between the leaves so that the bell hangs centrally below the B bead (fig 11).

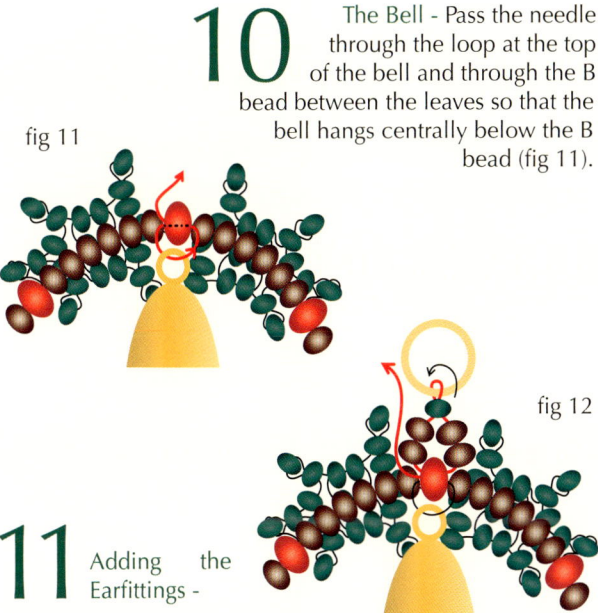

fig 11

fig 12

11 Adding the Earfittings -

Thread on 2A and 1C.

Pass the needle through a jump ring and back down the C bead and thread on 2A.

Pass the needle through the B bead between the leaves once more to centre the link above the B bead (fig 12). Pass the needle through the beads of this link again to make the connection strong.

Finish off this thread end neatly and securely. Attach the needle to the other loose thread end and pass through a few beads before trimming neatly.

Twist open the loop on the earfitting and attach to the jump ring.

Repeat to make the second earring.

12 Working in a well-ventilated space use a little clear nail varnish to seal the knot and to paint the thread loop through the jump ring to stop it falling through the gap in the ring.

Cracker Earrings

No tiny paper hats inside these crackers I am afraid, but I can give you a corny joke...
What is Santa's favourite pizza?...One that's deep pan, crisp and even!

You Will Need

Materials

1.0g of DB681 semi-matte silver lined squash Delica beads A
1.5g of DB683 semi-matte silver lined dark ruby Delica beads B
1.5g of DB610 silver lined violet Delica beads C
Four size 8/0 silver lined red seed beads D
Two 4mm blue fire polished faceted beads E
Two 4mm topaz fire polished faceted beads F
Two 4mm red fire polished faceted beads G
Two 4mm gold plated jump rings
Six gold plated eyepins
A pair of earfittings
A reel of red size D beading thread

Tools

A size 10 beading needle
A pair of scissors to trim the threads
A pair of round-nosed pliers
A pair of wire cutters
A small amount of clear-drying nail varnish

Each Earring is Made in Three Stages

A Peyote-stitched tube is made for the body.
A ruffle is added to each end of the tube.
A beaded chain is added to link to the earfitting.

1 The Tube - Prepare the needle with 1.5m of single thread and tie a keeper bead 15cm from the end.

Fig 1 shows the Peyote Stitch grid for the tube bead. Thread on the 12 beads as shown along the bottom edge of the grid.

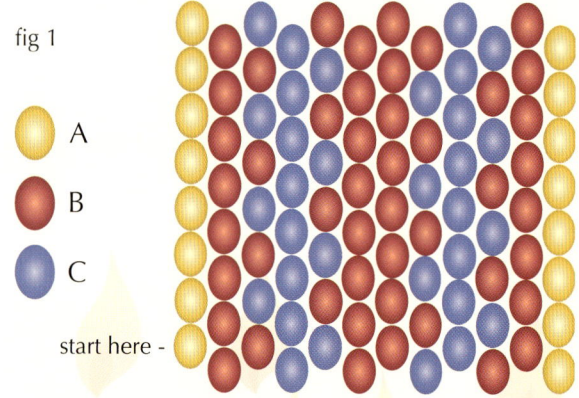

fig 1

A
B
C

start here -

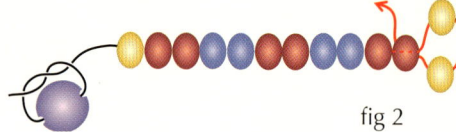

fig 2

2 Examine the grid and thread on 1A as indicated to sit above the twelfth bead just added. Pass the needle through the eleventh bead of the previous row in the opposite direction to bring the new bead parallel to the twelfth bead of the first row (fig 2).
Tension the thread through the beads to pull the 2A beads up snugly at the end of the first row.

3 Examine the grid and thread on the 1C bead as indicated to sit above the tenth bead of the previous row. Pass the needle through the ninth bead of the first row to pull the new bead alongside the tenth bead of the first row (fig 3).

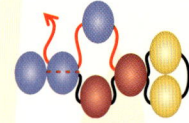

fig 3

You will notice that the first row is beginning to take on the keyhole profile as seen in fig 1.

Using the same technique as in fig 3 add 1B for each of the next two stitches, 1C for the following stitch and 1B for the last stitch of the row. The needle will be emerging from the first A bead of the first row.

Extra Info....

Peyote Stitch starts with a straight row. You then add alternate beads back along the first row to create a key-hole effect. The next row drops new beads into these keyholes and in turn, creates a new row of keyholes.

You will find a clear rule very useful to lay across the grid to help you to keep your place.

4 As indicated on the grid, thread on 1A for the start of the next row.

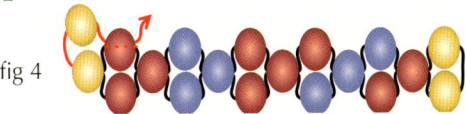

fig 4

Pass the needle through the last bead added on the previous row to bring the new bead into the keyhole above the first bead of the first row (fig 4).

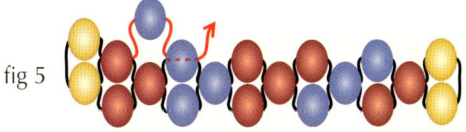

fig 5

Thread on 1C as indicated on the grid for the next keyhole. Pass through the next key bead along to bring the new bead into the keyhole (fig 5). This is Peyote Stitch.

Following the grid work to the end of the row.

Work the remainder of the grid in Peyote Stitch.

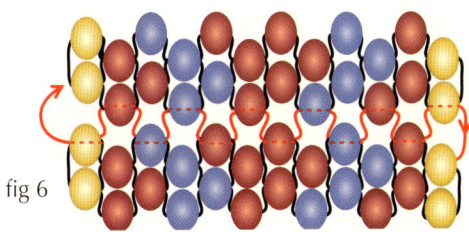

fig 6

5 Roll the beadwork into a tube so the key beads from the last row lock into the keyholes on the first row.

Pass the needle along the seam to complete the join (fig 6). Pass the needle back along the seam to make sure the join is firm.

6 The Ruffles - Each ruffle is supported by six of the eight beads at the end of the tube. The thread passes from these beads through a single D bead to pull in the end of the tube slightly. The D bead should finish in the centre at the end of the tube.

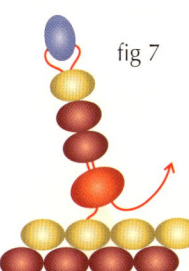

fig 7

7 If necessary, pass the needle through the beads to emerge from the end of the tube through one of the A beads.

Thread on 1D, 2B, 1A and 1C. Leaving aside the C bead to anchor the strand, pass the needle back down the previous four beads (fig 7).

8 Pass the needle down through the same A bead on the end of the tube and up through the next A bead around (fig 8).

Do not pull the thread too tightly as the D bead needs to centre across the end of the tube.

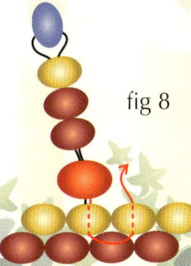

fig 8

9 Pass the needle up through the D bead and thread on 2B, 1A and 1C. As before leave aside the C bead to anchor the strand and pass the needle back down the previous four beads.

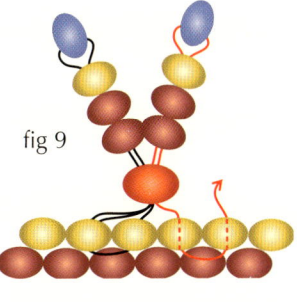

fig 9

Pass the needle down the next A bead around the end of the tube and up through the following A bead (fig 9).

10 Pass the needle up through the D bead and thread on 2B, 1A and 1C. As before leave aside the C bead to anchor the strand and pass the needle back down the previous four beads.

Pass the needle down through the same A bead on the end of the tube and up through the next A bead around (as fig 8).

Repeat step 10 once.
Repeat step 9 once.
Repeat step 10 once.

You have now added six strands (fig 10).

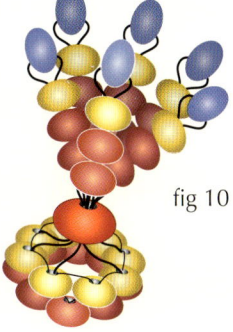

fig 10

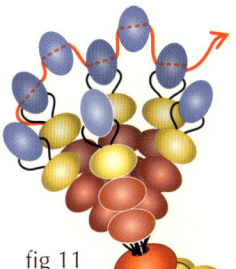

fig 11

11 Pass the needle up through the D bead and the beads of one of the strands to emerge from the top C bead.

Thread on 1C and pass through the C bead at the top of the next strand around. Repeat (fig 11). Add 1C into each of the remaining gaps to close up the ends of the strands into a complete ring.

Pass the needle down one of the strands and into the beads of the tube. Work the needle through the tube beads to the other end and repeat from step 6 to make a ruffle at this end of the tube.

12 The Beaded Chain - Pass the needle through the beads of the tube to emerge between the third and fourth beads from the end of a row (fig 12).

Thread on a jump ring and carefully attach to the tube with several small stitches - take care that the thread does not escape through the gap in the ring.

Finish off the thread end neatly and securely. Repeat with any remaining thread ends.

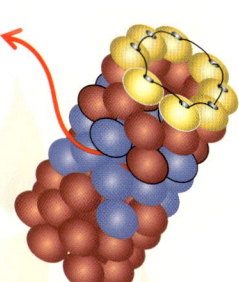

fig 12

In a well-ventilated space carefully paint the thread where it crosses the jump ring with a little clear nail varnish to make it strong and to prevent the jump ring from slipping.

13 Twist open the loop on an eyepin and link it to the jump ring. Thread on 1E. Trim the excess wire to 8mm and make a loop. Repeat to add an F bead link and a G bead link. Attach the earfitting to the top of the chain.

Repeat to make a second earring.

Rocking Robin Earrings

So cute and guaranteed to raise a smile, these earrings will lift the spirits of everyone around you - even if they are feeling a little tired after one too many Christmas parties or mince pies.

You Will Need

Materials

2.5g of DB769 matte transparent dark brown Delica beads A
1g of DB602 silver lined red Delica beads B
0.5g of size 15/0 silver lined gold seed beads C
0.5g of size 10/0 metallic gold seed beads D
Four size 10/0 black seed beads E
Two 10mm black fire polished faceted beads F
Two size 6/0 black seed beads G
Two 3mm gold-plated round metallic beads H
Four 4mm gold plated jump rings
A pair of gold plated earfittings
A reel of black size D beading thread

Tools

A size 12 beading needle
A pair of scissors to trim the threads
A pair of fine pliers to attach the earfittings
A small amount of clear-drying nail varnish

Each Earring is Made in Three Main Stages

The body is beaded with brown and red Delicas over a core made from larger beads
The wings, tail, beak, and eyes are added followed by the legs and feet.
Finally the link to the earring fitting is created.

1 The Body - Prepare the needle with 1.5m of single thread and tie a keeper bead 15cm from the end.

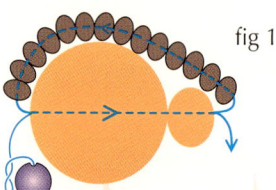

fig 1

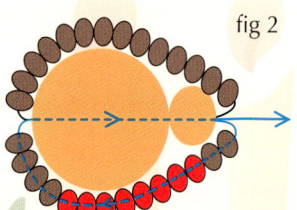

fig 2

2 Thread on 1F, 1G and 14A.

Pass the needle through the 1F and 1G beads to bring the 14A beads into a strap down the side of the larger beads (fig 1).

Thread on 2A, 8B and 4A and make a second strap on the other side of the F and G beads (fig 2).

Repeat to make two more straps of 14A completing four equally-spaced straps in total. The F and G beads should be sitting together snugly with the holes aligned.

3 Thread on 3A, 7B and 4A. Pass the needle through the F and G beads to pull a strap alongside the first B bead strap.

Make a second identical strap to pull to the other side of the first B bead strap so all three B bead straps lie alongside one another.

4 Thread on 14A. Make this strap to pull in-between two of the previous 14A straps.

Make a final 14A strap to pull into the remaining gap between the existing 14A bead straps.

The G and F beads will be quite well covered already. You should have three straps with B beads sitting together (with the 8B bead strap in the centre) and five straps of A beads.

The straps now need to be 'filled out' around the widest part of the F bead to complete the concealment of the core beads.

Extra Info....

The needle has to pass through the body beads lots of times in this pattern. It is important that you do not block the holes in the beads with knots. Do not tie any knots until instructed to. Leave old thread ends hanging loose and start any new threads with a keeper bead.

5
Pass the needle through the first 2A and 1B of the 8B bead strap and thread on 7B.

Pass the needle through the last 4B beads of the strap to emerge at the hole in the F bead (fig 3). Pass the needle through the F and G beads to pull the short strap into place.
Make sure the tension in the thread allows the new short strap to pull in snugly alongside the central portion of the original strap.

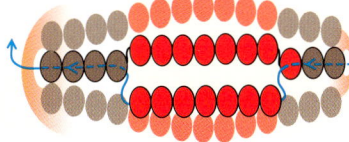

fig 3

You will need to add similar short straps to all of the long straps.

6
Start with the two long straps containing 7B beads.

Pass the needle through the first 3A and 1B beads of the first of these straps and thread on 5B and 2A.
Pass the needle through the last 3A beads of the long strap and the F and G beads to pull the new short strap into place between the B bead strap and the adjacent 14A strap (fig 4).

fig 4

Repeat with the other 7B long strap to pull the new short strap into the gap between this 7B strap and the adjacent 14A bead strap (fig 5). This tapers the shape of the red-breast.

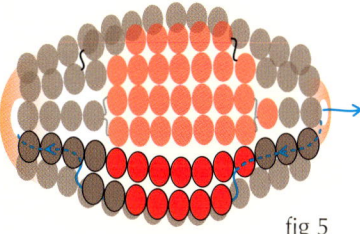

fig 5

7
Pass the needle through the first 4A beads of the next 14A bead strap around the work and thread on 7A. Pass the needle through last 3A beads of this 14A strap and the F and G beads as before to pull the new short strap into place. Repeat this stitch on the remaining four 14A bead straps.

Examine the overall coverage of the F and G beads - you may want to add one more 7A strap to the 14A strap that runs down the spine of the robin.

8
To neaten the covering and firm up the work, the straps are linked together with a series of square stitches.

Select one strap and pass the needle down through the first eight beads. Pass the needle through the middle two beads on the adjacent strap and back through the middle two beads on this strap to make a square stitch (fig 6).

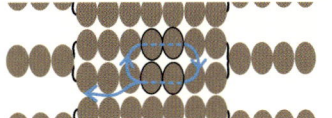

fig 6

Pass the needle through the middle two beads of the adjacent strap again to be in the correct position to start a new stitch (fig 7).

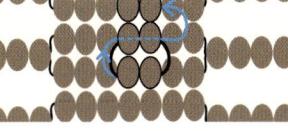

fig 7

Repeat figs 6 and 7 to work right around the circumference of the robin's body making the beadwork firmer.

The narrower, more tapered end of the body will become the head and the rounder end will support the tail of the bird.

Extra Info....
The needle will have to weave through the beads of the body to add the wings, eyes, beak, tail and legs. The holes in the beads might become congested with thread - if you cannot pass through the required bead find another path through an adjacent bead. Do not skip across rows and blocked beads as the thread will show and the beading may distort.

9
The Wings - Locate the two 14A straps that lie immediately to either side of the red breast. The middle 2A beads on these two straps support the wings.

Pass the needle up and down through the two-bead wide band around the circumference to emerge from the second of these two beads on the first band (fig 8).

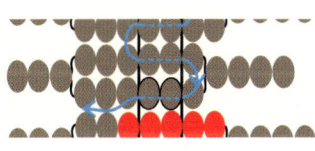

fig 8

10
Thread on 1A. Pass the needle through the 1A bead the needle emerged from on the strap and the new A bead to make a square stitch (fig 9).

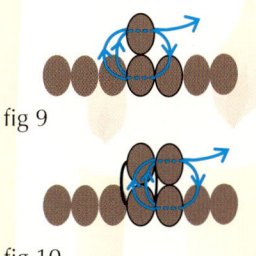

fig 9

fig 10

Thread on 1A and repeat the stitch to link this new A bead to the other A bead of the selected two A beads on the strap (fig 10).

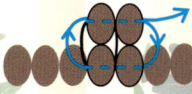

fig 11

Pass the needle through the 2A beads on the strap and the new 2A (fig 11).

11 Examine the needle position - is it pointing towards the tail-end or the head-end of the bird?

If it is pointing towards the tail-end you will need to add a two-bead stitch to start the new row.

If it is pointing towards the head-end you will need to add a single A bead.

To start with a two-bead stitch thread on 2A. Pass the needle through the A bead on the end of the previous row and back through the new 2A to complete the square stitch (fig 12).

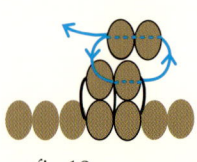
fig 12

Complete the row with a 1A square stitch (fig 13). To make the row firm pass the needle through the 2A of the previous row and the 3A of the new row (fig 14).

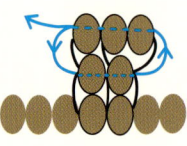
fig 13   fig 14

To start with a single A bead work a 1A stitch as in fig 13 followed by a two bead stitch as in fig 12.

Make the new row firm as in fig 14.

12 Reposition the needle through the beads across the red breast as before and repeat to make a second wing to match from the opposite middle 2A beads on that 14A bead strap.

13 The Tail - Pass the needle through the strap beads supporting the wing to emerge adjacent to the hole in the F bead at the tail end of the bird. Remove the keeper bead from this end of the work.

Examine how the A beads all come together as the threads disappear down the hole in the F bead.

Locate the ends of the two straps that support the wings - they should meet at the hole from opposite directions - the last 1A bead of each of these straps supports the tail (fig 15).

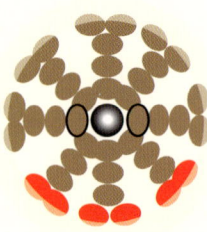
fig 15

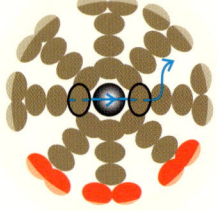

Pass the needle through the A bead at the end of the strap on the opposite side of the F bead hole so the needle is pointing away from the F bead hole (fig 16).

fig 16

Thread on 2A. Pass the needle through both of the end A beads on both straps to make a square stitch (fig 17). Pass the needle through the new 2A.

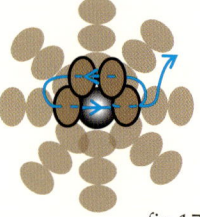
fig 17

14 Thread on 2A and square stitch these 2A to the previous 2A passing the needle through the new 2A to complete the row (fig 18).

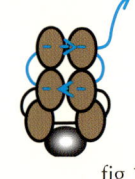
fig 18

Thread on 3A. Pass the needle through the previous row of 2A. Pass the needle through the beads of this 3A stitch again and work it back down to the body of the bird.

Pass the needle through the F and G beads to emerge at the tip of the head end ready to add the beak.

15 The Beak - Thread on 3D. Leaving aside the last 1D bead to anchor the stitch, pass the needle back down the second and first D beads to make a little spike of D beads (fig 19).

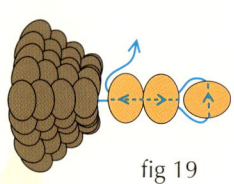
fig 19

Locate the middle strap of 14A running down the backbone of the bird. Pass the needle through the very first A bead of this row and pull firmly - this will bring the beak up tightly to the head and tip it up slightly to make a happy robin!

16 The Eyes - Examine the A bead straps to either side of the beak. Where the straps split to fill out the girth of the robin's body a little void opens up where you can see the gap between the F and G beads beneath the A bead covering. There is one of these voids on each side of the beak.

Stitch 1E bead into both of these gaps to create the eyes.

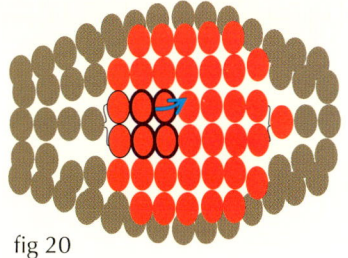

fig 20

17 The Legs - These attach to the two middle straps of the red breast.

Counting from the tail end of the robin pass the needle through the work to emerge between the second and third B beads of one of these straps (fig 20).

18 Thread on 7C. Leaving aside the last 1C to anchor the strand pass the needle back up the previous 2C (fig 21).

Thread on 1C.

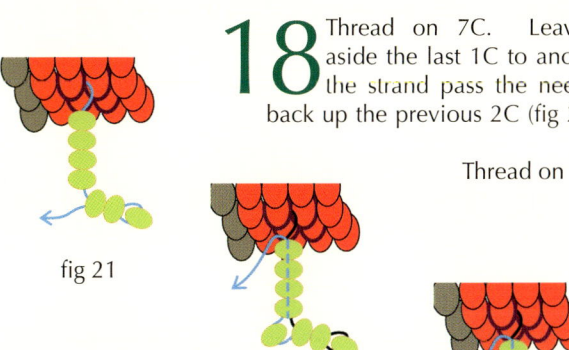

fig 21

fig 22

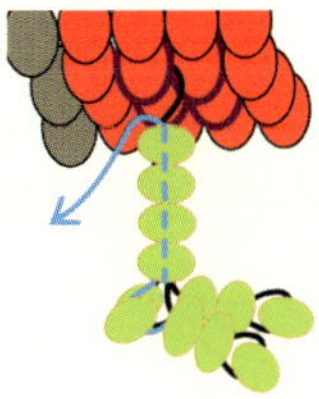

fig 23

Pass the needle up through the first 4C of the leg pulling the new C bead into place at the back of the leg to create a heel (fig 22). Make sure the toe is pointing towards the front of the bird.

Pass the needle under the bundle of threads between the B beads on that strap and back through the first 4C beads of the leg - do not pass through the heel bead.

Thread on 3C. Leave aside the last 1C to anchor the strand and pass the needle back through the previous 2C (as fig 21). Thread on 1C and pass up through the first 4C beads of the leg once more to add a second heel bead alongside the first (fig 23). Make sure the new toe is pointing towards the head and is making a neat V-shape with the first toe.

19 Reposition the needle through the B beads of the red breast to emerge in the matching position between the second and third B beads of the adjacent strap to begin the second leg.

Thread on 7C and make the first toe and heel as before passing back down to the red breast beads. Pass the needle underneath the thread bundle as before and back up through the 4C beads of the leg. Thread on 2C.

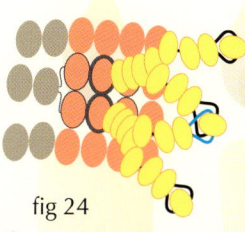

fig 24

Pass the needle through the end C bead of the closest toe on the first leg and back through the 2C just added to link the two feet together (see fig 24 showing the view from below with the link between the two toes).

Thread on 1C for the heel and complete the leg as before.

Make sure the toes are all pointing towards the front of the bird before moving on.

Rocking Robin Inspiration

Chirpy Chirpy Chick Chick Earrings

Make the robins with yellow Delica beads, orange legs and slightly wider beaks to make a pair of Easter chicks.

20 Adding the Earfitting - Reposition the needle to emerge from the A beads on the backbone of the robin.

You need to decide which 2A beads would best support the bird at the angle you want it to sit. You need to pick a pair of adjacent A beads across the straps down the middle of the backbone.

Pass the needle out through one of these beads and thread on 1H. Pass the needle through a jump ring (being careful to avoid the gap in the ring) and back down the H bead. Pass through the other A bead on the backbone. Repeat the stitch twice for strength. Finish off this thread end and any other ends neatly and securely.

Working in a well-ventilated space, paint the exposed thread loop over the jump ring with clear nail varnish to prevent it slipping through the gap. Stiffen the legs with two thin coats of nail varnish allowing it to dry thoroughly between coats.

Link the earfitting onto the jump ring on the robin's back.

Repeat to make a second robin.

Index & Suppliers

Ariel Tassel, 99-103
Astor Bauble, 30-35

beads, types of, 6,
    includes
    seed beads
    bugle beads,
    Delica™ beads
    fire polished faceted beads
    Twin beads, 7

beading needles, 7
beading thread, 7
Belle Époque Bauble, 62-67
brick stitch
    basic instructions, 10
    Belle Époque Bauble, 63-64
    Mistletoe Kisses Bauble, 49

Christmas Earrings, 104-111
    Holly Wreaths, 104-105
    Cracker Earrings, 106-107
    Rocking Robin Earrings, 108-111

Christmas Pudding Bauble, 68-75
Christmas Tree Bauble, 36-39
colours and finishes on glass beads, 6
Constellation Stars, 12-17

earrings, Chirpy Chirpy Chick Chicks 111
    Christmas Earrings, 104-111
    Easy Angel Earrings, 103
    Mistletoe Earrings, 53

findings, 7
Frosted Fir Tree, 18-21

Garland Bauble, 84-89

Inspirations,
    Beau Bauble, 90-91
    Chirpy Chirpy Chick Chicks, 111
    Clivedon Bauble, 35
    colour inspirations, 83
    Crafty Christmas Tree, 40-41
    Easy Angel Earrings, 103
    Galaxy Tree Topper, 17
    Garland Tassels, 91
    Mistletoe Earrings, 53
    Sinaloa Bauble, 60-61
    Tromsø Tassel, 47

Keeper Bead,
    attaching, 8

ladder stitch, 10
    Mistletoe Kisses Bauble, 49

materials, 6
Mistletoe Kisses Bauble, 48-52

Nordic Bauble, 42-47

peyote stitch
    Cracker Earrings, 106-107

Poinsettia Bauble, 54-59

right-angle weave
    basic instructions, 11
    Garland Bauble, 87-89
    Nordic Bauble, 44-45
    Poinsettia Bauble, 57-59
    Sinaloa Bauble, 61

Rivoli Bauble, 26-29

Sherwood Bauble, 92-98
square stitch,
    basic instructions, 11
    Belle Époque Bauble, 65-67
    Garland Bauble, 85-86
    Rivoli Bauble, 28-29
    Rocking Robin Earrings, 109-110

Sweetheart Bauble, 22-25

tassels, 47, 91, 102-103
thread conditioner, 7
threading materials, 7
tips and techniques, 8-9

tools, 7
Twin beads
    definition, 7
    basic techniques, 9

Vintage Bauble, 76-82

wire
    types of, 7
    making a wire loop, 8
    neatening soft wire, 15

All of the materials used in this book should be available in any good bead shop or online. If you are new to beading, or need more supplies, the companies listed below run fast, efficient mail order services, hold large stocks of all of the materials you will need in their stores and give good, well-informed friendly advice on aspects of beading and beading needs.

In the UK

Spellbound Bead Co
47 Tamworth Street,
Lichfield
Staffordshire
WS13 6JW
01543 417650

www.spellboundbead.co.uk

Spellbound Bead Co supplied all of the materials for the samples shown.

You can buy the beads for these projects loose (wholesale and retail), in counted bead packs or as fully illustrated kits.

In USA

Fire Mountain Gems
One Fire Mountain Way
Grants Pass
OR 97526 - 2373
Tel: + 800 355 2137
www.firemountaingems.com

Shipwreck Beads
8560 Commerce Place Dr.NE
Lacey
WA 98516
Tel: + 800 950 4232
www.shipwreckbeads.com